MIKE BREARLEY
& DUDLEY DOUST
THE ASHES RETAINED

MIKE BREARLEY
& DUDLEY DOUST
THE ASHES RETAINED

Hodder and Stoughton

LONDON SYDNEY AUCKLAND TORONTO

To Kari and Jane

By the same authors:
The Return of the Ashes

British Library Cataloguing in
Publication Data
Brearley, Mike. Doust, Dudley
The Ashes Retained

ISBN 0 340 24191 8

CONTENTS

ACKNOWLEDGEMENTS

All photographs in this book, unless otherwise credited, are by Patrick Eagar. The index has been compiled by Jim Coldham, statistics by Geoffrey Saulez. In preparing this book the authors would like to thank them all for their help, together with Wendy Wimbush and Enid Watson for their work in preparing the script, and Lillywhites Ltd., for their assistance in designing the cover.

Designed by John Tennant

FOREWORD

by John Cleese

I WAS DELIGHTED to get a letter from Mike Brearley from Australia last winter asking me if I'd be 'prepared to write the forward' to his next book. Delighted not only because I could leave the letter lying around to impress people; delighted not just that a former philosophy don could make such a basic spelling mistake; but delighted also because I like the man and found his first book *The Return of the Ashes* the most interesting book on cricket that I've read.

'Ah!' I hear you say, 'But what do you know about cricket? You're just a tatty old comic the publishers have wheeled out in the hope of a bit of cheap publicity.' This, of course, is undeniable. 'So why should we listen to your opinion on the subject of cricket?' you ask. Well, I'll tell you why. Because I once got Denis Compton out twice in an innings, *that's* why. '*Twice* in an innings?!' you cry. Look, please stop interrupting. I've only got 1,000 words and if you keep breaking in like this I'll never get it all in.

Now, I should make it clear that I believe that getting Denis out once in an innings would not be that much to write home about. A cause for momentary joy certainly, particularly in 1947, but not something that one would necessarily want on one's gravestone. After all, a lot of people have done it. Lindwall, Miller, Bedser, Laker and Bertie Buse, to name a few. But to dismiss the brilliantined genius twice in one knock is something else. Here is how it happened.

Denis came down to play against Clifton College, a West Country sports academy, in 1958. His son was a pupil there. So was I. I was in the team as a slow off-spinner, because during June I was more or less unplayable. This was because for these four weeks the pitches were in line with a huge red-brick building called School Hall. Being six foot five, my arm cleared the sight screen easily and so if I bowled the ball from the right end with the right trajectory the batsman was lucky to get so much as a late glimpse of it. During June, this was. Compton came in July.

He'd been in about ten minutes when I was called upon to bowl. He'd not had much of the strike and needed about four for his fifty. He was coming down the wicket in a way I'd never seen before. In first class cricket I'd seen him leave his crease as the bowler bowled. On this day he was setting off at about the same moment that the bowler commenced his run up. There was a danger with the quickies that he was going to strike the ball before it left the bowler's hand. I'm very sorry, I'm exaggerating. Let's just say he was as non-crease-bound as it is possible to be.

As an off-spinner I had one advantage over and about School Hall. That was our coach, Reg Sinfield, ex-Gloucs and England. He was quite my favourite person at Clifton, funny and wise and kind. I'm afraid he showed most of the masters up dreadfully. Anyway, Reg had told me to bowl very wide at any batsman running down the wicket, so just before my first over I said to the wicket keeper, one Pickwoad, '*Third* ball, I'll bowl him a very wide one. Be ready for it, we might get a stumping.' 'You can bowl him a wide one if you like,' said Pickwoad, 'but I'm not stumping him. I want to watch him bat.' This was a blow.

I don't remember what happened to my first two deliveries, but they were eventually retrieved. I ran up to bowl the third ball. Denis Compton left his crease and I bowled him a wide one; so wide that it surprised him, passing him yards down the wicket. It pitched, leaving him stranded, and proceeded at a gentle pace and comfortable height towards the waiting Pickwoad. Pickwoad calmly rotated his wrists through 180 degrees, and thrust the back of his gloves at the ball. The ball shot up in the air. 'Damn!' cried Pickwoad toward the master-in-charge, umpiring at square leg. But to my amazement the ball landed, spun sideways and bumped against the stumps, dislodging a bail, with the King of the Sweep still yards out of his ground. I'd got him.

Time passed. I became aware of a strange stillness. It occurred to me that no one had appealed. Denis had wandered back to his crease and now stood there, slightly puzzled. Pickwoad was replacing the bail. The other fielders seemed absorbed in their personal problems. Pickwoad picked the ball up and tossed it back to me. 'Bad luck,' he called.

Then I realised I'd blown my chance. If I'd appealed straight away it could have been put down to youthful excitement. But to do so now was cold-bloodedly to spoil everyone's afternoon. I'd got Compton out and no one would ever know. It was a sad moment. I turned, walked back to my mark, ran up and bowled the next ball, a slow high full toss on the leg stump. Spectators started taking cover.

Whether Denis was distracted by the sight of a bowler openly weeping in his delivery stride, or whether he took it upon himself to right this particular wrong, I shall never know, but painstakingly he hit a catch to mid-on. Mid-on was Ken Whitty, playing in his first match for the XI, and consequently the only other man in the ground with an interest in the catch being taken. Had the ball been edged to Pickwoad, it would no doubt have been thrown over the sightscreen for six. Whitty grabbed glazedly at the ball and suddenly stood there triumphant, the ball securely wedged between his chin and his forearm. Compton, D. C. S. c White b Cheese, the *Bristol Evening Post* later announced.

I hope this establishes my right to pronounce this book a good read. It's about an extraordinary series, of course, full of the most bizarre twists and turns of fortune, and with a deliriously happy ending. Mike and Dudley Doust tell the story well, with just the right mixture of narrative, character insights, cricket politics and humour. The anecdotes always have a point and the greatest delight of all is the sheer amount of hard fact. I've followed cricket for years but I never realised how much I didn't understand till I read this account of tactical battles, of the reasons behind field placings and bowling changes, of the technical strengths and weaknesses of individuals and how they are countered or played upon. Most books have a bit of this but not enough. This book has a lot and every word is fascinating.

Brearley is a nice man. I've got to know him quite well in the past eighteen months. He's got a lot of qualities I envy. A quiet but sympathetic watchfulness, a little like a writer's watchfulness, but less judging, more generous; an almost unexpected toughness and competitiveness, never displayed for its own sake, but there when the job requires it. And instead of just loyalty towards the people he plays with, a real affection, a smile of enjoyment crossing his face as I ask 'What's so-and-so like?'

He's got his faults too, but I've only got 1,000 words.

P.S. Pickwoad now lives in Canada. Serves him right.

CHAPTER 1

In the Air

IT WAS AFTER England won the last Test of the summer, beating New Zealand by seven wickets at the end of August, that Alec Bedser asked me to have a word with him outside the dressing room at Lord's. He is chairman of the selection committee, and he said the selectors wanted me to captain the side on the 1978–79 tour of Australia. I accepted. I was excited by the challenge of remaining captain of the side, and began to look ahead to the task of retaining the Ashes we had won from the Australians in 1977.

Still, I had misgivings. I had just finished an appalling season with the bat, easily my worst since 1965, and it is an ordeal to undergo failures in public, as one does in cricket. I had batted poorly in the final two Tests against Pakistan that summer, and in the first against New Zealand at the Oval I had scored only 2 and 11. At this point I decided to give myself one more chance. If I failed again as a batsman early in August at Nottingham, I would say to Bedser, 'I don't want to hold the selectors to their decision to pick me for all three New Zealand Tests. If you want to try someone else for the Lord's Test I shall be perfectly happy.' At Nottingham I scored a half century and their confidence in me – and to a lesser extent mine in myself – was sufficiently restored to take me on for another term as captain of England.

As captain, unbeaten in 17 Tests, I felt I had earned my place; as a batsman, though, there were problems to solve. The trouble possibly dated back to January 15th when, in a one-day match in Karachi, a rearing ball broke my left forearm. I carried a plate screwed to the bone for the next fourteen months. I am not sure how much of an effect the injury had on my batting. In any case, an abundance of advice was offered during the season. It came daily through the post, and in the pubs I visited in connection with my Middlesex Benefit. One gentleman wrote to say he had never been able to hit a cricket ball properly until someone told him to swing the bat down over his back foot. He said he realized it was a bit of a cheek for a village green player to write to the captain of England, but he thought if this advice had 'added a decibel to a mouse's squeak, how much could it do for a lion's roar?' A West Indian, who must have read that I sometimes hum a passage from the Rasoumoffsky Quartets when I bat, spoke to me in a pub. 'Man, you've got to change your symphony,' he said. 'The ball ain't coming down in tune with the one you're humming.'

In the fortnight before we left I went almost daily to the Indoor School at Lord's. There is a camera and a video-cassette machine there, as well as a bowling machine which is quick but annoyingly inclined to break down, especially after you hit a couple of fours. With these aids the MCC coach, Don Wilson, gave me great help. He emphasized the basics, keeping still, playing straight, playing sideways on. I not only batted against Don and members of the Lord's ground staff but my Middlesex team-mates Phil Edmonds and John Emburey. I was happy to watch myself batting at length with the help of a machine that produced playbacks: I became more confident.

Who would make up the rest of the team for Australia? Early in the summer, speaking as the existing rather than the prospective captain, I made a suggestion about the composition of the party.

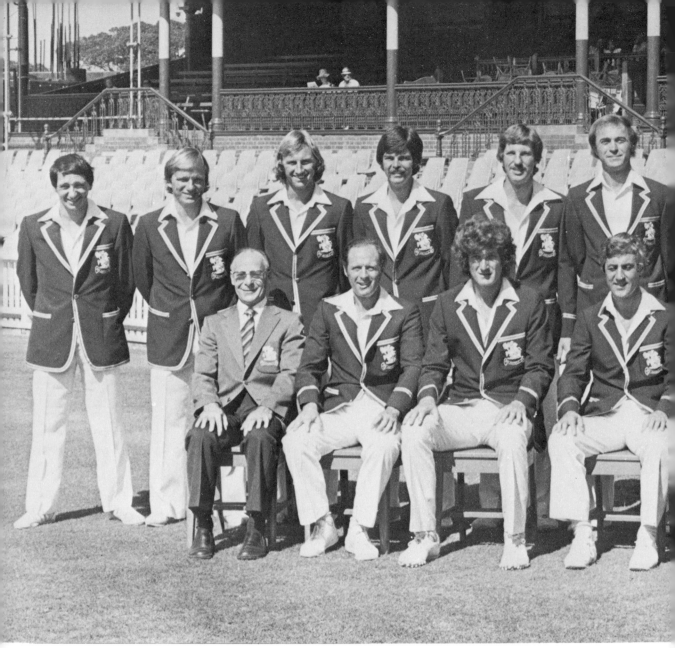

Long before the managers or captain had been chosen, I suggested to Donald Carr, secretary of the Test and County Cricket Board, that regardless of the individuals involved the assistant manager's job mainly consisted of running the practice. Therefore, it could be done by a current, senior player who could be the seventeenth man, able to be considered as a player in an emergency. Someone like Keith Fletcher, David Brown or Ray Illingworth might be ideal in this dual capacity. I suspected that the traditional make-up made the party top-heavy with management.

The suggestion was rejected. In retrospect, I suppose the dual role might cause problems; the individual and the other players might be sensitive about how much opportunity he would be given to establish a place in the side. However, I hope the idea is not utterly dismissed. The official decision came in August, when the TCCB announced that Doug Insole would go as manager, Ken Barrington as assistant manager and Bernard Thomas as physiotherapist.

The selectors, Bedser, Charles Elliott, Ken Barrington, John Murray, Peter May and myself met in early September to select the players. A number of them chose themselves. Bob Taylor was

named as wicketkeeper. Four quick bowlers, Bob Willis, Mike Hendrick, Ian Botham and John Lever, were chosen; whether or not the party contained sixteen or seventeen players, it was agreed that we would certainly need another seam bowler. Chris Old was the one we wanted, but it is no secret that Chilly is subject to physical breakdowns. Russell Davies, the columnist, captured Old in his amusing, acid pen-profiles of the team members in the *New Statesman*. 'Left arm never fit at the same moment as right shoulder, inner ear, bladder, etc.,' wrote Davies after the selections were announced. 'Would be wonderful player if all of him could turn up at the ground on same day.' Once we were satisfied as to his fitness he was certain of his place, though we stipulated that he should see Thomas at once and work out a rigorous training programme.

That made six, including myself. David Gower and Geoffrey Boycott were obviously in as batsmen. Graham Gooch and Clive Radley, as well as the spinner Phillippe Edmonds, also picked themselves on the strengths of their recent performances in the Pakistan and New Zealand Tests. We now had to find at least one more spinner, possibly two, one more batsman, possibly two, and a reserve wicketkeeper. The question to solve at this stage was whether to take sixteen or seventeen players. It seemed foolish, at least to me, to take seventeen when sixteen would want all the match-practice they could get.

It was quickly agreed that we would take sixteen, which meant we had room for four more. Emburey was chosen as a second spinner. However, in my opinion, he and Edmonds could not both play in the same Test. If they did, our tail would begin at Number 7, since besides the two spinners we would need Taylor and two other seam bowlers to follow Botham at Number 6. Rather than being short of a batsman or a bowler, I argued that Miller should come as a second all-rounder. He had rarely had an extended chance in Tests to prove himself as a spinner as we had so often not needed more than four main bowlers. He was duly named, which left two places to fill.

We had a long discussion over Roger Tolchard, David Bairstow and Paul Downton. I argued that Taylor's superiority as a 'keeper together with his exceptional fitness record made it more likely that we would need a spare batsman for Tests than a spare wicketkeeper. This argument, backed by the fact that the second 'keeper had not played in a Test in the previous two tours of Australia, and had not played as a 'keeper in the tours of the last two winters, prevailed, and Tolchard was chosen, narrowly ahead of the Yorkshireman.

The selection of the last batting spot stimulated an even livelier discussion. It came down to either an old stager like David Steele, Fletcher or John Edrich or, on the other side, the young Chris Tavaré of Kent or Derek Randall. The old stager, it was felt, would add solidity to the team, whereas Tavaré was promising and Randall unpredictable but certainly a potential match-winner. Randall had not played Test cricket the previous summer and had averaged 44.70 in county championship matches. He had scored 174 in the Centenary Test in Melbourne; but one swallow does not make a

summer. Randall finally won the vote for the last spot – but it was close. In the light of the result, this proved to be a happy choice. Bairstow and Tavaré, as an early order batsman, were to be the paid reserves. We also named unpaid reserves who would stand by for the openers and for Emburey and Edmonds.

So there we were, on the night of October 24th, on the flight to Australia, a party of twenty – three managerial men, sixteen players, and the scorer, Geoffrey Saulez, a retired accountant who has travelled with many MCC teams. We scarcely had settled into our seats when Insole, as though to ratify the selections by confirming them indelibly with signatures, began to pass round autograph sheets to be signed by each of us. We must have signed these sheets, on and off, during most of the flight; in all we signed perhaps 2,000 sheets to be given to fans and friends over the next sixteen weeks in Australia.

The players, shortly after take-off, began squirming in their seats, changing out of their England travelling uniforms into more comfortable slacks, track suit bottoms and tee shirts. It was to be a 22-hour flight and we looked like a group of schoolboys, eager to get out of our official uniforms. Derek Randall kept his on. Surprisingly, he sat still, neither shuffling up and down the aisle nor jabbering to himself as he does in a match. He was content to sit there, he said later, drawing inspiration from the orange, red and navy-blue striped MCC tie and, even more so, from the light-blue tour jacket with its emblem depicting St. George slaying the dragon.

Unlike Randall, Bob Taylor was soon circulating. We call him 'Chat' because he makes the most of the functions as well as the cricket on a tour. At last, on his third England tour to Australia, he was going as number one 'keeper. He met another long-standing understudy: an air steward who said he had been kept out of the Queensland side for years by John Maclean, who now, he thought, had probably missed his last chance to keep wicket for Australia. Oddly enough, the sociable 'Chat' also bumped into a former Victorian 'keeper, Bill Jacobs; they had spent weeks together when Bob toured Australia with the Rest of the World side which was managed by Jacobs. Wicketkeepers are a tribe of their own. It is such a specialized job that to talk shop they often fall

ENGLAND TOUR TO AUSTRALIA
1978-79

Captain—J. M. BREARLEY (Middlesex) ....

Vice Captain—R. G. D. WILLIS (Warwickshire) ....

I. T. BOTHAM (Somerset) ....

G. BOYCOTT (Yorkshire) ....

P. H. EDMONDS (Middlesex) ....

J. E. EMBUREY (Middlesex) ....

G. A. GOOCH (Essex) ....

D. I. GOWER (Leicestershire) ....

M. HENDRICK (Derbyshire) ....

J. K. LEVER (Essex) ....

G. MILLER (Derbyshire) ....

C. M. OLD (Yorkshire) ....

C. T. RADLEY (Middlesex) ....

D. W. RANDALL (Nottinghamshire) ....

R. W. TAYLOR (Derbyshire) ....

R. W. TOLCHARD (Leicestershire) ....

Manager—D. J. INSOLE ....

Asst. Manager—K. F. BARRINGTON ....

Physiotherapist—B. W. THOMAS ....

Scorer—G. G. A. SAULEZ ....

into conversation with their opposite numbers.

On the first leg of the flight I sat with the man who was our first walking wounded, Ian Botham. Two days earlier he had cut his left wrist, dangerously close to the tendon, on the glass door of a pub. Now he sat with his arm in bandages and a sling. Ian had been examined by Thomas, who felt he would miss only about three weeks of cricket in Australia and would be fully recovered in good time for the First Test, in the first week of December, in Brisbane. Ian is the most straightforward of men, enjoying country life, shooting and fishing. Yet a fundamental and amusing mystery surrounds him. How does he pronounce his surname? Is it with a long 'o' (as in 'boat'), as in his father's nātive Yorkshire, or with a short 'o' (as in 'pot'), as in his own native Somerset? Ian used to say he didn't know which was right: he now opts for the 'o' as in 'boat'.

There were no mysteries surrounding his intentions in Australia. He was keen first that England should slaughter the Aussies and, second, he had his eye on Andy Roberts's record of taking his first 100 wickets in only 21 Test Matches. (In fact, the record is held by the nineteenth-century fast bowler, Lohmann, who reached the target in 16 Tests.) Ian already had 64 Test wickets in eleven matches and, needing six a match in Australia, the goal to him seemed attainable in 17 Tests. I admired his ambition and optimism, two of his most valuable virtues, though I had doubts as to his so quickly breaking what he took to be the record. As it was, I had to cut his food when the tray came round.

I tried to eat little on the way out. Also I was interested to see if by avoiding dehydration I might reduce jet-lag. An American doctor, in a book called *Food for Sport*, had written that due to inordinately dry air and rapid ventilation in an aircraft you lose more than a full quart of water in a 3½-hour flight. Therefore, all the way to Sydney, I was filling and re-filling a pint bottle with water from the little tap at the rear of the plane. I never felt fitter in my life. Bernard Thomas had given each of us a programme of exercise to follow in the late summer. He worked on Gooch's knee-action, for instance, and Miller's posture and Hendrick's arthritic hip which gave him intermittent trouble as a bowler. Botham's programme was complete rest. For me, Thomas was interested in 'corrective running'; he felt I wasn't pushing off with sufficient thrust from my back foot. He also gave me stretching exercises, and for the first time in my life I could touch my toes without bending my knees.

Willis, as usual, was also very fit, although he was not altogether comfortable, his 6feet-6inch frame folded up in an economy seat. He had taken five-mile runs every day near his flat in Birmingham. We did not think much of it then, but it was ominous that he wasn't completely happy with his boots. He carried five pairs in his luggage. In hindsight, it seems ironic that a dear, elderly lady, who was travelling to Australia to see her grandchild for the first time, should have offered to massage his feet on the flight. She joked about usurping the job of the team physiotherapist.

Miller, Emburey, Gower and Botham are the card players in the team. Botham later mentioned the game of pontoon they played on the flight, and, being an unrelentingly competitive player of any game, his recollection of it was wholly in character. 'We didn't play for much money at all, as I remember,' he said. 'But what little there was to win I won.'

Gower also spent some time chatting to Hendrick about the merits of turning themselves into limited companies. When their cricketing days were over, what might they do with their futures? Gower, only 21, had not given it much thought. Hendrick, just turned 30, reckoned he fancied running a pub somewhere in rural Derbyshire or going into farming. His wife is from a farm family. Otherwise, Gower slept. He is one of the most accomplished sleepers in the side, and in the air he spends much of his time in a sort of suspended animation, like an animal waiting for the spring. I envy him this *sang-froid*, yet still it bothers me. I would like to see other feelings come through more obviously – excitement, anger, fear. He told me later, putting it rather as a rule of life, that one must always keep one's cool. As I got to know him better on the tour I was glad to see that he occasionally broke this rule.

The team does not travel in a tight exclusive block of seats, and there was the inevitable, devout Yorkshire follower on the plane. Yorkshire produces a curious mixture of the blunt and the adoring, and this son of the White Rose came into the latter character. Boycott handled his blandishments well, before returning to his customary

ALL-SPORT, ADRIAN MURRELL

chore of writing notes for his book, for newspaper articles, and for letters to the Yorkshire Reform Group, who were advocating his reinstatement as captain of the county side. In lighter moments Geoff sat talking with Edmonds. These two have helped each other in the nets over the last year or two, and they banter away with jokes based largely on their respective backgrounds, Yorkshire on one side, Zambia, Cambridge and Middlesex on the other.

Later I spoke to Boycott about his harrowing six weeks leading up to the tour. He said it had been the worst period of his life. His mother, with whom he had lived, had died after a long illness. Their house belongs to the Coal Board, so it was uncertain not only about whether he had a home but also about whether he could continue to live there. Then there was his continuing dispute with Yorkshire who had deposed him as captain and replaced him with John Hampshire. He said to me that leaving Yorkshire (if he did) would be a divorce for him; he had been married to the county since he was seventeen. The third blow had been the announcement that he had been selected for Australia as a player only; he had been passed over as vice-captain in favour of Willis.

I remember saying I thought getting away from England, batting and scoring runs would be the best way of recovering from these blows. He said later, when finally we were collecting our luggage at Sydney, that already he was happy for being in Australia. He might well have been speaking for the whole team.

Before we left, Bob recorded a pop-song called 'Owzat' by Bob Willis and the Wickets. As vice-captain, he showed the same enthusiasm as he does in his job as fast bowler. A man of strong views, powerful silences, and manic flights, he is prepared to sustain an unpopular view regardless of resentment. He also is excellent company and was a linch-pin of the tour, on and off the field.

CHAPTER 2

Bradman, Bouncers and Botham's Bad Dreams

AT SYDNEY WE changed planes and flew on to Adelaide, where in warm and pleasant spring sunshine we were met at the airport by Sir Donald Bradman. He is a spry, twinkly-eyed man of 70, a stockbroker, who for the past forty years has lived in Adelaide. He invited Insole, Barrington, Willis and myself to lunch two days later and there, over a restaurant meal of well-cooked grills, he shed light on the current Australian cricket scene.

Sir Donald talked about Bob Simpson and Jeff Thomson, the captain and vice-captain for the recent tour of the West Indies, who were now, it seemed, not going to play against us. Simpson had wanted to have his place as captain guaranteed for the whole series, as had been done against India a year before, but this was refused, presumably because of doubts about his batting against our fast bowling. And Thommo, having joined World Series Cricket, was awaiting a court decision after the Board's application for an injunction to prevent him playing in any but Board-sponsored matches for the duration of his contract. The question was whether the Board's contract was valid, since it did not guarantee him any money. Bradman thought the Board would win; soon after he was proved right.

Some weeks later Thomson stated that he wanted to play against the 'Poms' for Queensland, but the State did not pick him as he had not been to practice and was unlikely to be available for their Shield matches. His absence from practice might seem a

Sir Donald Bradman makes a point at Adelaide. We spoke for more than two hours with him on various aspects of the game.

contrived excuse, but a Queensland selector told me, 'We need Thommo for this match like a hole in the head.' Certainly the State felt their first priority was to build a team for their Sheffield matches, and they had several inexperienced fast-medium bowlers whom they wanted to blood. As it was, Thomson announced he would spend the summer fishing to pay off his debts. He did not do so, but that is another story.

By chance, our one glimpse of Thomson in action coincided with our first glimpse of Rodney Hogg. Queensland played South Australia at Brisbane in the Gillette Cup the Saturday following our lunch with Bradman. Thomson was Man of the Match,

with 6 for 17, while Hogg did not take a single wicket in his side's easy defeat. We were watching on Bernard Thomas's minute portable TV set, but despite the fuzzy reception from Brisbane we were able to confirm Bradman's cautious estimate, that Hogg was indeed 'a bit slippery'. Whether he was really quick Bradman wouldn't, or couldn't, say.

He did say that he thought bowlers had not become quicker over the years. He rated Tyson as the fastest bowler he has ever seen, and Larwood quicker than present-day bowlers. I find this hard to believe. Javelin-throwers and shot-putters, like other athletes whose performances are measurable, have improved steadily over this period. I suspect that bowlers have too. Bradman agreed, however, that many were quick enough to justify the use of helmets by batsmen. He thought helmets should not be allowed for fielders, though, since they might be enabled to gain an advantage and field too close in. 'Mind, I never worried about fielders being close to me,' he said. 'In fact, they were better off being five yards back, as they'd have a better chance of getting me out. I always used to tell them, "It's okay by me you being so close, but let me warn you, if I can hit you I will."'

The conversation continued energetically for over two hours. Sir Donald had strong and interesting views on all aspects of the game. I found him cautious, honestly able to laugh at other people's misfortunes, and shrewd. I liked him. Forever being asked his views on the game, he was at pains to point out that he was no longer a selector or Chairman of the Board: others should be the spokesmen for Australian cricket.

Adelaide itself, with its superb practice facilities, was perfect for the start of our tour. We soon impressed observers as a fit and dedicated team. Ken Barrington organized the nets efficiently, and made sure that each day all the main batsmen had a long net against our main bowlers and that the tail-enders had local bowlers. Later in the tour Barrington would go on ahead to arrange practice sessions at the next venue. We relied a lot on local bowlers. Throughout, we were helped to find them by the ground authorities. Their overall standard varied. Occasionally, they were near to State standard, but more often they were students on vacation, intensely keen, of limited ability. Yet Test batsmen often prefer at least some of their practice to be against ordinary bowlers, especially on irregular pitches.

Another asset to us was the number of young English county cricketers in Australia. Only over the last two years has this opportunity become widely available. We were fortunate to have cricketers of the calibre of Gatting, Larkins, Tavare, Roebuck and Agnew. We welcomed them into the dressing-room at all times (despite our strict ruling about its being forbidden to all outsiders), and they must have learned a lot from their involvement.

The selectors – Insole, Barrington, Willis and myself – met to discuss our policy for the early stages of the tour. We had four four-day State games and four one-day up-country matches before the first Test. There are two possible approaches to pre-Test build-ups. You can formulate your likely Test team and aim to give these players the optimum chance to establish their form by match practice; or you can try to keep everyone in the party happy and involved by spreading the cricket as widely as possible. We decided on the latter method; we knew that any of the sixteen players could be picked on merit for a Test, and we were conscious of the need to keep everyone as involved as possible. We remembered too the unhappy situation a year before, when I broke my arm just before the third Test at Karachi, and Mike Gatting had to come into his first Test without any recent first-class cricket behind him. Botham's injury meant that he would be on the sidelines for three weeks, which gave us that much more scope to fit in players during the early matches; we tried to help him not to get bored by putting him in charge of the autograph sheets, but it failed to keep his interest. Even so, the enforced rest may have been a blessing in disguise.

Any complacency we may have had – and the defeatist Aussie press seemed ready to fan it – was salutarily squashed by the events of the first State match. South Australia had not won a match for two years, but now they beat us by 40 runs. They were delighted.

During this match we had our first sight of Rick Darling, a strong runner as one of Australia's opening batsmen. He was rumoured to hook rashly and indeed he was out both times in the match this way, our bowlers purposely bowling short to him. We paid for this tactic, however, later in the tour.

Most of our bowling was done by the spinners, Edmonds and Miller, who both bowled excellently. Edmonds bowled as well as ever; nothing in his performance against South Australia suggested his later loss of form. Miller flighted the ball more than usual, especially in the first innings when the ball hardly turned. More importantly, after several conversations with Max O'Connell, the umpire, he changed his approach to the wicket. 'Dusty' had normally run in at an angle, and would swing away sharply to avoid treading on the pitch. He also came in quickly, and bowled in his run, without pausing to gather himself. The need to veer away immediately after letting go of the ball also affected his action: he was bowling with his chest square on to the batsman, and with his arm slightly low. O'Connell told him two things: first, that he was not allowed to cut the edge of the popping crease in his approach (i.e. he would have to come in straighter): and second, that he was often blocking the umpire's view after he let the ball go. Such unsighting might cost him an LBW or caught behind. So Miller experimented. He came in straighter, and slower – and at once felt more relaxed and in control. He felt that his arm was higher, as he did not have to bowl across his left leg, and this enabled him to be more accurate and to drift the ball away from the batsman. When I spoke to Dusty later I asked him why it had been O'Connell that had persuaded him to change so fundamentally, when others had made similar criticisms in the past. He said that he knew O'Connell was likely to stand in several Tests, so that if he was to do well he would have to be able to satisfy O'Connell's demands; and that, unlike many English umpires, Max was concerned and insistent, keeping on to him to such an extent that the point finally got through. For a couple of nights he lost sleep thinking about the problem. Then, after a number of sessions in the nets, he decided to gamble with the new method in the second innings, when early on he had Nash stumped off a perfectly flighted outswinger. He said O'Connell's tip was the key to his bowling success on the tour.

After the first morning, the ball did little for the seam bowlers. We were, moreover, already hit by injury. Old dislocated a finger and was in pain: but Bernard Thomas met him in front of the members' stand and with a dexterous twist and pull replaced the joint. Willis, more ominously,

was already having trouble with his feet. A blister had gone septic. In his single-minded quest for fitness (and his usual early-morning insomnia) he had made it worse by carrying on too long with lonely five-mile runs.

One fast bowler did make an impact on the game, and that was Hogg. After having Gooch caught at the wicket off a nasty lifting ball, he came in at Radley. He bowled one a little short, outside the off-stump. It flew, and came back off the pitch, hitting Clive an ugly blow on the forehead. In falling he hit the wicket. He had seven stitches, but remained cheerful. He is a tough competitor, who was most annoyed at having dislodged the bail. He said, 'If they all bounce like that, I've no chance.' It would have been true for all of us.

It is hard to know how such an accident affects different players' confidence. After talking to Thomas and to Clive himself, I decided to keep him at Number 3 in the second innings. He played wildly at Sincock and was caught at cover. That one ball from Hogg probably ruined Radley's tour.

One role of nicknames is that they make fearsome enemies less threatening. 'Hoggy' quickly earned his share. From now on, he was variously 'Quentin', 'Road', or 'Hedge', after other well-known 'hogs'. We noticed that he liked to bowl in short spells, perhaps because of his asthma; that he only bowled really quickly with the new ball; and that he bowled very straight. He also shouted at Bob Blewett, the captain, if there were no fielders where the ball went (as often in the case of Gower, who played his strokes fluently), or if he thought he was on at the wrong end. We wondered, in short, whether 'Edge had the necessary 'eart.

Our next stop was Melbourne, where we saw other Test bowlers – Hurst, Callen, Laughlin, and Higgs – as well as the Victoria captain, Yallop. In the cold damp weather the MCG looked even vaster than we remembered it during the Centenary Test. England's fielding now matched that of any side in

Clive Radley struck on the head, Adelaide, 4 November. Clive just touched the off-stump with his pad, dislodging the bail. This blow marked the start of the emergence of Rodney Hogg, whose face shows concern, and the displacement of Radley whose Test average at that point was 48.10. Despite the disappointments of his tour, Clive always shared in others' successes.

Ken Barrington steers slip catches to Botham and Hendrick during a practice session. Lever, Tolchard, and Randall are involved with another group to the left. The ball would be thrown at chest height outside the line of the body, and the 'nicker' would steer or cut it to the waiting fielders. Barrington and Radley, both adept cutters, were especially good in the role of 'nicker', though they needed batting gloves, and occasionally had to take evasive action if the 'thrower' lost his line. Lever was the most dependable at throwing. We practised this almost daily, both deep, as for fast bowlers, and close-in, with the ball thrown underarm, for spinners. This is the best practice for slip catching, and the Australians soon copied us. Towards the end of the second Test our fielding practices had become more and more dedicated. I wondered what the reason was, until I realised that there was an increasing reluctance to go to the lively net wickets. After the seam and bounce of Brisbane and its nets, and two weeks at Perth where the seam-bowlers had everything in their favour, batsmen found respite in training and fielding. And bowlers rarely mind missing the occasional net practice. Botham and Hendrick, two of our main bowlers, were also our two best slip-fielders.

the world; but we still found ourselves out-thrown by the Australians. They learn to throw at baseball, and are accustomed to the Australian-Rules football pitches doubling as huge cricket fields. Thomas's pre-Tour training instructions included practising throwing, especially for Radley who has a weak arm and was used to fielding in the slips. Now Gower and Old both had sore elbows and could not throw far. Our strong throwers were Lever, Botham, Hendrick, Gooch, Edmonds and Emburey, most of whom as it happened usually fielded close to the bat.

If the pitch at Adelaide had been untypical, Melbourne was even more so. It resembled Faisalabad in Pakistan – flat, brown and lifeless, set in a lush heavy outfield, so slow that a four along the ground was almost out of the question. The game was rain-affected, but we managed to derive some benefit. Our bowlers, as usual, were accurate. As at Adelaide, we dropped a few catches. Randall played well for his 63, and I scored my first hundred for 17 months. I did not mind the fact that it took so long, just over six hours, partly because the conditions were entirely against fast scoring, and partly because I was keen that our younger batsmen should get used to the idea of playing long innings. In county cricket, a side rarely bats more than 5½ hours (100 overs), whereas in Tests a batsman who gets in must set his sights on an 8- or 10-hour innings. I doubt if Gooch, Gower, Botham, Miller or even Randall (except in his Centenary Test 174) had ever batted longer than five hours. Hurst and Higgs bowled well, while Callen showed flashes of the ability that had enabled him to take wickets at a remarkable rate in State matches. We were struck by the players' football-style cries of encouragement: between Alan Hurst's deliveries I could hear, 'Come on the Vics, get quick now, Al-Pal!' We were also puzzled, at times, by Yallop's field placings: he seemed unable to put pressure on the batsmen, especially when Higgs was bowling.

The one-day match at Canberra was one of the most pleasant social occasions of the tour, while we also won the game easily by 179 runs, Willis taking four for ten. There was a magnificent stand between Tolchard and Boycott, who each got hundreds. Tolchard set the tone with quick-footed driving, and Boycott matched him, even going down the wicket to the medium-pacers. Sometimes Geoff needs the stimulus of an improviser at the other end. I remember the Nottingham Test of 1977 when he and Alan Knott had their superb stand, again both batsmen scoring centuries; after Knott's arrival Boycott's batting became altogether lighter and more adventurous.

At Sydney we had a convincing win against N.S.W. Bob Willis captained the side, while Botham played for the first time, scoring a fifty and taking five wickets in the second innings. The bowlers – Willis, Botham, Hendrick, Miller and Emburey – all looked good. Lawson bowled fast for N.S.W., while Hourn, with his chinamen and googlies, spun the ball past the bat frequently. Randall again played well, as did Gooch, after a torrid first hour.

Bob Willis and I had a (friendly) argument over dinner during this match. He feels, rightly, that top-class cricket is largely a matter of consistency. As a bowler, he is acutely aware of the waste involved in casual batting – in throwing away wickets. Like Rugby forwards irritated by fancy play among the backs that has them traipsing back to their own corner flag, fast bowlers – the power-house of a team – need respite, and have scant sympathy with batsmen who specialize in pretty 20's. On this occasion, Bob's targets were Randall and Gower, who he felt weren't applying themselves. His pet phrase was, 'They've got to be spoken to.' I am wary of 'speaking to' people too much. Like a parent, one can too easily become purely restrictive. Players of flair like Randall and Gower must to some extent be given their heads. The following retort by the poet Roy Campbell to critics who had praised certain fashionable novelists is to the point:

> 'You praise the great restraint
>   with which they write
> I'm with you there of course
> They use the snaffle and the bit all right,
> But where's the bloody horse?'

Nevertheless, I did talk to Randall, and arranged to see Gower when we arrived in Brisbane. Randall had given his wicket away for 110. I asked him what he had been thinking. He said it was hot, and there was nothing at stake in the match. I said this was unacceptable. It would be hot in the Tests; what was at stake was our learning to dominate all the sides we played against and to destroy the bowlers' confidence; and above all he could have played himself into even better form and confidence by scoring 200. So he *was* 'spoken to'.

I asked Gower to come to my room as soon as we had settled in to our town-centre hotel in Brisbane. Doug Insole was there too. Gower had a beer, we had a soft drink. My main concern was to hear what he was thinking about his batting and the problems of Australia.

I had wondered if he was at times a bit casual, even 'flip' about it; when he got out for a breezy 13 at Melbourne, caught and bowled by Julian Wiener, an opening bat who occasionally bowls off-breaks, his comment was, 'You can't let a bloke like Wiener bowl at you, can you?' He felt that he should never allow himself to be dictated to by second-string bowlers. Gower had been built up – with good cause – as the most elegant young English player since Cowdrey; he had played well at Adelaide, scoring 73 and 50 – though, as usual, scattered amongst the pearls were some airy-fairy shots outside the off-stump. I had no wish to suppress his instinctual flair; and I appreciate now as then that he is bound to play and miss more than others as he plays so many cover drives. We must have talked for half-an-hour; I was impressed. He had given thought to the problems. As he said, the biggest change from English pitches was likely to be the higher bounce in Australia – though we had seen little of that so far. He wondered how much he would have to change his technique to balls just outside the off-stump. 'I score a lot of my runs to third-man and square on the off-side; so I don't want to cut out too much,' he said. He was also aware of his habit of leaning too far towards the off-side, which tended to make him play across the ball on the leg-stump, and hit it in the air. Doug Insole and I pointed out the need to think in terms of long innings, and for him not to be too ambitious with his square shots until he had felt the pace of the pitch. Gower added that he had enjoyed batting with Boycott, but had been a little disconcerted by Geoff's saying, more than once, between overs, 'If only I could hit the ball like you.' He thought it an odd attitude from so senior a player, and a man who had scored 100 first-class centuries.

We wanted to pick more or less our full Test team to play against Queensland. The main doubt was whether to give Radley one more chance to re-establish himself; in which case Gower would have stood down for the State match, as he had played in all the other games. The conversation we had with Gower made us even keener to keep him playing. In the event, he scored only 6 and 1. By the end of the match he was down-hearted. 'If you want someone to make you a quick three, send me in, skip,' he joked. Randall played well again, as did Boycott, though not at his best. I was pleased with my two innings. Queensland were a competent side, with Maclean, Dymock, Cosier and Carlson. Also playing were Ogilvie (who had been on the tour of the West Indies) and an aggressive left-arm bowler called Balcam. We won this match comfortably too, though we had various worries by the end of it. Boycott still lacked rhythm. And he was spending much of his time composing statements to the Yorkshire members, to the newspapers, to – it seemed – everyone. Gooch twice played himself in well, and then got out casually. Botham had had little batting; the middle order was fragile. Miller in particular looked all at sea; so much so that Willis said, 'How can he learn to bat on those slow wickets at Derby?'

Randall was worried; his wife's pigs weren't eating. As Botham said, loss of appetite is serious when it comes to pigs. We had a birthday cake for Botham and Barrington. Ken's present was an old ball with bits of string hanging from it, while 'Guy' was given a bunch of bananas: Boycott had given him the nickname 'Guy the Gorilla' on the previous tour, and it had stuck.

This lead-up to the first Test had been marked by a spate of head injuries. I could not remember so many in so few matches. It was not, however, that a high number of bouncers had been bowled. In the one-day match in North Queensland, against Bundaberg, an ex-State player called Scott Ledger had his head split open while trying to hook Lever. He had several stitches, then bravely, or perhaps rashly, returned. First ball he ducked into another short ball, this time from Hendrick, and was hit on the other side of the head. We speculated, unkindly, on the reception he would get at the casualty ward. . . . In the State game we were not sorry that Thomson was not playing. The groundsman moved the pitch the day before the game, and the new one was very grassy. There were another two nasty head injuries to Broad and Ogilvie. The whole spate of injuries precipitated the hasty purchase of helmets. In the two days after the State

match all the team, except for Boycott, Randall and three of the fast bowlers, decided to buy them. They arrived from Sydney in time for the Test. The injuries also, probably, contributed to Botham's macabre dreams, in which he was bowling at Ian Chappell. He would hit him on the head, and the head would slowly split open. Botham had not yet hit anyone during the tour; he seemed to relish his dream. He at least was ready for the Tests.

CHAPTER 3

Preparing for Battle

A TEST TEAM is usually chosen the day before the match. This gives the selectors a late chance to view the pitch and gives the players that much more time to recover from any injury. At Brisbane, however, we made our selection at lunchtime on Wednesday. The English Press had asked us to do this if it were at all possible because, given the 10-hour time difference between Australia and London, it would allow them a day to write their previews before they were into the match. As it was, we felt we knew where we stood on the selection. Also, once the team is settled you can organize the practice explicitly round those who will actually play.

Much of the selection had gone on before the Queensland match a week earlier in Brisbane. At that point we decided that Clive Radley would not play unless somebody was injured, since he had not faced any fast bowling since he was hit on the head by Hogg. Willis, Edmonds and Miller were in, and that left one bowling place to be filled by Old, Hendrick or Lever. If Hendrick gets a greenish wicket he is as good as anyone in the world, but he is mainly a one-pace seamer who moves it off the pitch rather than in the air. Lever is the most experimental of the three, able to swing the ball each way, bowl a good bouncer and vary his pace. But whereas he is especially good for the first three or four overs, when the ball is new, Hendrick and Old can bowl just as well when the ball is ten or twelve overs old. As for Old, he also has variety; he can seam the ball and swing it and, altogether, has more aggressive flair. We backed Old, reckoning that when bowling well he was the best attacking bowler of the three.

Still, a recurring doubt hung over Chris. He had been saying he was not fit, fussing about a strained back and looking as though he would not be at all sorry if we came up to him and said, 'Look, Chris, you're not fit and you shouldn't play.' In his history of Test matches, however, we could not think of one occasion when he had had to go off through injury, even though sometimes he was not totally fit when he started. He often has some injury just before a Test – after all his success, can he still fear failure? – but I do know that once he starts a match he sticks at it well. The difficulty is to get him to begin in the right frame of mind. So, at practice on the morning of the Test selection, I said, 'Look, Chilly, if we decide to select you you've got to play as though it's the only Test match you're going to play on the entire tour. And once you've started you're not coming off after three overs.' I reminded him of the Centenary Test in Melbourne in 1977 where he bowled magnificently for two hours with a strained groin. He looked relieved that we were taking this firm line. Ironically, it did turn out to be his only Test match appearance.

The four selectors met for lunch in the team room of the hotel. Bernard Thomas, who is always present throughout selection meetings, gave us advice on the fitness of the players, and once he said he could find nothing mechanically wrong with Old, that problem was solved. Chilly was in, and we could give him no further option in the matter. The rest of the team picked itself.

However, there was still the question of the batting order. Willis thought I should go in first, and gave two reasons. First, in his view, Gooch was not as good against the bounce of the new ball and could get caught in the slips fending one off. Second, he felt that Gooch was more likely than me to dominate the bowlers if he got in in the middle of the innings with the older ball.

My view, shared by Insole and Barrington, was that the best possible order, if it worked, was for Gooch to open with Boycott. Geoff is often a slow scorer whereas Gooch is liable to attack and get on top of the bowling; and since I was on form I might add some solidity between Randall and Gower. Moreover, Gooch had gone in first in two Test matches in England and had scored 91 not out and 55 against Richard Hadlee and not a bad New Zealand bowling side. I had also scored a few runs at Number 5.

Another part of my reasoning recalled something that Brian Close has said for a long time: it is hard to go in first and captain a Test side as well. After a hectic session in the field, or, indeed, after all the business of tossing up and deciding what you're going to do if you win the toss, it is helpful to be able to unwind for a while by going in at Number 4 or 5. The majority view prevailed, and the team for the First Test, in batting order, was: Boycott, Gooch, Randall, Brearley, Gower, Botham, Miller, Taylor, Edmonds, Old and Willis. Lever was twelfth man.

We had nearly forty-eight hours to think about the match and get settled from the time of the announcement. I do not think this is a bad thing, although it is an eternity compared to the days of D. R. Jardine. Later in the tour I met Harold Larwood who recounted what selection was like under Jardine's autocratic captaincy. 'When we visited Australia Jardine would have all seventeen members of the party changed into gear before the start of the match, both wicketkeepers with their pads on, opening batsmen with their pads on,' Larwood recalled. 'Then when Jardine would come back from tossing up, fifteen or twenty

Umpire O'Connell calling no-ball during the first Test, as Hogg bowls to Taylor. Notice the seam almost upright as the ball approaches the batsman. Hogg wears a toe-cap on his right boot. He leans forward after delivery, so much so that on occasions he would fall forward on to his knees. Randall was the non-striking batsman; despite his remarks at the team dinner, I do not think he began his redrawing of Hogg's line quite so early in the tour.

minutes before the start, he would hang the team list on a hook on the wall. Everyone craned their necks to see who was playing. Jardine was so cagey he wouldn't let the Australians have any early information at all.'

The next formal meeting prior to the Test match was the team dinner. This again took place in the hotel, on the Thursday night, the eve of the first Test match. These are important meetings where we discuss the opposition, player by player, our own tactics, the weather, the pitch, anything that seems relevant. I remember talking about specialist fielding positions. It is a good thing if the players who are to take up first and second slip stand next to each other regularly. They get used to each other's ways, know where to stand and what to go for. As Botham would be ·bowling a lot, I decided to have Gooch at second slip. Botham was silent, too shy perhaps to dispute the idea. Gooch had fielded well at first slip against New South Wales, when I was not playing. As it happened, he was to drop a couple of catches in this Test, and three days later Botham told me his feelings on the matter: that he himself should be at second slip, whoever else was there when he was bowling.

Another question was how to make best use of Phil Edmonds in the field. Edmonds is a fine close fielder, especially on the leg-side. Often, though, we did not have a short-leg when our quicker bowlers were on, or perhaps only for one of the batsmen, so the specialist short-leg found himself back by the square-leg umpire – in Edmonds's case, usually in conversation with him. Is this a waste of a good catcher? Or is it too fussy and disruptive to keep moving one of the slips to square leg and Edmonds from short-leg to fourth slip? We plumped for the fussier course. At this meeting I also tried to get the quick bowlers to tell me whether, in general, they preferred a mid-off or a third man when we decided to have one man less in the slip cordon. Old prefers a mid-off, so that he has the confidence to pitch the ball further up and try to swing it. Botham reckoned that if the ball was swinging he would like to leave mid-off open to induce the drive. He is always prepared to risk fours in search of a wicket.

There followed a rambling discussion of no-balls. The topic came up because, in the previous match against Queensland, the bowlers, particularly Willis and Old, bowled a great number – even though the

Chris Old in action (above). Notice the head looking down the pitch behind the high left arm. Old bowled superbly on the tour when fit, and sometimes, as in Tasmania, when he was not fully fit. No sunbather or beach-lover, Chris found it hard being away from his home and family for the fifth consecutive winter. (Opposite page) Gary Cosier's ungainly power is well illustrated in this cut over the slips. Yardley and he play this unorthodox shot to good effect, leaning back inside the bouncer and playing the ball to fine or square third-man.

umpires hadn't called them all. One of our fielders had stood at mid-on and watched Willis bowl four consecutive no-balls at the beginning of an over. None was called. This was not because the umpire had been unable to see them, but, more worryingly, because he seemed to think it better to ignore them. As we were going off the field the umpire

Toohey ón-drives. He has opened up well to hit the ball on the leg-side, but his right hand has taken over and has dragged the bat round, rather than allowing it to flow out in the direction of the ball. Toohey was to be out playing this way in both innings of the Melbourne Test. A congenial player, his nickname is 'Rats' after ratatouille.

concerned said, 'I had to let some of them go by or we would never have got on with the game at all.' Hogg, too, had bowled several no-balls in South Australia. Old pointed out that if a bowler is constantly worried about stepping over the line when he runs in he soon loses his rhythm. It was decided that in order to ensure that the umpires applied the law strictly the non-striking batsman should make an obvious show of watching the crease. Randall suggested we go even further. He wanted us to keep re-drawing the crease with the bat.

Another topic of conversation was whether as the non-striking batsman you should be firm about stopping the bowler when he is running in, if his fielders are moving around on the leg side. Someone said that keeping his mind on moving fielders was all well and good but, in doing so, he might disrupt his own concentration. I became tetchy. 'Look, I'm telling you,' I said, 'if somebody's moving round you stop the bowler because that's your job. That's what the striker doesn't know and that is the end of the discussion. This thing has been worth talking about but not for twenty minutes.'

We did finally discuss the Australian side for the match, though their inexperience meant that we knew relatively little about them. Here are the – necessarily sketchy – assessments that we made.

Graeme Wood, aged 22, left hand batsman and physical education teacher from Western Australia. Wood, an opener, was unknown to most of us. Gower had played the previous season in Western Australia, though, and had seen Wood in action. He felt Wood was a good player all round the wicket, especially off his legs. He could hook if you bowled short. We did not realise, although we learned it the next day, that the weakest part of his game was calling and running between the wickets.

Gary Cosier, 25, vice-captain, right hand batsman, right arm medium pace bowler and promotion officer for a Brisbane building firm; a Queenslander. Although he did not look like an opener, he seemed a better player than when we saw him in 1977, where he was clumsy against the spinners. We had just played against Queensland, and he had got 27 and 0. He was a powerful player, who punched the ball hard off both feet. He stood up to drive balls of a good length where many English batsmen would have crouched defensively. Though he is an ungainly batsman, his strength and unorthodoxy had earned our respect: we were not sorry when he was dropped after two Tests.

Peter Toohey, 24, right hand bat and qualified food technologist for a brewery; a New South Welshman. He sounded their most promising Test player and, indeed, we heard that the Australian Packer players considered him the best Australian batsman outside their own ranks. He had been successful against India in Australia a year earlier, playing in all five Tests for an average of 40.90 runs, and in the West Indies had a Test average of 59.30. I had not played in the State match against New South Wales, but Willis, Hendrick and Botham had, and they reckoned he was vulnerable just outside the off stump. Willis had bowled to him with a seven-two offside field, a man at deep point, five slips and a cover, a field he rarely uses; but they got Toohey out outside the off stump in each innings. In many ways he reminded us of Doug Walters. Like him, he is a good cutter and a good hooker, but he hardly moves his feet at all; again like Walters, he would be vulnerable to the out-swinger.

Graham Yallop, 26, captain, left hand bat, in family iron-casting firm and a string of Melbourne sport shops; a Victorian. Yallop had batted for a short while on a slow wicket in the match against Victoria in Melbourne. He was reputed to be a good player of spinners, which was later confirmed. We judged that bowling at his off-stump and just outside and across him could be the way to get him out. He tended to play too square on, and would push the ball out towards cover with the bottom hand.

Kim Hughes, 24, right hand bat, publicity officer for a building society in Western Australia. We saw a little of him in England in 1977 and, as Willis pointed out, he was a nervous starter and liked to get off the mark as quickly as possible. We therefore decided we should be very much on our toes to stop a first run. I remembered how Underwood had flummoxed him in the fifth Test in 1977, when Hughes batted 50 minutes for one run. He had pushed forward to almost every ball, moving too early and therefore often getting his left leg too close to the line of the ball; the result was that he tended to pop the ball up off pad and bat. However, that was his first Test innings, and I for one knew well the shaky knees of that particular ordeal. We found out an interesting quirk of Hughes's later in the series: he often did something particularly

stupid first ball of a session, or of an over or of a new spell. Also, he tries to get well forward, towards the off-side, and when you're lunging forward as he does it is hard to read the line and to let the difficult ball go. We decided to pitch the ball well up to him, on the off-side, and occasionally well wide, in the hope that he would chase after it.

Trevor Laughlin, 27, left hand bat, right arm medium pace bowler, promotion officer for an insurance firm; a Victorian. What we learnt about him and the means by which we learnt it illustrate how much help we got throughout the tour from English players in Australia but not in the England party. The Leicestershire fast bowler Jonathan Agnew, who had played grade cricket against Laughlin in Melbourne, suggested he was weak if you bowled to his hip, short of a length but not bouncer length. We used this information at Melbourne, where it had limited application because the pitch was so slow. But we saw enough to note that Laughlin did at first fend the ball off his hip firmly and uppishly towards short square leg, where Edmonds would have caught him if he had been a little deeper. After a couple of early escapes, Laughlin adopted a different method, hooking hard but high. Next day, he went for the hook early on, with fatal results.

John Maclean, 32, right hand bat, wicketkeeper, graduated civil engineer from Queensland. Here we made a mistake. In the Queensland State match Maclean scored much of his second innings 94 by sweeping the spinners or by whacking them to long-on or mid-wicket. I was therefore reluctant to employ the spinners against him. We remarked, too, that rather than coming straight down on to a ball of full length, he came round it, with the bottom of his bat away from his body. We thought a yorker on middle or leg stump might get through his defence. As it happened, we never dismissed him in this way.

Bruce Yardley, 31, right hand bat, right arm off-spin bowler and cricket ground curator (groundsman) in Western Australia. Although he had been around for a long time we knew little about Yardley. Gower had seen him in Western Australia, and while we knew he played a few shots outside the off stump we had to wait to find out more about him in the match. We knew that he had performed well as an all-rounder in the West Indies, and that he pushed his off-breaks through quickly.

The tail – 'Ogg, 'Urst 'n 'Iggs, as John Emburey, then all of us, called them – was clearly vulnerable. Hogg had some ability with the bat, but we had mainly bowled spin at him in Adelaide, because of the pitch; we thought the quicker bowlers would get him out. Botham and Emburey knew Hurst and Higgs well from their stay a year before in Melbourne: Ian thought three balls would suffice for Hurst and two for Higgs – and hoped to be bowling at the time! Higgs had, in fact, reached his 150th first-class run in the same match as he reached his 150th first-class wicket; then his batting fell off so much that he only scored 33 runs on his way to his 200 wickets. Jeff Thomson, captain of the side against Jamaica, promoted him to No. 10 for that match in the hope that a miracle might enable him to score the 17 needed to keep up his all-round level; but Higgs's arrival at the crease coincided with Michael Holding's taking the second new ball, and he was out second ball. During our series Jim worked so hard at his batting that we feared him more than we ever did that other notorious record-holding non-batsman, Chandra-sekhar.

We then looked at the same three in their role as attacking bowlers:

Rodney Hogg, 27, right hand bat, right arm fast bowler, insurance representative from Victoria who was now playing for South Australia. Considering the fact that Hogg took 41 wickets in the series, we misjudged him at this point. We were unsure how long he could keep going, especially as he had difficulty with his breathing and suffered from asthma. We thought that if we could see him off for a while his head might go down.

Alan Hurst, 28, right hand bat and right hand fast bowler, a physical education co-ordinator for a group of Victorian primary schools. It was our opinion that Hurst, like Hogg, could get dejected if things didn't go well and, in fact, at times in the past he had bowled so badly he couldn't get the ball anywhere near the stumps. His sling-like action was such that if his timing were not right the ball might be dragged down the off-side or way down the leg side. If he did get it right, his action enabled him, as it did Les Jackson, to swing the ball away and sometimes make it come back sharply off the pitch.

Jim Higgs, 28, right hand batsman, right arm leg-spinner, civil engineer for a city council in Greater Melbourne; a Victorian. Higgs is a big spinner of the ball who was fairly accurate for a leg-break bowler but who only occasionally bowled a googly. I made the point that at Melbourne on a slow pitch he had made the ball bounce sharply at times. I said this mainly to Boycott as he had not played at Melbourne; he replied, rather spikily, that as an opener if he stayed until Higgs came on most of his problems would have been solved anyway.

Phil Carlson, 27, right hand batsman and right arm medium pace bowler; in family farming goods market in Queensland. We speculated (correctly) that he would be twelfth man. He looked a useful bowler, with a good bouncer, and he could swing the ball either way. He could be surprising, we thought, and we shouldn't underestimate him because nearly all of us had had trouble with him in the Queensland match. As far as his batting was concerned, he could perhaps be bounced out. We should avoid pitching balls up to him as he was a good driver.

We got to the end of the meeting with some relief. Before we broke up Boycott made a suggestion. He felt that the meeting had not only gone on too long but ended too late. At least in his case, he wanted to get his kit sorted out and to go to bed early. In future we ought to have our pre-Test meetings at about 6.30, so that any tension that might arise between players, or excitement about the Test match to come would wear off, and we would then have time for a leisurely meal together. It was a good idea. We adopted the practice throughout the remainder of the tour.

The meeting finally broke up about 10 o'clock. I was depressed. I was fed up with players making niggling points and putting each other down. I walked with Doug Insole through the hotel lobby and down the stairs and out into the street for a stroll round the block. We bumped into Jeff Thomson, a local Queensland boy, who was having enough of his own troubles in cricket. I asked him how things were going and where he had been. 'I've just been to a meeting of sports fishermen at the hotel,' he said, 'and I fell fast asleep.' At that point I might willingly have changed places.

CHAPTER 4

Brisbane: First Test. Willis hobbles through

PARACHUTES WERE TO drop into the grounds before four of the Test matches, colourful stunts in reply to the spectacular gimmickry that had been organized for the Packer matches. At the Woollongabba one parachutist carried a Union Jack, another the Australian flag, and a third bore a special coin provided by the Governor of Queensland. Of greater cricketing interest was the fact that they came down out of a cloudy sky. Cloud-cover, especially over the grassy and slightly damp pitch, would obviously help the fielding side, but the weather forecast – copies of which the Queensland secretary was considerate enough to drop in to the captains before play each day – predicted that the sun would soon break through. We were also well aware that six days was a long time; the cracks already visible on the pitch might widen enough to encourage spinners by the last day.

Yallop spun the coin in front of a battery of photographers, another echo from Packer. Willis had said, commenting on my bad record at winning tosses, 'Why don't you call tails for a change?' So I did – and the coin came down 'heads'. Yallop chose to bat. I did not mind losing the toss; two hours later I was delighted to have done so. In conditions that might favour seam bowlers early on, a captain is not sorry to have the decision whether to bat or field taken out of his hands. Either way it is a gamble. Oddly, he is more likely, if things go wrong, to be criticized for putting in the opposition than for electing to bat. I have never understood this attitude. At Brisbane in 1954 Len Hutton put Australia in; they scored 601 for 8 declared, a thunderstorm made the pitch unplayable, and England lost by an innings and 154 runs. Ever

since, that match has been quoted as a cautionary tale for English captains in Australia. Decisions to bat first, on the other hand, though they may have catastrophic consequences, are rarely held against one. Yet one hazard of putting in the opposition is now removed: pitches are covered overnight and against rain, so the Australian 'sticky dog' is a thing of the past.

The toss over, other decisions had to be made. Who should open the bowling? Willis and I had discussed this at length. He would obviously open downwind. A case could be made for either Botham or Old partnering him. Overseas, the ball often swings for only three or four overs; if so, Botham should bowl. However, he is such an attacking bowler, so prepared to chance being hooked or driven, that he and Willis (who is similarly attacking) can be expensive. If batsmen get away to a flying start you can be forced to operate semi-defensively at a time when you want to attack, in order to get the game back on your terms. I decided to open with Old, since I thought the ball would move off the seam.

We had a fairytale beginning. Wood – who, like Boycott, scores many singles – played Willis's first ball down on the off-side, and called for a quick run, though the ball went to Edmonds' left hand. Cosier responded and Edmonds, whom I had put in the gully, ran across, picked up the ball and threw it at the stumps. Had he hit them, Cosier would have been out. On the fifth ball, after each player had scored a run, Wood made the same blatant error. He pushed the ball slightly square of cover, and called for a run. Gower, who is quick and accurate, ran in and threw the wicket down underarm.

In box: Gower, fielding at cover to the left, has just broken the stumps to run Cosier out in the first over of the first Test. Taylor, umpire French and Willis look on.

Left: Randall's flamboyant effort narrowly failed to run Yallop out on the third afternoon. He had darted in from mid-off when Yallop called for a short single, and rather than aim at a single stump had flung himself at the wicket.

Gower and Randall fielded brilliantly; yet their fielding, like their batting, was totally different in style. Gower is economical of movement, but when the chance comes he strikes with deceptive speed. His presence on the field is scarcely noticed until the moment comes when he runs someone out. Conversely, Randall is always noticed, shouting 'Come on, England,' making slightly derogatory remarks just out of the batsmen's earshot, and teasing them into a run. If they are in two minds, he will sometimes let the ball lie and stroll past it waiting to pounce. Randall is a loud cat on a hot roof in this cat-and-mouse game, while Gower is quiet – and a very cool cat, too. Later, and for some situations, I learned to use them differently. When an off-spinner bowled at Wood, for example, I wanted one of my best fielders at deep square-leg for the sweep and another at mid-wicket to stop the drives and to cut off the short single. I went for Randall in the deep, as he is electrically quick and a fine catcher, and Gower close in, for his steadiness and the accuracy of his short-range throwing.

Cosier was just out. At the time we were unsure whether the throw had beaten him, but it proved to have been a good decision; the photographs show that when Cosier's bat was just over the line the bails were well clear of the stumps.

In his next over Willis bowled two beautiful balls at Toohey which came back and over the stumps. The batsman let them go, but not without misgivings. The next ball was further up. Toohey shaped to drive, missed and was bowled middle and off. Australia were five for two wickets. Wood went next, caught behind off Old: 14 for three. We were in a commanding position. But things were not quite perfect. The conditions were ideal for Old – his first spell of six overs cost him just seven runs – yet he was not bowling as aggressively as he could, nor as he had bowled at me recently in the nets. He was still worried about no-balls. In fact, he bowled a couple before he left the field at 12.15 after again damaging the finger he had dislocated in the match at Adelaide.

Old's injury meant that I had to change my bowling plans. I had intended to bring Botham on for Willis, but instead he now came on for Old. Botham had not yet bowled much on the tour because of his cut wrist. Into the wind, the ball began to swing prodigiously for him. Bill O'Reilly, the former Australian Test bowler, said he had never seen the ball swing so much in Australia. Botham trapped Hughes with an outswinger in his first over, and soon after Willis took the wickets of both Yallop and Laughlin. Thirty-five minutes before lunch Australia were 26 for six, and it looked as though we might get them out for 30. The Press, who are keen on such things, started thumbing through the record books. In Sydney in 1887–88 Australia were all out for 42 and in Birmingham in 1902 they scored only 36 in an innings.

Willis was tired, but his tail was up, and he protested when I took him off and bowled Gooch for an over before lunch. My reasoning was that Willis needed as much rest as possible because he would have to bowl again immediately after lunch.

I could not bowl Old then as there is a recent law which states that if a player is off the field for more than 15 minutes he may not bowl on his return for the same amount of time as he has been absent. So I needed Bob to carry on for at least another forty-five minutes.

It was not until just before tea that we finally dismissed Australia, for 116. Conditions had gradually eased – though the clouds continued until tea – and our bowlers had tired. Botham swung the ball so much that he found it hard to control his direction. Yardley, Maclean and Hogg fought tenaciously in their different ways. Hogg was the most frustrating. When we pitched the ball up he drove hard and sometimes high. The shorter deliveries he stepped back from and cut. Our frustration was sharpened when, after Hogg had received just one bouncer, from Willis, Umpire French told the bowler that he was not to bowl bouncers at a non-recognized batsman. At that point I had the first of my many on-the-field discussions with the umpires. I argued that the question of recognition was the responsibility of

the fielding captain, not the umpires; he could recognize any batsman in the opposing team if he thought it right. Besides, Hogg had already scored 26, evidence enough that he was a competent player. He himself had plainly not expected exemption, as he had come out in a protective helmet. I told French that Yallop and I had agreed before the match that in this game numbers 9 and 10 (Old, Edmonds; Hogg and Hurst) were to be allowed some leeway, but were not exempt from bouncers if they stayed in for a while; and that Willis and Higgs were to be wholly non-recognized. French appeared to be satisfied, and the issue was dropped.

It continued to be a hot potato for several more Tests. Much of the furore stemmed from the incident in June 1978, when Bob Willis hit the Pakistani nightwatchman Iqbal Qasim in the face. The respective responsibilities of captains and umpires were then clearly spelled out, and in all Tests that I have played in since I have sought some lines of agreement with the opposing captain. One principle has found general acceptance; that anyone sent in as nightwatchman to protect front-line batsmen must expect to be treated as a fully-fledged batsman.

Willis in particular, Old and Botham had done a fine job for us. We now needed as large a lead as possible. Gooch was soon out, adjudged to have hit a ball that flew via his pads to gully. We came off for bad light, but soon returned. At once, in rather murky light, Boycott was caught in the slips off Hogg – the third time Hogg had had him in three innings. It was now 5.30, and we were 38 for 2. The custom is to send in nightwatchmen when there are 20 minutes or less left before the close, but on this occasion I sent Taylor in, confident that bad light would soon persuade the umpires to come off again. Decisions about bad light are among the hardest for umpires, and the hardest for spectators to understand. The Queensland Government has not helped by ignoring the Daylight Saving Time adopted by the other East Coast States, so that in Brisbane daylight arrives triumphantly at 5 a.m. I had had my curtains changed, with little effect.

The second morning was ideal for bowling, especially after a shower had interrupted play. The sun lifted steam off the damp outfield, and the seam bowlers made the ball move considerably. Randall and Taylor battled through until after lunch, Randall looking well set. One topic of our team dinner arose during their stand; as Hurst moved in to bowl to Randall, Wood moved back at square-leg, and Taylor promptly drew the umpires' attention to the fact. Yallop was told firmly that this was unfair, and the ploy was not used again. The Australians, wisely, now cut out the bouncers to Randall after he had hooked several for four, and instead tried to tie him down. This method succeeded: he was brilliantly caught in the gully driving Hurst, out for 75. Randall normally excels at manipulating crowds, but this time a long spell of slow handclapping seemed to upset him.

I was out cheaply to a good piece of bowling by Hogg. The ball was about fifty overs old, yet Hogg made it lift from just short of a length to brush my gloves, and I was caught by Maclean down the leg-side. It was a ball that would not have taken me by surprise if I had been opening the innings. Taylor went without addition to the score, so that three wickets had fallen for nine runs, leaving us at 120-5, with our youngest players, Botham and Gower, yet to get off the mark. These two, however, proceeded to share in a sixth-wicket partnership of 95, the highest and easily the most exciting stand of the innings. Botham's 49 was peppered with good luck – he often played and missed, and was also dropped – but he hit some magnificently savage shots. One pull, in particular, off a bouncer from Hogg with the second new ball, went first bounce for four over wide long-on. As for Gower, after his recent batting failures he went in, one would assume, under tremendous pressure, but he never lost that look of nonchalance, and his 44 revealed his coolness and aplomb. He was beginning to look settled when he followed a wide ball from Hurst. After the last two wickets added 60 important runs we were all out for 286, giving us a first innings lead of 170. Both Hogg and Hurst had stuck well at their job, and shared all ten wickets, although Hogg was a little lucky to get myself, Botham and Edmonds caught at the wicket on the leg-side, when most of his fielders were on the off-side.

Our innings had been a patchy, workmanlike affair, yet it put us in a position of strength from which we ought to win the match. When the Australians came in again, shortly before lunch on the third day, we got away to an even better start than in the first innings, Willis bowling Cosier first

ball with an inswinger that went through the gap between bat and pad. Next over Botham had Toohey LBW so that Australia were two for two wickets. Botham shared the new ball this innings, as we had runs to play with and the grass was now less lush. However, he was not swinging the ball – the delivery that dismissed Toohey was dead straight – so I quickly replaced him with Old, saving Botham to replace Willis downwind, since Botham is a versatile bowler who can either gain maximum movement by cutting down his pace or go all out for speed.

At 49, with Australia still 121 behind, Old dismissed Wood. One more wicket, and we would be past the specialist batsmen. Willis roused himself for a tremendous effort at Yallop and Hughes. I had watched him at lunch in the dressing-room, writhing his way out of his boots, and painfully peeling off the bloody socks. Blood was coming out through the big toe-nail of his right foot; but worse was the deep blister at the base of the fourth toe on his left foot. He sat – as he did each interval while we were fielding – in his string vest and trousers, staring ahead. He ate a few ice-creams and drank tea. His seat was surrounded by a mounting litter of boots, old and new. He had discovered that his feet were of different lengths, and that the shorter one was also wider. A Melbourne cobbler named Hope Sweeney had spent hours with him during the Victoria match measuring his feet and trying out different boots. The problem had started with the retirement of a Northampton shoe-maker a year before. This shoe-maker, Albert Whiting, had made boots for generations of cricketers at his workshop behind the county ground, and Willis had gone through three previous tours of Australia in Whiting's boots without serious problems. Now he was wearing boots that had not been specially made to measure, and he was in constant pain.

The lunch break passed quickly; Bernard Thomas had powdered and patched Willis's feet as well as possible. I saw Bob staring ahead, muttering to himself the words, 'Come on, really come on, you can do it.' That afternoon he bowled as well for five overs as I have ever seen him. He might have had Yallop out ten times. We put Edmonds at silly point, right under Yallop's nose. Edmonds stared at Yallop; Yallop avoided his eyes. He popped one up just out of Phil's reach. He edged one, also from Willis, to me and I caught it at face height: no-ball.

Next ball we thought we had him caught behind, hooking: not out. Yallop rode his luck courageously and well. He played two or three good pulls and some straight drives. He twice square cut Botham for four.

At the other end Hughes played even better, the best Australian innings of the series. He got under way with two hooks for four and one for six, all well struck but in the air and close to Boycott at long-leg. When we put another fielder back and tempted him with more bouncers, he resisted the bait, ducking out of the way. He played correctly and with control. To everyone but Willis he concentrated on getting well forward and if anything outside the line of the ball, accumulating many runs off the seamers by letting the ball run out towards mid-wicket, or down to fine leg. He made remarkably few mistakes.

Throughout this long innings the breeze was coming from mid-off or long-leg. Such a breeze helped Miller more than Edmonds, since he naturally drifts the ball away from the right-handers. He bowled beautifully, giving nothing away, while Edmonds bowled the occasional loose ball. Miller several times deceived Yallop in the air, almost having him caught and bowled, or caught at short extra-cover, driving. Hughes looked increasingly sound against all our bowlers, and the third day closed with Australia 157-3, only 13 runs behind. They had fought back magnificently.

Hughes sweeps Miller, on his way to his century. Kim Hughes played a magnificent innings. He was generally content to play Miller defensively, but here he sweeps what must have been, judging by the position of Taylor's hands, a dangerously straight delivery. Miller was using the wind well at Brisbane, setting the ball off just outside the leg-stump and making it float back on to the line of middle-stump. English off-spinners have in the past grown desperate in Australia when this type of delivery has hit the front pad and been given not out. English umpires used to be more willing to give the batsman out on these occasions. We found that this Australian side swept less than most, so the umpires were not often asked for their decision. Apart from the chance of an LBW, we also thought that if he swept we might get Hughes out caught, either just forward of the square-leg umpire, or at deep square-leg.

We were ready for the rest-day. After play, several players got rid of their tension at a barbecue given by the Queensland Cricket Association. Randall, Miller, Tolchard, and Cosier all sang at the microphone. A few drinks were drunk; indeed, 'Both' walked into a lamp-post outside the town-hall on his way back to our hotel. He escaped without injury, but he said he was going back after breakfast to see how the lamp post was.

It was shortly before this mishap that I had been talking with Botham, and it was now that he told me that he was upset at what he thought was his demotion from second slip. He maintained that the ball goes more often to second slip than to any other slip-position; and that he had had a good record there for England. I agreed with him: I also felt more confident standing next to him, so I decided to tell Graham Gooch that I was going to move him away from second slip for the time being. The Australians had rotated their slips more than once already: throughout the series, we were to find that they made constant changes in these specialist positions.

Richie Benaud, when captain of Australia, used to invite the press into their dressing-room at close of play. I have always felt that the dressing-room is a private place, where players can let off steam about outsiders (including umpires and journalists) to their hearts' content. Besides, I need more privacy myself. So I arranged with the press that I would make myself available the day before each Test – when we announced the team – on the morning of the rest day, and immediately after the end of the match. This arrangement worked well. At 9.30 I went to the team-room in the hotel to meet them. There were usually 10 or 12 journalists there, and we would often have enjoyable and even jokey meetings. I now started by saying that I did not have much to offer. One Australian journalist said, 'Why not give us a ballad?' I happened to have read recently a couplet that reminded me of David Brown and the 1976 season in which Warwickshire put Middlesex in to bat four times, and lost all four games, and David was batting at the death each time. The rhyme went as follows:

'The captain's name was Mister Brown
He played his ukelele while the ship went down.'

I did not, I went on, think our ship would go down: but the odds were only a little in our favour.

The turning-point of the Test: Yallop c and b Willis for 102. Willis broke the fine stand of 170 between Yallop and Hughes with this low one-handed catch. The faces speak for themselves. Yallop is wearing one of the new-style helmets that many of us wore in this Test. Botham, back at second slip after our rest-day conversation, and I are wearing typical fielding headgear.

The press tried to get me to comment on the umpires, but I was resolute that I would not do that, either to praise or to blame them. Within the side, though, we did talk about appealing and the effect on the umpires.

Our appeals had sometimes sounded half-hearted. For instance, when Yallop may have touched that early hook off Willis, the uncertainty of some close fielders was reflected in the appeal. The conversation round the bat went: 'Did he hit that? I wasn't sure. I'm sure he gloved it. Could have been anything.' We remembered the Test against Pakistan at Lord's six months before, when Haroon Rashid, beaten by an outswinger from Botham, hit the ground as the ball went by the outside edge; the 'click' could have been either bat on ground or bat on ball. Several of the slips stifled their appeal because they were not certain he had hit the ball. I thought David Constant, one of the game's best umpires, was about to give Haroon out but he did not; one factor leading him to think again may have been the ambivalence of our appeal. The Australians have always appealed with total conviction, whatever their personal views.

Now, we said to each other, we must not give such cues to the umpires since we would probably lose by them. However, we never were able to give up entirely the habits of county cricket, a game played, I suspect, with less fanaticism than Australian State games.

On the rest day our players did as they pleased (except that I had forbidden a proposed deep-sea fishing trip. Wrestling with a 200lb marlin, possibly in a choppy sea and a temperature of 100 degrees, would not have been ideal preparation for cricket). The Australians seemed more inclined to go on trips en bloc on the rest days, and the local press were surprised that we had nothing planned as a group.

One person who did have a plan was Boycott, who had arranged privately for a net session. As it was, there was heavy rain. Some of the team went to *Jaws Two* (some kind of second best to deep-sea fishing) while Boycott, Willis, Emburey and I went to the preview of *The Return of the Pink Panther*, where Doug Insole's nickname 'The Chief Inspector' was conceived. The Manager has a penchant for the movies, and especially for Peter Sellers's French accent.

The trouble with rest-days is that you need a day to wind down; then by the time you have properly relaxed and are ready for a rest they are over. On the morning of the fourth day the dressing-room atmosphere lacked the edge of the earlier days. I made the exercising compulsory (especially as the nets were too wet), and asked Thomas if he would liven people up with a longer session than usual. He had us dashing about, to key us up mentally and physically, rather than only have us do the usual set of exercises. We also had a concentrated session of slip practice directed by Barrington; and Botham came back to second slip.

The day's play was utterly absorbing. The match reminded me of the third Test against Australia at Trent Bridge in July 1977; there Australia started the fourth day eight runs behind with eight wickets in hand. In both games the pitch was at its easiest, the weather fine, the struggle tense. In both, too, we finally dismissed the opposition after tea, and faced a moderate, though not easy target. In each, the slowly developing contest, with runs and wickets equally crucial, typified the unique fascination of Test cricket.

Hughes and Yallop played through to the new ball with little trouble. Willis, looking increasingly like a brave but wounded camel, was still the likeliest to break through, but it was not until his last over that his – and our – luck changed. Yallop played a reasonable straight drive; Willis, following

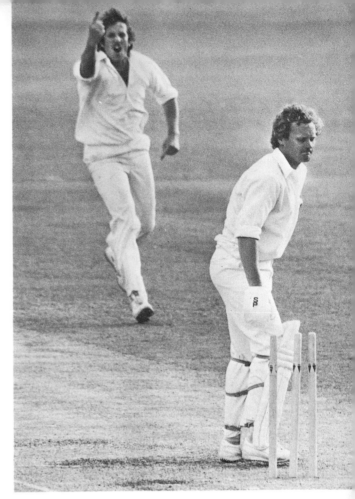

Botham bowls Hogg for 16. Botham's gesture reflects partly his enjoyment at winning another round in his personal duel with Hogg, and partly his reply to the goading by Willis from mid-off. On at least one other occasion anger spurred Botham to take a wicket: when Umpire Bailhache instructed me to tell Botham not to bowl any more bouncers in an over against Dymock in the first innings of the fourth Test. He proceeded to bowl yards faster, and within two balls had burst through Dymock's defence.

through, bent, instinctively stuck out a right hand, and caught a fine catch. Yallop was out for 102. On such threads of skill and luck Test matches, even series, hang.

Now one end was at last open. Laughlin did not last long. Maclean was again stubborn, but we could see better now how, in the pressure of a Test Match, with four fielders round the bat, he looked clumsy and vulnerable to off-spin. He lasted an hour or more, but then was LBW trying to sweep a ball that was too far up for the shot. Yardley played well; I caught him low to my left off Miller for 16. Some people thought the ball had not carried, but I was completely confident it went straight into my hand, as was O'Connell at square leg. French, whose decision it was, had his impression confirmed when he glanced at his colleague: throughout the tour they collaborated well. Hogg now came in at 261-6, and proceeded to apply himself. By now the ball was soft, the pitch dead, the bowlers tired. Willis was at mid-off when Botham bowled at Hogg. He decided to use stronger medicine. 'Call that quick?' he taunted Ian as he walked back to his mark. 'You're slow-medium. How can you let *Quentin* pull you?' It worked. Botham, angry, came in with venom, and took two wickets that same over. Finally, Hughes, who had played admirably, fell for 129 trying to score a few extra runs with Higgs at the crease. It had been an innings of immense maturity and promise for Australia.

Just 170 were required for victory. Boycott and Gooch survived until close of play, when we were 16-0. The pitch was now taking a little spin. The bounce had in general become lower, with the occasional ball keeping very low if it landed on one of the cracks. We talked before play began, as indeed we were to talk again later in the series, of the need to play forward against the quick bowlers, to lessen the possibility of being LBW or bowled.

Australian umpires are reluctant to give batsmen out LBW if they are hit on the front leg. Boycott, Gooch and I all tended to play back too much.

It was not through lack of bounce, however, that on the morning of the fourth day Hogg struck. Immediately he surprised Gooch with steep lift, and had him caught at slip. Randall and Boycott played steadily, until Randall called Boycott for a short single to mid-off. Toohey quickly threw down the stumps to run Boycott out. The score was 37-2. Almost immediately Randall was lucky to escape two LBW appeals off consecutive balls from Hurst.

Our feeling was that Australia's main chance of victory lay with the spinners, though Hogg and Hurst could always be dangerous. Yallop's tactics were odd. Hogg, whose natural role is as a strike bowler, performing for short spells with the wind behind him, was now mis-handled. Yardley bowled, initially, with no mid-wicket and with four or five men on the off side when his off-breaks turned sharply. And Higgs when he at last came on, with less than 100 runs needed, bowled with only one fielder in a close catching position.

I was well caught off the bottom edge by Maclean as I tried to cut a ball from Yardley that did not rise more than a foot off the ground. When Gower joined Randall with the score 74-3 we could have struggled. However, they soon played as if they had no cares, easily and fluently, and we had no fears comparable to those of the later stages of the Nottingham Test, when tropical storms over Sleaford were rumoured to be approaching. By mid-afternoon of a warm, breezy day we were home. We had won the first Test by 7 wickets.

Botham and Lever pour champagne over the Man of the Match while Miller, Hendrick, Boycott and Tolchard look on. After the six days' ordeal both sides would drink champagne or beer in the winners' dressing-room.

CHAPTER 5

The 120 Per Cent Man

A tour party in years past included a bagman, to keep an eye on the luggage, and occasionally a trainer to rub the odd sore muscle. Cricket, however, is now in the age of sports medicine, and Dudley Doust spoke with Bernard Thomas, the lively, much qualified physiotherapist who has become such a valuable member of English parties overseas.

IN THE OLD days, when touring sides travelled to Australia by boat, they usually wrote ahead and put any problems of a medical nature in the hands of their hosts. 'At each ground we were provided with a fellow to look after us. If he was unqualified, he was a "rubber", and if he was qualified, he was "masseur",' recalls Bill Bowes, who travelled to Australia once in the 1930s. 'Jardine, though, always insisted on a chiropodist. He was interested in our feet.' It wasn't until Hutton's 1954/5 tour of Australia that a chartered physiotherapist regularly went along with the team, and, in all those years, no man has served longer in this capacity than Bernard Thomas, M.C.S.P., M.S.R.G.

Thomas has not missed an official England tour since he joined the side for Cowdrey's tour of Pakistan in 1969. It was on that tour that he earned the nickname, 'Bolt'. As the story is told, a bus carrying the team passed under a low, up-country bridge with a terrible scrunch. The luggage had been hit. Thomas, a former international gymnast, squirmed through a tiny window, hung precariously above the road, and tied the luggage back in place. Since then he has been called 'Bolt', in vague reference to 'Bernie the Bolt', a selfless little Midlands television character of the day.

At 53, Bolt can still walk on his hands, or swing round the rings of the gymnasium in the prosperous clinic in Birmingham. On tour, he looks as fit as anyone in the party, and in the honourable tradition of the sergeant major will rarely ask a player to do calisthenics he will not do himself. Thomas received his training in an Army physical training course at Aldershot and later at the Wolverhampton Royal Hospital School of Physiotherapy. Since 1964 he has looked after the Warwickshire cricketers, a happy relationship which contributed to his decision to turn down an offer to join Kerry Packer's World Series Cricket at its outset. 'I'd become deeply involved in Warwickshire and England cricket,' he said. 'And morally I thought I'd have to withdraw from it if I went with Packer.'

On tour, Thomas carries comprehensive kit. Into two cases he packs exercise weights, a first-aid bag that includes inflatable splints and a resuscitator, a wide range of cotton, bandages, liniments, sun creams, sun glasses, pills, and three pieces of electro-medical equipment. The workings of these machines are specially compelling to a visitor to the dressing-room. Take the Bio feedback machine. It is a small device, which measures the blood supply to a player's skin, and, in turn, his tension. 'Players show their tensions in different ways. They go to the toilet, talk non-stop or sit quietly in a corner,' said Thomas. 'But if they are over-tense they are tight when they go into bat.' On the tour he used the Bio feedback machine a half-dozen times to help ease this tension in players. The machine does no more than *measure* tension, but, with its electrodes clasped in his hand, the player can watch a needle fall on a gauge, hear a softening bleep as he is encouraged to relax his shoulders and breathe

Hendrick stretching a ham-string on Thomas's convenient shoulder. Constant exercise has made Mike more reliable and consistent.

slowly and deeply. 'We don't only use the machine in field situations,' Thomas added. 'We sometimes use it to help a bloke sleep at night.'

The second machine is called a 'nerve impulse stimulator'. It was used, for example, on Taylor at Perth. In the second Test he suffered from a torn rotator muscle in the crutch, a 'strained groin' probably caused by awkwardly dragging his right leg as he moved to his left to catch a ball. With the nerve impulse stimulator, Thomas gave him 'pain-block' treatment, reducing his pain by implanting two needle electrodes of the machine about half an inch into the groin area for about ten minutes. 'The treatment was successful in that it broke down the pain,' said Thomas. 'But, as one knew, it couldn't help absorb the bleeding in the area. For that we had to turn to ultrasonics.'

Which takes us to the third, ultrasonic machine. Its high-speed vibrations hasten healing by improving blood circulation and breaking down scar tissues in the damaged area. Taylor needed it in this instance, but, more often, it is used on the bowlers. They frequently suffer from chronic shoulder injuries, mild inflammations of the tiny tendons of the shoulder joint which are caused by the rotation of the arm during bowling. Medically, the complaint is called a 'tear in the rotator cuff'; but among sportsmen it is known widely as 'throwing your arm out'. Apart from bruises and blisters and finger damage, a thrown arm is the most common injury among cricketers. Fieldsmen suffer from it, but mostly it bothers bowlers. 'It is odd,' Thomas explained. 'It rarely prevents a bowler from bowling, yet it often prevents him – as well as regular fielders – from properly throwing in from the outfield. You see lots of old pros lobbing the ball in underarm. The cricket fraternity is alert to this because a batsman, if he is on his toes, can often take a second run to a bad-shouldered fielder.' A converse to this, of course, is that a fit fielder can sometimes lure a batsman into a run-out by first feigning a bad shoulder with a few feeble throw-ins from the deep.

Another complaint on the tour, felt chiefly during the fourth Test at Sydney, was the blazing heat. Thomas, for a start, issued the players with barrier cream and four other grades of sun oil. 'If a player on sun oil Number 2 is over-exposed and gets a reaction one day,' he said, 'we'll put him on Number 5 the next day.' The oil naturally is spread on the face, neck and wrists but, Thomas pointed out, not on every tour. 'When there is a lot of reflected heat off a sandy, white wicket, as in Hyderabad, you advise a player to put cream under his chin, ears and especially his nose.'

Thomas issues an abundance of sports tablets, but he rarely gives them without dextrose or glucose as well. 'A Salt tablet in isolation can cause slight burning and discomfort in the stomach,' he said. Thomas also made handkerchiefs from cotton slings soaked in iced water and often sent in a player with one round his neck to keep cool. Sometimes, as when the temperature touched 105 in the shade during that Sydney match, even salt, glucose and enormous drinks of water were insufficient. Such was the case when Hendrick came off, exhausted and dehydrated. He was stretched on a treatment table. A doctor was summoned. Hendrick was found to be not seriously ill, and, much needed on the field because Willis also was off ill, he went into a shower where he stayed for twenty minutes. 'We kept him under luke-warm water,' Thomas explained. 'It would have been medically wrong, and inefficient, to use cold water. Cold water would have brought his blood to the skin, so to speak, and in that circumstance we couldn't afford to take his blood from his muscles which were in a state of dehydration.' Hendrick returned to the match, and in a very short time was able to take the new ball.

In past years a common injury that dogged bowlers, chiefly the fast bowler, was stress fractures of the metatarsal bones caused by constant pounding of the front foot, a complaint also known as a 'march fracture'. Thomas had not yet, nor was he to treat such a fracture on the entire tour. 'I saw lots of metatarsal stress fractures a few seasons ago,' said Thomas, 'which were brought on by the use of new, light-weight boots. Now we've gone back to sturdier and better anatomically-supported boots for our bowlers.'

It was boots, in fact, that brought on the most nagging injury of the tour, Willis's septic toes. At least three specialists were seen and, medically, there seemed to be no quick solution to the trouble. At one point it was thought Willis would simply have to hobble through the tour before having a toe amputated. The patient may not think so, but such an amputation is not necessarily as serious as it sounds, for in the past there have been successful four-toed players. A Perth chiropodist, however, solved the problem. He came up with a 'sling' that kept Willis's raw toes apart. It saw him through the tour.

England otherwise suffered only two serious injuries in Australia. They were both head injuries incurred by batsmen. At Adelaide in the first week Radley was struck on the forehead by a rearing ball from Hogg, while Tolchard, more seriously hurt, fell with a shattered cheekbone in January during the upcountry Northern New South Wales match. It is of grim interest to hear Tolchard's befuddled recollection of his injury.

'A big wind was blowing down the pitch and, as the bowler came in, I thought for a split-second that it would blow dust into my eyes, then I wondered what it would do with the pace of the ball. It pitched half-way down the wicket and I picked it up well enough as it lifted at me, dead-straight. I tried to hook it and missed it completely. Usually those balls will slide straight past your head or shoulder but this one, a big red blob, came *bang* into my right eye. I remember trying not to fall on

'Tolly' sporting the moustache he grew on tour. He batted well virtually every time he was given a chance, and may well have forced his way into the Test team had it not been for his nasty injury at Newcastle. In this photograph, taken in the second match against South Australia, he plays a characteristic shot to leg; judging by the position of his left foot, I would guess that this ball was outside the line of the off-stump. The balance is perfect, so that the head will have been kept still. Tolchard has his hands close together, but very low on the handle. Until recently he was David Gower's landlord in Leicester; he maintains that the phone will still ring now that Gower has left.

my wicket (he did) and then there was a lot of blood and we were in the ambulance. Bernard kept telling me to keep my eye closed and I was lying there with my hands clasped over my chest. I'm not a religious person but I was playing it safe – praying that I wouldn't lose my eyesight.'

Over the years Thomas has seen too many head injuries not to recognize the traumas they can bring upon their victims and, although both England players appear to have survived with their psyches intact, he watched them closely following their blows. For reasons of medical ethics, Thomas cannot discuss these particular cases, but interestingly he said that dazed cricketers, swimming above consciousness, often ask three questions: did I fall on my wicket, do I have to bat again in the game and how badly am I hurt? 'If he's medically able, whether he likes it or not, we try to get the player in to bat if there is a second innings,' said Thomas. 'We don't want to give him an excessive amount of time to think of his injury before he conquers his fear of it.' In fact, Radley who indeed fell on his wicket in the first innings, resumed his place at Number 3 in the second innings but was soon out; Tolchard by his second innings was in the Newcastle Infirmary, in no state even to watch television. His right cheekbone was star-shattered, 'like a tapped hard-boiled egg', as Thomas put it, and there was fear that a muscle that moves the eye might be detached. A surgical balloon was inflated under the compressed fractures and Tolchard remained a month in hospital. When he was dismissed, still shell-shocked but physically recovered, he rejoined the team and Thomas, ever watchful, intentionally roomed him with the friendly, extroverted and boisterous Botham.

The assignment of room-mates, in fact, is another of Thomas's responsibilities. He is reluctant to room county team-mates together, in fear of cliques being formed and is quick to detect the faintest whiff of incompatibility among players and accordingly will change their rooms. Further, Thomas has become the trusted advance-man on shopping forays, whether it be to the best market stall in Lahore or the leading discount boomerang shop in Sydney. His major job, though, has been the less dramatic one of keeping his players in peak basic fitness. This too is a complex assignment, and Thomas is confidently altering his exercise programmes day by day, man by man, with a keen eye for the physical peculiarities of each player. In his mind each bears a tab of identification: one has a posture problem, another a remarkably low pain threshold, another, a bowler, has a stiff upper spine that sometimes gives him, Thomas feels, a dispirited look that must comfort the enemy. 'I want the entire team to be 120 per cent fit,' is his goal. Brearley praises Thomas's work in this regard, and especially with the bowlers who, due to regular stretching exercises, have in recent years largely avoided the common bowlers' plague of muscle injuries. In general, the captain also places high value on the psychological as well as the physical well-being that Thomas has helped to instil in the side. 'When I hear Bernard shouting "Up-two-three-four, Up-two-three-four,"' said Brearley, 'it makes me laugh and I feel the day has begun.'

CHAPTER 6

Perth: Second Test. Geoff-the-Ripper comes good

THE TEAM ROOM on the 18th floor of the Sheraton Hotel commands a splendid view of the Swan River and the clean sharp lines of modern downtown Perth. It seemed remarkable that the city, with a population swelling towards a million people, had been the site of Test cricket for less than a decade. In old times the seafaring England sides would dock at Perth, and find their cricketing landlegs before heading to Adelaide and the major cities of the East coast. Perth's first Test, a drawn match before 85,000 spectators, took place during the 1970-71 tour and included only Geoffrey Boycott from our own team.

It was at Perth that one of the few unsavoury incidents of the tour took place, an episode which became notorious because somehow the local press got hold of the story. On December 10th, the Sunday before the beginning of the Test, Boycott, who had been under increasing emotional stress caused by the mounting crisis over the Yorkshire captaincy and by his lack of batting form, cracked. The crack came during the second innings of the match against Western Australia and, as it happened, only a few hours after Boycott learned that the Yorkshire committee had received a vote of confidence in their decision to replace him with John Hampshire as county captain.

In our first innings Boycott had been given out LBW, and in the second innings had also been given out by an umpire when the ball bobbed up to short square leg off Yardley. In Western Australia's second innings, after Hughes had been given not out LBW playing half-forward to Botham, Boycott walked towards the bowler's end from cover. He called umpire Don Weser a cheat. Weser

asked him to repeat what he had said; Boycott did so. At drinks twenty minutes later Weser told me of the incident, saying he was going to report Boycott to the Umpires' Association. After play, Insole told Boycott to apologize to the umpire, Geoff did apologize, shaking Weser's hand. The

Boycott's stance, facing Hurst, looks more open than usual; this may have been a factor in his not scoring many runs in front of the wicket on the off-side.

Boycott was under pressure early in the tour, some of it self-imposed, as he could not let matters drop. After the result of the Yorkshire vote became known, he accepted the situation, and appeared to relax and enjoy the tour more. He played an invaluable innings of 77 in the Perth Test. Immediately after that match, we had a three-day game against South Australia. In the first innings, he looked uncomfortable, on yet another awkward pitch. On the third day, we were clearly going to be set a target in the fourth innings. On the way to the ground, I asked Geoff whether he fancied going in first and letting all his inhibitions go; I said that I wanted to give Radley and Tolchard a chance at 3 and 4, and have Gooch at 5 (as he would be batting lower down in the next Test). Miller also needed a knock. Boycott showed no inclination for the attacking role. In the event, the run-race was so delicately balanced, that it seemed right to put each hard-hitting lower-order batsmen in before him; he ended up at no. 11. He took this excellently, joking about Wilfred Rhodes starting his career at number 11 and ending at no. 1, while he was doing just the opposite. And before he went in, he said, 'It feels very strange: usually I go in with someone else and come back by me'sen; now I'm going in by me'sen and coming back with someone else.' Boycott was the sting in our tail.

The true professional. Geoffrey, as ever meticulous about his gear, sorting out his batting gloves at Perth. Boycott's gloves are specially made for him, with the padding extending right over the tips of the index and the third fingers of his right hand. The picture also reveals his affection for the cap.

incident was taken no further.

Nevertheless, Boycott was considerably upset by the affair. He rejoined the manager on the balcony of the pavilion and asked to be dropped from the second Test. Insole convinced him that even ticking over at 75 per cent of his potential, Boycott was needed in the England side. My impression at the time was that Geoff was relieved to learn of the outcome of the Yorkshire affair and happy that he no longer had to fight an uneven battle against the county committee. He seemed less tense, more willing to enter into the everyday events of the tour. The other players helped, with the friendly banter and horseplay of the dressing-room. Someone put ice cubes in his socks. Botham challenged him to several mock wrestling matches. Boycott even began to joke about an imminent move: he would go to Nottinghamshire, he said, taking Edmonds and Emburey with him, and together they would lead the side to the 1979 county championship. He had been given until January 31st to decide whether to play for Yorkshire, and sought my opinion; I said that I could not advise him whether to stay with Yorkshire or leave them, but that whatever he did he should continue playing cricket at a high level, for that was the work in which he was so marvellously gifted.

We won that match against Western Australia by 140 runs, the first defeat for the State side in thirty consecutive matches. Our seamers bowled throughout both Australian innings; Hendrick had a wonderful match, taking 8 for 34, while Botham took 8 for 53. Tolchard had an apprehensive start but batted well, scoring an unbeaten 61 and holding seven catches. The team went up to Albany two days later where in a 40-over match against a Western Australia Country XI Gooch boosted his confidence for the forthcoming Test with a score of 112.

After practice one day, I had lunch at the home of John Inverarity, the Western Australia captain who in 1976-77 taught at Tonbridge School in Kent. Inverarity had been in the team under Ian Chappell during the Australian tour of England in 1972 and had been on the short list of possible Australian captains for the current Ashes series. I consider John an astute judge of the game and was interested to hear his views on Hendrick. He was emphatic; he said that Hendrick had been the best of the three seamers (Lever and Botham were the others) who had dismissed his team for 52 and 78. Hendo had bowled at his best, to a perfect line and length, making the ball bounce and move off the seam.

Inverarity's comments brought to mind that at the start of the tour Hendrick had asked Barrington and me for advice: why did he beat the bat so often without getting wickets? We reckoned that he pitched the ball marginally short, so that when it moved off the seam it often did so too much. I remember Ken demonstrating this. It took place during the first week of the tour in Adelaide. Ken, who enjoys participating in these little instructional sessions, became the batsman. He stood at the crease, reaching tentatively forward. 'I used to hate it if I had to push forward for the ball, rather than play back.' He said. 'Pitch it up there, and you'll have the batsman in two man's land.' His phrase 'two man's land' became a catch-word for the tour; but the advice helped Hendrick, who thereafter was less worried about batsmen occasionally driving him. Another point we had made to him at Adelaide was the matter of his getting out to the nets late; Hendrick always seemed to have some adjustment to make to his boots. The truth was, we learned, that he liked to practise his own way, that is, to bowl a good spell off a full run-up against good batsmen before finishing and showering. Our discussions with Hendrick had a salutary effect: afterwards he went through his exercises and running with special keenness, so that despite being omitted from the first Test he was in peak fitness and had lost no ambition for the Perth Test.

At lunch, Inverarity also talked about the unusual winds at Perth. The prevailing wind was from the west, from fine leg, and it was often strong. John said Australia had lost a Test against West Indies in December 1975 there because they had picked a side with four main bowlers, all of whom wanted to bowl with the wind – Lillee, Thomson, Walker and Mallett. If the wind changed, it normally went right round, to the east or south-east, so the effect was similar. Reflecting on his comments, I wondered how this might apply to us. Again, Miller would be helped more than Edmonds, since the wind the spinners would bowl into usually came from fine-leg rather than third man. In these conditions, as we have seen, Botham and Old would be able to swing the ball away, and both could bowl effectively and persistently into the wind.

At our selection meeting we again discussed Old. He had yet another niggle in the back; but this time we were a day nearer the match, and the competition had stiffened. We decided that Hendrick should have his place. Willis would almost certainly be fit (he was smiling now); if not, we would reconsider Old. As fourth seamer, if needed, I preferred Lever to Old, for his variation of swing and approach (left-arm over the wicket inswingers as opposed to right-arm over the wicket outswingers).

Again it was cloudy on the morning of the match. We decided to leave out Edmonds, and to put Australia in. One factor in our thinking was the lushness of the outfield. Far too many groundsmen left too much grass on the pitches, and did not allow them to dry completely, as they feared that otherwise a pitch might break up. Add rich, green outfields, watered to make them look good from a distance, and you have a recipe for cricket that is dominated by seam-bowling, slow moving and impossible for many spectators to understand. There are fewer and fewer spinners playing in Test cricket these days, their places being taken by the faster bowlers. Every sixty-five overs the pace bowlers have the advantage of a new ball which will always hurry through, bounce more and often swing. Lush outfields not only reduce the scoring rate but enable the shine to be kept on the ball longer. Groundsmen must play their parts in redressing the balance, so that captains pick – and bowl – their spinners, and this aspect of the game is encouraged.

Australia too had left out a spinner, Higgs being replaced by Geoff Dymock, an experienced left-arm medium-fast bowler not unlike Lever. He, Cosier and Hughes were the only survivors from the previous Ashes series. They also dropped Laughlin, replacing him with Rick Darling who would open with Wood, Cosier going back to Number 6. Yallop won the toss (I had reverted to 'heads') and chose to put us in.

We had a disastrous start. Hogg took two quick wickets, Gooch caught behind and Randall impetuously trying to hook. I came in with the score at 3 for 2. Boycott and I partially repaired the damage with a two-hour stand. As I stood at the non-striker's end, and watched him avoid yet another hostile ball, I felt a wave of admiration for my partner, wiry, slight, dedicated, a lonely man doing a lonely job all these years. What was it that compelled him to prove himself again and again

among his peers? Although we added only 38 runs, we had survived the main onslaught, when the ball seamed, swung and bounced alarmingly. We had faced little of Hogg early on, for Yallop had taken him off after four overs when his analysis was two wickets for no runs; perhaps on this occasion Hogg's own wish for short spells was being given too much deference. I was finally caught off Dymock for 17 off a ball that came across me. 41 for 3.

The highlight of the first day's play – perhaps of

Gower's temperament was excellent. After being hit in the throat by Hogg, he could carry on as if nothing had happened. The shot is a typical one square on the off-side. The back foot points to cover, the head has stayed still, and the bat has followed through fully. He often scored fast. As Hogg said of him, 'All of a sudden, you look round and see he's got 20; you think to yourself, ''where the hell did he get those runs?'' ' We often felt the same way.

49

the Test – was Gower's century, scored in 3½ hours and reached just before stumps. Hogg bowled at his best in this match, and the pitch gave help to the bowlers, though less so by now than in the morning session. Early on, Gower edged him just wide of third slip, off the shoulder of the bat. As Gower said, 70 per cent of Hogg's deliveries were coming up chest-high. One ball hit Gower in the neck, just under the helmet. I feared the blow might unsettle him; yet the very next ball he played with easy timing for four on the offside. David's attitude to batting is delightfully uncomplicated. Ask him to talk about a 'creamy' off-drive off Yardley, and he shrugs slightly and says, 'The ball just seemed to go off the bat.' He played his shots with perfect timing and minimum movement or fuss.

Technically, he had improved fast on the tour, especially against the lifting ball. After the hotel conversation at Brisbane, we had had several net practices on pitches not unlike the Perth pitch; I remember Gower having a torrid time against Old and Lever, but learning to relax, keep still, and stay inside many of the lifting deliveries.

With the second new ball, Hogg bowled three consecutive balls that cut away and went through at chest- or shoulder-height. Gower started to play at them, then took the bat inside. He said later: 'I had no chance of hitting them, because they did so much.' But in the next over he hit Hogg for two fours square on the off-side – one off the back, the other off the front foot – a mark of his class. This sense of timing also saw him reach his century after a flurry of scoring shots just three minutes before the close of play, with a sweet straight drive off Hurst. Gower's 101 had drawn us back from the abyss and we ended at 190 for 3. It must have been a frustrating day for the Australians. They had bowled and fielded well, but perhaps they had not had their slips in the right places. First slip stood almost behind the wicketkeeper and very deep, second slip closer but also too fine, with the result that instead of covering two positions they were covering one and a half. Moreover, all the slips tended to stand too deep, particularly for Boycott, with his excellent defensive technique: thick edges from a less able player, more inclined to push firmly at the ball with a tighter grip, would have carried further. Geoff played his own game and had not hit one boundary all day in scoring 63 not

out, getting singles to the leg-side and limiting his stroke-play on the off-side. Still, his spirits were high, and with good grace he accepted a wisecrack that had been passed by an Australian observer. 'Boycott has done for Test cricket,' said the Aussie, 'what Jack-the-Ripper did for door-to-door salesmen.' In fact he had provided the foundation of our eventual win.

Gower added only one run next morning before falling, fittingly, to Hogg, bowling round the wicket. Gower's had been a virtuoso performance, scoring 102 runs in 254 minutes off 221 balls with nine fours. Hogg continued to bowl magnificently, and put paid to any of our suspicions about his stamina. Dymock bowled well, just as we expected, giving us nothing at all. Hurst, looking a little desperate for wickets, was patchy. Once Gower was gone, Yardley bowled better. He more easily found his line to the right-handers. Miller, however, read his length better than others and, with Lever and Taylor chipping in, saw us beyond the 300 mark on a pitch where we could well have been bowled out

for less than 100, and where 200 would have been a good score. In fact we were all out at tea-time for 309.

I opened the bowling with Lever and Botham. This was probably the first time in his international career that Willis had not been given the new ball in the first innings. My feeling was that if Lever, who is a fine swing bowler, was to be an attacking force, he must bowl early, and from the end Willis would use. Moreover, Lever likes bowling at left-handers, and in the recent State match had first bamboozled then dismissed Wood. When Lever had Wood LBW in his second over (after beating him three times in his first), Willis exuberantly congratulated him – then, more quietly, agreed with me on my choice. However, Bob too needs the new ball for its extra bounce; so as the ball was not swinging much for Lever, I took him off after he had had only three overs, and Willis continued until close of play from that end. He was near his best throughout, clean-bowling Hughes for 16 and Yallop for 3. In the last over of the day Darling was

Darling is run out for 25 in Australia's first innings. Umpire Bailhache is perfectly placed for his decision. Toohey had turned the ball behind square; Hendrick (on edge of picture) had half-stopped it, and Botham ran back from short square-leg. Darling called for a run, Toohey sent him back, and Botham's fast low throw came in above the stumps, where Miller had quickly got into the perfect position for taking the ball.

run out. Miller was bowling. Toohey turned the ball round the corner. Hendrick half-stopped it. Darling called for a single, Toohey sent him back. Botham ran back to square leg, threw the ball at the stumps and Miller had the bails off in a moment. It was a fine piece of cricket, and a high note on which to end the day: 60 for 4.

Next morning Willis and Hendrick took up the attack. Willis got Cosier out, but it was a near thing. Willis was making the ball come in to the batsman from the off. For Cosier he had a fine-leg and another man half-way back, behind square, for a mis-hook. We also had four slips and a gully. Cosier now looked as though he might pop up on the leg-side, either fending off a short ball (rather than risking the hook) or pushing forward. Botham suggested the fourth slip should go to short square-leg. I thought he might well be right, but was reluctant to weaken the slip cordon. I left things as they were. Next ball Cosier edged straight to Gooch at fourth slip. Three more wickets fell, two before and one after lunch, and at 128 for 8 Dymock came in to join Toohey.

Toohey played easily his best innings of the series. He had trouble with Willis, but skilfully chose which balls to leave. When we pitched the ball up to him he did not fail to drive, with that strange stiff left leg and characteristic flick of the wrists. We decided to give him a single at the start of the over, and to attack Dymock; but there are drawbacks to this ploy. Once for example, Toohey turned Hendrick to long leg. The ball went between two deep fielders, so the batsmen ran two. Next ball he took a single. Then a leg-bye enabled the batsmen to change ends again. So four runs had been scored, none of which might have accrued with orthodox fields, and the batsmen were back at their original ends. However, we did succeed in keeping Toohey from most of the strike; he received only 22 balls while Dymock faced 53. Our problem was getting Dymock out. Again, the ball was now soft, and the sun had eased the pitch. As Dymock's assurance increased I said to Bailhache that I thought he warranted a bouncer or two. Bailhache agreed, but told me to make sure they were occasional. I also reverted to orthodox field placing for Toohey; when the fielders all go back the tension goes, and it is hard for the bowler to run in with the same aggression. This change was costly, however, for they took 10 runs off an over from Lever, including straight drives for four and three by Toohey, and 14, all pulls by Toohey, off the next by Botham. This was the 65th, so with the new ball due next over Botham's attempts to prove to Toohey that he could not play the bouncer were particularly inappropriate.

We took the new ball. As he handed it to me, Umpire Brooks said: 'We don't think you should bowl bouncers at Dymock with the new ball.' I said that I could not agree, and that it was my responsibility. He replied that it was his responsibility to ensure that tail-enders did not get hurt. In my view

the mere threat of a bouncer often makes the tail-ender play differently, and less well: I said I would not instruct bowlers not to bowl bouncers. Brooks said: 'If that happens, then we will do what we have to do' – which I took to mean, report what happened to the Board. While this surprisingly amicable argument was going on, Willis, waiting to bowl, was trying to find out from me who would bowl the following over. He said, 'Don't give it to Guy, he could go for 20 and over.' At this moment Botham was fuming, Willis was angry with Botham, Lever was aggrieved that he had come off for Willis, and the umpires were threatening to report me. I felt under siege from all directions. To restore some calm and sanity to the proceedings, I told Hendrick to get loose for the next over. Fortunately he bowled Dymock with his second ball. Fifty-seven runs had been added for the ninth wicket. Hurst was soon out, though not before a ball from Willis had hit the off stump hard enough to leave a red mark but not hard enough to dislodge a bail. Toohey was left undefeated on 81. The bowlers had again done a fine job, especially Willis with 5 for 44, and Australia were all out for 190.

Since dismissing Wood, Lever had bowled very little. In most Test matches I have found that one bowler is under-worked, especially when we are dismissing the opposition relatively quickly. In England, the man I had least used was Miller. At Brisbane it was Edmonds, and later in the series Willis was to be idle for long periods. Such un-employment can be depressing to a bowler; he feels under-valued in comparison with his colleagues. A vicious circle can emerge: a man is not put on because he does not, perhaps, bowl at his best; he does not bowl at his best because he is not put on. Bowlers, like batsmen, need to find a rhythm, which often comes only from performing in the middle.

At Perth, Lever was bowling well, but in the Australian first innings I found it hard to bring him into the attack. Willis and Hendrick were at that time our main strike bowlers, and both preferred to bowl from the end where the wind helped Lever's swing. When I did bring Lever back he did not immediately find his length, and was driven, first by Yardley then by Toohey. After a second two-over spell I took him off to give Willis the new ball. Something similar was to happen in the second innings, though the ending was happy, for Lever and for England.

There is no way of avoiding such situations. A captain must try to show his regard for all the players, and it is hard to do so when he keeps coming to the same conclusions as to who should bowl. I felt especially uneasy with Lever, who contributes so fully on tour whether he is himself in the centre of the picture or not.

We batted for two hours on the third evening. Hogg bowled three consecutive bouncers at Boycott, who ducked into the last one. The ball glanced off his cap and went for four leg byes. The Australians also thought they had his scalp when Dymock beat him outside the off stump; they were sure he had edged the ball and were up in the air with delight. Umpire Brooks, however, gave him not out. The pitch by now was relatively benign and Gooch ended the day on an aggressive note against Yardley. We closed at 58 without loss, Boycott 23, Gooch 26.

We started the fourth day with a lead of 177 aiming, optimistically, for an overall lead of 400: of these I reckoned 80 runs for the loss of perhaps two wickets might be an adequate target for the morning session, considering that the humid and overcast atmosphere was not conducive to batting. We got the runs, 92 of them, but at the cost of four wickets: Boycott's, Gooch's, mine and Randall's, although Derek contributed an amazing little innings, full of exotic and dangerous shots, before his charmed life ended at 45. We now were 135 for 4, and I asked Gower and Botham not to be too ambitious in the next hour. However, Gower's comparatively restrained innings ended soon after lunch when he was caught behind off Hogg, who had thus dismissed him twice in the match from round the wicket. I do not think that Hogg is given full credit for the variety of his talents.

The ability of a fast bowler to bowl round as well as over the wicket is an asset. Clearly it provides variation, while the purpose may also be to make use of the different ridges or bumps there may be on different parts of the pitch. It also forces the left-hander to play. Hogg mainly moves the ball into the right-hander off the pitch, so that he aims to pitch the ball outside the off stump; when he bowls to a left-hander that same ball is not so dangerous, as the batsman cannot be out LBW. If he pitches the ball on the stumps, though, it will often miss the off stump. So Hogg can bowl to hit the left-hander's stumps more often when he goes round the wicket. Many pace bowlers are unable to do this because the need to run off the pitch takes away the power in their action. Hendrick and Old, for example, hate going round the wicket, while Botham and Willis are happy to do so, and frequently used this approach during the series, especially against Wood.

Gower's dismissal by Hogg left us at 151 for 5. Botham now went gaily on, driving with power, until he tried to hit the off-spinner Yardley straight but was caught at deep mid-off. We were 176 for 6, well short of our intended target. Miller and Lever then stabilized the innings for a while. They added 25 slow but useful runs, by which time I was keen that Lever should chance his arm against Yardley before Hogg returned with the new ball. I signalled to him to do so, but before facing the spinner again he was out to Hurst. The tail went cheaply, and we were all out for 208, well short of the goal we had

Second innings: Botham drives Yardley, to be caught at deep mid-off. He was similarly dismissed in the sixth Test. Afterwards he said that he had been trying to hit the ball dead straight. The photo shows that he has gone 'inside-out'.

The Dismissals of Wood

In the first innings (below, left), Wood is given LBW for 5 by umpire Brooks, off the bowling of Lever, a dismissal that particularly gratified me as it vindicated my unorthodox choice of bowlers. In the second innings (below, right), Wood was given not out: Taylor and the slips were certain that he edged this ball faintly, but Gower, at silly point, heard nothing, nor did Botham, who turns round more in hope than expectation. I would never criticise such a decision: if players closer to the batsman than the umpire cannot hear a noise the umpire cannot be expected to know; besides, we might have been wrong. Botham regularly went round the wicket to Wood, partly because Wood found it harder to know what to leave when the ball was coming in from a wide angle, partly because there was a line of cracks outside the off-stump which caused the ball to do odd things occasionally; the cracks are visible as slightly darker patches in the picture. They would be too wide of the off-stump if Botham had bowled over the wicket. I tried having a silly point for a while because Wood looked soundest when playing forward rather than back to the good-length ball, and when he did so he sometimes edged the ball onto the pad and out on to the off-side. I hoped the close fielder's presence might incline him to play back.

The third picture was taken a moment after Brooks had given Wood out, caught at the wicket off Lever. The delighted Willis hugs his friend, while Wood waits incredulously.

Controversy about umpiring decisions is not new. It was unusual, though, that an umpire should announce his retirement from Test cricket while still standing in the match. Tom Brooks did just this, at lunch on the last day. Perhaps Tom was over-conscientious. He felt anguish that a bouncer might injure a batsman through his own failure to intervene; and was determined to stamp out swearing or 'sledging' in games in which he officiated. I had also been told the shows of dissent by bowlers made reluctant to answer their appeals in the affirmative. But I had the highest regard for his straightforward honesty.

It was ironical that the news of his retirement was printed in the same column as the announcement that the TCCB was not continuing its programme of appointing overseas umpires for first-class cricket in England, as Brooks was one of four umpires who participated in 1977 and 1978. Incidentally, Max O'Connell was hoping to be invited to England on this scheme. I think it a short-sighted decision not to do so, as in the intense programme of county cricket umpires can gain much experience.

set ourselves. The match was in a position where, with a good start, Australia could win. In eight hours they needed 328 runs. On the other hand, the humidity was now to our advantage, and we fancied getting some wickets before stumps. In fact we got only one man out before a tremendous thunderstorm ended play ninety minutes early and left Australia the task on the last day of scoring 317 runs. I did not think they could do it.

The morning dawned bright – by the end of play Australia had had the advantage of batting on the only two bright days of the match – and the game continued to be tense and hard-fought. They survived for half an hour before Hughes was brilliantly caught throat-high by Gooch at fourth slip. Wood played reasonably for an hour but with much less confidence when Botham came on.

Yallop at once survived two hard chances off Willis and was very uncomfortable. He and Wood had added 22 when Hendrick, who had replaced Willis, had Yallop caught by Taylor down the leg-side. At once, Hendrick and Taylor struck again, when Toohey was adjudged caught for 0 in the same over.

At this point we were buoyant and optimistic. Cosier looked vulnerable in defence, and occasionally swished without contact outside the off stump. However, he struck the ball hard whenever the opportunity offered. He pulled Botham rustically over long-on, and cut Willis impudently over first slip: the longer he stayed the more assured he seemed. At the other end Wood continued on his erratic but successful course. For once Botham bowled throughout a Test without taking a wicket, and for once he was desperately unlucky. He caused Wood to play and miss outside the off stump several times; he troubled him with balls that kept low, and the occasional lifter from the same uneven area that Hogg had made use of against Gower. Wood hooked him two or three times for four, but when he tried to pull a ball that was not very short he skied it to mid-wicket, where it drifted away from Boycott in the breeze towards square-leg. Looking into the sun, he missed the chance. Wood promptly tested him with another almost identical catch, with the same outcome. Botham took these misfortunes philosophically, though his placidity was not encouraged when another delivery, which Wood chipped to Boycott, who this time caught a simple catch, was called 'no-ball'.

Despite these ups-and-downs, Wood and Cosier took the score to 141 for 4. The balance had swung back somewhat – and we now had problems in the field. Taylor had pulled a groin muscle, and was much less mobile than usual. Randall, too, had an injury, to his back, which led him to field below par in two sweaters on a hot day. With three hours left, Australia should now have achieved a draw: it was even conceivable that they might have snatched an improbable win, or at least that we would have been forced back on the defensive for the last hour or so. Certainly, the new ball would have become available only during the last hour. Willis, Botham and Hendrick were all tiring. At last Lever was given his chance with the wind coming from mid-off. At the other end, Miller had been bowling into the wind, and was making the ball 'drift' well. Wood, worried by him and by the close fielders, had been reduced to one or two slogs to the leg-side. However, they were playing well, and we were beginning to worry, when the astonishing collapse occurred. Cosier was LBW sweeping Miller; the ball missed his front leg and hit his back leg, plumb in front of middle stump. Wood departed next over, caught at the wicket for 64, off Lever. A few balls later Miller bowled a superb quicker ball and Maclean edged it straight to me at slip: the Australians had slumped to 143 for 7. Yardley was brilliantly caught, low and left-handed, by Botham at slip; Hogg was bowled by another of Miller's quicker balls. Suddenly Lever was coming in to bowl to the last man, Hurst, and within a few balls he had bowled him. The last six wickets had fallen for 20 runs, and we had won the Test by the flattering margin of 166 runs. We were 2-0 in the series, and the headlines in Perth suggested that the Ashes had already been lost, and won.

Ian Botham in the nets. He had the same air of relaxed confidence when at the crease.

Hogg was the undoubted hero of the series for Australia. He ended with 41 wickets at an average of 12.85, a record for an Australian bowler in a series against England. Here he traps Derek Randall LBW for 2 in the second innings of the third Test at Melbourne.

CHAPTER 7

Melbourne: Third Test. 1066 and all that

ONE OF THE umpires came into our dressing-room at Melbourne with a box of six new cricket balls. We had lost the toss, the Australians had elected to bat and we were being asked to choose two balls, one for the start, the other in case we should take a second new ball, which became available after 65 overs. As usual, our seamers took the box to the window for a better look in the light. They first searched for darker balls, not only because they are harder for a batsman to see but because for some reason they swing more in the air. They also looked for balls with an exceptionally high seam or a bad bit of stitching since these irregularities can cause balls to bounce freakishly off the wicket. The final, more elusive quality they sought was compactness – they looked for balls that somehow felt smaller, harder and so more lethal than the others. They did not have much luck. The Australian 'Kooka-burra' balls on this tour were remarkably uniform: machine-stitched rather than hand-stitched for the first time in Test-match history.

The team that went into the great bowl of the Melbourne Cricket Ground showed one change from the previous Test. John Emburey came in, his second Test appearance, in place of Lever. He was to find himself bowling after only 70 minutes, as the faster bowlers did not start at their best, and the pitch quickly lost any early life. Willis and Hendrick were both hooked – Darling, especially, quickly gets into position to hook and cut – and the luck did not run our way.

You make your luck, of course, and though we were aware of the dangers of complacency at being 2-0 up in the series, our out-cricket on the first day lacked its usual edge. We missed run-out attempts.

For example, early on Darling was stranded and Randall narrowly missed the stumps when he might have had time to run in with the ball from cover; Miller, backing up at backward short leg, might have darted in for a second attempt, but did not do so. On another occasion, Hendrick, following through, missed an underarm throw at the stumps from point-blank range after Wood had been sent back. Wood and Darling, however, seemed intent on ending their partnership with a run-out, and finally they managed it. They lost a wicket at 12.30 with the score at 65-0. Wood drove Emburey to mid-on and took two or three paces down the wicket before saying 'no'. Darling was lured down the pitch, and was still yards out of his ground when Boycott's throw came in to Emburey. Many of us in the field did not realize that Emburey, who had his back to the batsmen, had no idea that a run-out was on the cards, and only flicked off the bails, casually, as a safeguard.

Next ball Hughes was given out, caught behind: 65-2. Taylor kept skilfully on a pitch that was to become increasingly awkward for 'keepers, but the groin injury he suffered at Perth still bothered him. Bob's immobility contributed soon after lunch to the first of my two dropped catches at slip; the edge from Yallop went between us, and I hesitated for a moment before going for the catch. I also missed Toohey off Botham. I felt worse about dropping these catches than I was to feel about two low scores with the bat. Two days before, I had been stupid enough to bat in nets that had been rained on overnight and was hit above the eye when a medium-paced ball bowled by the Leicestershire fast bowler Jonathan Agnew lifted from a length.

The England players looking at the pitch the day before the match. Between Lever and Gower is Jonathan Agnew, and in the centre of the picture is the author with a plastered eyebrow. What will the pitch do? The larger picture shows part of the answer: Emburey, in our first innings, is bowled by a Hogg delivery that scarcely rises off the ground.

The cut took six stitches to close, but my vision was good. It was only after dropping Toohey that I wondered about the effects of the injury on my reflexes and confidence.

During the first innings I possibly fell into the temptation of over-attacking before assessing the pitch fully. The bowling was not up to its usual standard, and perhaps we were too ambitious with the number of slips. Even on the first day the pitch was so lacking in life that thick edges did not carry to third or fourth slip, and these fielders might have been better employed at third man, or saving ones in front of the wicket. We missed two other chances, both from Wood, during that opening day. On the credit side, Hendrick brought off a marvellous diving catch at second slip to get Yallop out, and Randall an equally good one to dismiss

Toohey, when he mis-drove Miller on the leg-side. Yallop had played the spinners exceptionally well in his innings of 41, driving hard and straight and with a freedom I had not previously seen. And Toohey looked dangerous before getting out for 32 with the score at 189-4.

At this point Allan Border, who had replaced Cosier, came in to play his first Test innings. Naturally we crowded him, with four close fielders for the off-spinners, and I also brought deep square-leg in to stop the single; but after a nervous twenty minutes without scoring Border swept two fours. We took the new ball an hour before the close of play, but the two left handers, Border and Wood, played it with confidence.

The day ended with Wood straight-driving Botham for three to reach his century. He had had many close calls, not least when Emburey bowled a superb ball which 'went on with the arm'; much too close for Wood to cut, it came in from outside the off-stump, touched his pad, and then the stump. Incredibly, the bail did not fall. Twice in consecutive Tests we had struck a stump but failed to dislodge a bail, an event that normally one would see perhaps once in fifty matches.

Wood is a player who keeps to his limitations, as a close study showed. He hooks well, and tucks the ball off his legs. Against the spinners, he occasionally chops the ball down towards short third man; but mainly he relies on the sweep or on-drive. His bearing, his moustache and hair cut, his unsmiling, pale face, even his close-fitting shirts, call to mind the mannerisms of Greg Chappell, and though Wood will never be as complete a player as Chappell he has some of the latter's balance and grace. At stumps, Australia were 243-4, easily their highest first innings score so far in the series from either side, with Wood on 100.

The next day we reminded each other that after one more wicket the longest tail of the series began, for Australia had brought in Higgs to replace Yardley. I opened with Hendrick and Miller. Border, we felt, 'showed the slips a lot of bat'. Hendrick seemed the most likely of our seamers to probe relentlessly at his off-stump, and sure enough, on the last ball of the first over, Border, who had already played and missed, edged Hendrick to me at first slip, where – to my relief – I took a low catch. 247-5.

I wanted an off-spinner to bowl at Wood, who is more comfortable against the quick bowlers. It would have been Emburey; but Maclean's arrival changed matters, and I asked Miller to bowl instead. Miller had been Maclean's tormentor, and had already dismissed him three times in two Tests. First he was to bowl at Wood. We started with a five-four leg-side field; short-leg, deep backward square-leg, square-leg, mid-wicket and mid-on. The off-side field was slip, silly-point (where we thought we had had Wood caught before he reached 50), extra-cover and mid-off. This field left short third-man open to let him try his chop-shot early on. Wood played a maiden over. Next over I suggested to Miller that we take Emburey away from square-leg to allow Wood to play the 'lap' – a risky shot that he had played when well-set the previous day. I thought Emburey should go to

I drop Yallop off Hendrick at Melbourne. The ball went at a nice height for catching, between Taylor and me. Despite my initial hesitation, I saw the ball well and should have caught it.

short extra-cover; we might get Wood caught there driving at the ball. Dusty said, no, put him at short mid-wicket, the corresponding position on the leg-side, where he is more likely to look to drive. An over later, Wood, fretting to score, drove the ball hard but waist-high and straight to Emburey in that position: 250-6. We were learning about the Australians now, and knew that Hogg, in common with many fast bowlers, either blocks the spinners or slogs them; when he had gone for the big hit he had dragged the off-spinners to wide long-on or hit 'inside-out' to long-off. So we put mid-off and mid-wicket back, and kept three close catchers. Perhaps it was lucky, or perhaps the field led Hogg to drive half-heartedly, but a couple of balls later he was caught at extra-cover: 250-7. Hendrick, who was bowling with nagging accuracy, at once bowled Dymock, off the inside edge, and Hurst, both for ducks, so Australia were 252-9. Finally, Botham, brought on in place of Miller to get Higgs out, bowled Maclean, so the last six wickets had fallen for eleven runs in less than 1½ hours. Australia were all out for 258.

We faced this total with high hopes, despite the fact that the occasional delivery was shooting. What we had not bargained for was Hogg, and the splendid support he was to get not only from Hurst, Dymock and Higgs, but from the 40,000 spectators. (40,000 had come on the first day too, with a total of 136,000 over the five days.) As Hogg came in to bowl, they roared for their new fast-bowling hero as they had done in the Centenary Test for Lillee. 'Will-is, weak as piss' gave way at the City end to 'Kill, Kill' and 'Hog-gy, Hog-gy'. He bowled fast and straight. In his second over he bowled Boycott with a ball that came in from the off and kept low; three balls later another ball nipped back, and I was LBW. Both of us had been only half forward. We had scored three runs for the loss of two wickets.

So Gooch, who had been moved to number four in the hope that he would be spared the new ball, found himself at the crease in the third over of the innings, just five minutes before lunch. He played extremely well. In his previous Test innings of 43 at Perth he had shown more aggression and confidence, and he had played excellently against South Australia for a quick 64. Now he put into practice the basic requirement for survival on this pitch: he played well forward. He had learned a

similar lesson the previous summer, at The Oval, when having been LBW for 0 in the first innings playing back to a ball of fullish length from Brendon Bracewell, he played forward in the second innings and scored 91 not out. It may sound an easy thing to do, to play forward to quick bowlers, but many batsmen find that if they commit themselves to the front foot too early they lose balance, play across the ball if it comes down the line of their front pads, and get into trouble against the short-pitched ball. Gower, by contrast, managed to play well at Melbourne without going forward more than usual. Gooch adopts this technique easily; he may even find in the future that the method of going early on to the front foot against quick bowlers suits him, as it did another tall, powerful driver of the ball, Tom Graveney. At any rate, this was the technique Gooch used promisingly in this match, although his dismissal did illustrate one of its dangers. Playing forward to Dymock, he pushed too firmly at a short-of-a-length ball outside the off-stump, fencing at it rather than letting it go or allowing it to come to him, and was caught after some juggling by Border at second slip. He had made 25, and the score now read 52-4.

Gower and Botham came together with the score at 52 for 4; Gower took 17 off three overs from Higgs, but this burst of scoring was isolated. He was then LBW playing back to a near-shooter from Dymock, who had earlier made two balls lift to

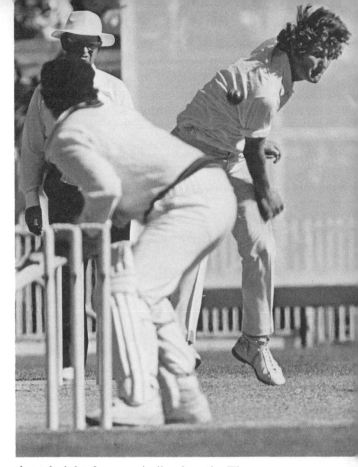

The famous Willis curtain-rail: this unique shot gets its name from the invisible curtain-rail going from square left to cover point and passing at hip height four feet in front of every batting crease at which our 6′ 6″ batsman stands. For along the rail, from leg to off, Willis runs his bat on soundless runners, after taking a big stride forward to reach them. The face of the bat points towards cover; it starts its movement along the rail outside the leg-stump, and runs along until, its owner hopes, it comes into contact with the ball travelling along its path at right-angles to the motion of the bat. Contact is made with remarkable frequency; Willis is a very awkward batsman to remove. Above right:
Willis, his face registering concentration and effort, bowling to Border at Melbourne; first day, second new ball.

chest height from a similar length. The score was then 81 for 5. When captain I rarely leave the dressing room, which at Melbourne is a dingy underground area beneath the stands, originally meant more for the briefer needs of Australian Rules footballers than the extended visits of a Test cricketing side. Instead, in the cleaner light and air of the members' stand, I watched as a detached spectator. The members, courteous and informed, were nonetheless perplexed by the rapid, inexpensive fall of wickets that day: by the end 14 were to have gone for 122 runs. I could only suggest that the answer lay more in the pitch than in either the bowling or batting. We watched Botham fighting, with admirable patience, to survive against Higgs. He was clearly happier against Hogg, whom he twice hooked savagely. Then Higgs tempted him with a slower ball, and Botham mistimed his drive, to be well-caught at cover by Darling. When Taylor was bowled by Hogg with only a single added I thought I had better end my contemplations, and hurried back to the dressing-room. Before the close Emburey too had been bowled by Hogg. The measure of Australia's control during the last session was that in 110 minutes Miller managed only three runs, and one of them was from a mis-field.

By close of play we had reached 107-8, a position that it would require a miracle to reverse. The next day was rest day, a proper moment to consider any New Year's resolutions and the unhappy prospect of a disappointing start to 1979. My day started with the routine press conference which, perhaps coincidentally, included an Australian television team to record my views on the poorest beginning England had yet made in the series. I spoke of the wicket with some delicacy for it is difficult to mention a passing truth without it appearing as an alibi or a sorry piece of 'Pommie wingeing'.

New Year's day was even hotter than the first two days. We fought back well. Willis, with his extraordinary batting technique, scored 19, making full use of the 'curtain-rail', and the last two wickets added 42 runs. We closed at 143.

In their second innings the first five Australians played well, but got out trying to accelerate the scoring. Their opening stand of 55 was broken when Randall caught Darling at extra-cover. Then Botham, resourceful as ever, dismissed Wood for 34, as the Australian opener tried to sweep a slower ball that was even slower than Emburey's stock ball. Not long after Botham received an unpleasant blow on the arm at short-square leg when Toohey struck out at Emburey. I thought of Harold Larwood's story in which D. R. Jardine was hit on the shin while fielding at Melbourne; after a few minutes, blood started to ooze through his trousers and down over his boots. Someone said, 'Skipper, you'd better go off and get that seen to.' 'What,' said Jardine, 'and let 90,000 convicts know I'm hurt?' Botham, as hard a competitor as anyone, was not too proud to rub his arm or to be happy to move out of the firing-line. He had the last laugh, as a few balls later he made a fine catch at mid-wicket to dismiss Toohey, also off Emburey. That made it 136-4. Botham's contribution to the day was not yet finished. He had Hughes caught at extra-cover for 48, with another slow loosener, after Hendrick had pinioned him with four vice-like maidens; he also dismissed Hogg. Australia ended the day at 163-7.

Next morning we again quickly dismissed the tail, Hendrick and Emburey doing the damage. We had taken the last seven wickets with the old ball for 31 runs, and Australia were all out for 167, an overall lead of 282. At the start of the morning's play we did not take the second new ball, though it was available at once. The old ball had become so ragged and soft that the slips were virtually decorative, and on a normal pitch we would have been waiting anxiously for the chance to ditch such a ball and take the new one. There tends to be a clearer contrast in Australia between the new and the old ball, and therefore between early all-out attack and later defence, whereas in England the changes seem more gradual. 'Kookaburras' keep their shape better than English balls, but not their hardness. On this Melbourne pitch, brown, dead and uneven, a new ball would have gone off the bat faster than the old rag, and have given the batsman a bonus.

It failed to do so for us, however, for once again England made a disastrous start. Once again Gooch came in before lunch after two wickets (Randall and myself) had fallen in the first three overs. He played with even more authority, this time in partnership with Boycott. It is a pity that so many spectators are unable to appreciate the tension of contests in which bowlers are mainly game by those who have mindlessly dismissed such cricket as 'slow': you might as well criticize Jane Austen for not being Agatha Christie. The cricket during this period was absorbing, as it had been for almost every hour of all three Tests. Boycott and Gooch carefully took the score to 71 before Gooch was given LBW to Hogg, well forward this time. Gower, too, played superbly. He and Boycott slowly advanced the score to 122, when, in the last over before tea, Hurst, who had been under-bowled, had his seventh appeal for LBW against Boycott answered by a raised arm from Umpire O'Connell. We depended heavily, again, on Gower and Botham. They showed maturity, so that when our score reached 163-4 the odds against us had diminished almost to evens for the first time since the start of our first innings. Then, an hour after tea on the fourth day, Dymock had Gower LBW in a similar way to the first innings.

Defeat was now almost certain, and by close of play had become inevitable. Higgs dismissed

Wood, attempting to sweep Botham's outrageous slower ball, is bowled behind his legs. This fact is not yet registered on his face.

Botham, for the second time in the match, and Miller, while Hogg took Taylor's wicket: 171-8. Later in the evening the four Middlesex players and Gooch barbecued steaks and sausages at the public cooking place on the banks of the River Yarra. We looked vainly in the clear sky for clouds.

Once the die is cast, one can face a defeat more philosophically, or so I thought. Hogg wrapped up the tail to finish with 10 for 66; and after the presentations I was called upon as usual to answer questions for the television cameras on the ground. The jeering insults that accompanied the interview suddenly became too much, after the five days of barracking, and I turned and snapped at the crowd. 'That's the sort of thing we've had to put up with for days.' I was asked if I intended to stand down from the next Test, as Denness had four years before. I said I had not given it much thought, but such thought as I had given to that question had been that I should not step down. Larwood said to me in Sydney: 'If anyone had asked Jardine that question, he'd have punched him in the face.'

In retrospect, the match was decided by three factors: the toss of the coin, Hogg's bowling and Wood's 100. The value of his century may be measured in part by the fact that no-one else on either side reached 50. Willis's dearth of wickets – 0-68 – was due in part to his style of bowling; he pounds the ball down from a great height, and needs some response from the pitch to achieve his dangerous bounce. Hogg by contrast delivers from lower, and makes the ball skid through quickly, but he also deserves credit for the sense and fire with which he bowled. After the presentation, the press conference and bag-packing, I had a light salad lunch with Higgs, Toohey and others. We discussed Hogg, and remarked that he and Thomson would have been a highly effective combination. We agreed, too, that it is difficult to imagine any other fast bowler – the exception being Michael Holding at The Oval in 1976 – who could have bowled better on such a pitch. Certainly, at a similar stage of his career, Lillee would never have bowled with such controlled pace or length. Hogg had now taken 27 wickets in three Tests at an average of exactly 11 runs per wicket.

CHAPTER 8

Self-doubts

OF THE MESSAGES I received following our defeat at Melbourne none made its point more swiftly and bluntly than a letter from a man on the south coast of England. 'Losing to the Australians just isn't good enough,' wrote 'G.G.', who otherwise remained nameless. 'You ought to be shot.' Nobody was going to shoot anybody on the tour, unless it was with Botham's water pistol; but since the first day of the third Test I had not needed such invective to call into question my own role in the team: my run of low scores spoke for itself.

It was the second time in six months that I was considering standing down. In the previous summer I had almost come to the point of suggesting to the selectors that they consider another captain for the final New Zealand match, despite having appointed me for all three. Now I had the example of Mike Denness to consider as well. At precisely the same point in the 1974/5 tour, he had stepped down as captain. His batting record had been 65 runs in six innings; mine was worse – 37 runs in six innings.

There the parallels ended: we were 2–1 up, while the 1974/5 team had been 2–0 down. Moreover, likeable as he was, I think Denness had neither been an easy communicator with his team, nor tactically astute. For my part I believe I had improved during my 18 months in the job. I had become more confident about my own tactical judgement. I was more aware of the different ways individuals could help the team effort, especially off the field. And I enjoyed captaincy. On the field, I continued to be absorbed in the business of handling the bowlers, considering how they might bowl from different ends to different batsmen, planning the field-placings and looking ahead to the next over,

hour or day. And although in this exacting job there will be times when you find it hard to motivate yourself let alone others, they were rare days when I did not feel like captaining a side.

Nevertheless, the feeling of inadequacy, once it emerges from its burrow, is hard to kill or to drive back underground. It worms its way into your consciousness in the middle of the night, and obstinately refuses to listen to reason. An irrational inner voice says: 'If I am no good at batting, painting etc. then I am no good as a person.' This argument is crazy, but creepy, in that if a person allows it to insinuate itself into his mind its presence there will make him both worse as a performer and weaker as a person. The defect in character does not lie in batting badly, but in *believing* that batting badly is proof of a character defect. There is certainly no need for failure in one's specialist role to affect one's efficiency as a captain, unless one allows it to.

I do not think my poor form with the bat did particularly affect my captaincy, but without doubt it reduced my overall value to the team. I needed other opinions about remaining in the side, and before the end of the Melbourne Test I spoke separately both with Willis and with Insole. Willis was firm: he insisted that I was worth my place in the side as captain, especially on the field. Insole was even more emphatic. 'Don't be stupid, don't let the idea enter your head,' he said in his friendly but dismissive way. We did not pursue the matter.

I was grateful too for some unsolicited support from Ian Johnson, who had captained Australia in England in 1956, and had, he said, faced similar problems. I was also reassured when Hendrick said

Setting the field, Melbourne. Much of a cricket captain's job is done in football by the manager. It is much easier for the latter to 'play god' because he does not have to perform on the field. However low the captain may feel about his own performance, he still has to exert authority. Here I am setting a field for Hendrick, on the fourth morning of the match. The batsmen are Dymock

(far end) and Maclean. At Perth a business studies course team watched us in the field, and told me that I communicated a good deal with the bowlers by touch, and with everyone by eye contact. Inset: Somebody loves me! This is Erica Medhurst who came to see all our matches in Adelaide. This picture was taken a day or two before Christmas.

much later on the tour: 'Well done for sticking at it; it must have been hard when you were struggling with the bat,' and I took this to be the voice of the players. Captaining a side, I had long realized, is like teaching at a university, in that unless you are a genius you will always have students who are better at the subject than you. Gower, for example, is a much better player than I ever was (or will be!), yet I can say things to him about his batting which may well be helpful, and be received as such.

By the time we left for Sydney, I was convinced I should carry on. I could joke with Radley that I was not sure whose position I preferred; mine, where I was exposed to the risk of further failure, or his, where he had no chance to prove himself. But I was glad about the decision. However, all this did nothing for my batting. Barrington tried to reduce the pressure that builds up round a batsman who is not scoring runs by telling me a story about the time he had been out four times in six balls. A writer asked him how it felt to be out of form. 'Out of form?' he replied. 'I haven't been in long enough to be out of form.'

I attempted yet again to analyse my batting problems. The margin between success and failure is slight. I had started the tour with a row of good scores, and the work with Don Wilson in the Indoor School at Lord's before we came out to Australia seemed to have stood me in good stead. And there was no obvious pattern to my dismissals in the six Test innings so far. Naturally, I wondered whether my broken left forearm had left some damaging legacy, physically or psychologically. The fracture itself was well healed, but perhaps during my summer batting drought the left arm had been weaker, leading me to more 'bottom-handed' as a batsman. In the past I had always been 'top-handed' – that is, the left hand had been the dominant one. I dragged the bat down with the left hand rather than punching the ball with the right, which made me a better off-side than on-side player. Some of this freedom was certainly lacking, but I doubted whether the broken bone could be blamed for the loss. Nor did I think that there was any lingering apprehensiveness that might have arisen because of the injury. Early in the tour I had played the lifting ball well enough and, on the advice of the surgeon, I wore a small arm-guard whenever I batted, so I felt well protected.

Before the second innings at Melbourne Willis

offered me some practical help. He bowled briskly at me in the nets, shouting from time to time, 'Play it *straight*. Down the wicket. Mid-off! Mid-on!' In the past summer, Richie Benaud had given me similar advice. He pointed out that when I played the ball it nearly always went off square to the wicket. He said that Ian Chappell, when practising through his bad patches, tried to hit every ball back towards the bowler, and visualized playing each ball straight down the pitch. I found that useful.

Benaud mentioned another device Chappell would use to get out of his bad patches. He would try to concentrate, concentrate *fiercely*. Was I a fierce concentrator? I said, no, I thought I played my best when I was relaxed and at ease, aware of things going on round me. Benaud's comments, and my replies, had come to mind clearly during the Perth Test. On the second morning I woke up with an aching jaw. I could not remember hurting myself or biting down on anything. Only afterwards did I realize what the cause was: that during my two-hour innings against the moving ball I had been working intensely on my chewing gum. In that same innings an incident illustrated that I was not concentrating, or at least that I was not properly preparing for my job. While batting I noticed a piece of string hanging from the bottom of the handle of my bat. I asked Robin Bailhache if he had any scissors. He only had a knife, and as I was trying to sever the string I cut my finger. It was not the kind of injury a Boycott would suffer.

As for purely technical advice, Benaud's were not the only tips I was offered during the summer. Brian Close thought my left hand was too far towards the front of the handle, and this prevented me from properly swinging the bat. Alec Bedser added that when I played forward I was anchoring my back foot flat to the ground, with the result that I did not lean into my shots. Len Hutton noticed two faults: I did not go forward far enough and, secondly, when I did play forward my back foot was moving across the stumps towards the off, rather than staying round leg-stump. Ted Dexter said that when I tried to force the ball off the back foot I did not stay sideways-on long enough; I tended to throw my left hip and leg out and push away from my body with my right hand. To me, this seemed not only technically valid in itself but particularly relevant to my present problems.

On the other hand, in the nets one day, Dexter said he thought my basic swing was fine, but suggested I try breaking my wrists in the follow-through. He was asking me to be Dexter, whereas I am more like Colin Cowdrey in this respect in that I don't follow through beyond the point where my arms are still straight (though the picture on the back cover of the present book is an exception). Ted accepted this but, as with Benaud's remark about Chappell's fierce concentration, it illustrated an interesting problem in teaching a sport. The advice given applied to how Dexter, or Chappell, might play the game, not to how I most naturally play it.

This diagnosis of a disease without regard to the nature of my previously healthy state also applied to advice given by Robin Marlar in the *Sunday Times*. He wrote as though I could not hope to score runs with such a high early backlift and with hands apart on the handle. Yet I had been doing both these things for the previous four or five seasons. In fact, the high backlift had been a factor in that initial improvement; it had helped my balance and my ability to deal with the rising ball. As for hands apart on the bat, Cowdrey, Edrich and Asif Iqbal are amongst those who have succeeded with this method. In all, my Middlesex team-mates Radley and Mike Smith, as well as our coach, Don Bennett, felt I had not basically changed my technique.

It is curious how sometimes you do not realize the tensions you are under and, even when you do, how difficult it may be to deal with them. Towards the end of the 1978 season I had had on more than one occasion a fantasy image that appealed to me strangely. I had a picture of one of those seeds that come out of a sycamore tree in autumn, spinning down slower and slower in bigger and bigger circles. Unwinding: I both needed to and was beginning to unwind.

When a sportsman performs at his best, I feel, he plays with relaxed concentration. The questions are how to concentrate without tension, and how to relax without looseness. I am convinced that you can be helped to achieve these goals, and that sports medicine is incomplete if it ignores psychology. Dr. Arthur Jackson is a medical hypnotherapist who lives and works in Sydney. I had first met him socially after the Centenary Test in 1977; it had been at a barbecue (at his house) that Greig had dropped the hint, which I did not

fully understand, about a new era of cricket in Australia. At that time, Jackson was already helping Willis with hypnotherapy and with cassette tapes that enabled him to relax and sleep. Under hypnosis, by encouraging him to reflect on his better performances in cricket, he had had some success in reinforcing Willis's confidence in himself and increasing his motivation. Bob talked to me about this during our long flight home, and I became interested in the possibilities of this method.

Jackson had worked with other players, and also with the New South Wales cricket team. I wrote to him from England to ask if he would be willing to hypnotize me; and he came to see both Willis and myself when we went to Sydney in November. I was not, I think, what he called a 'deep trance-subject', but I did become utterly relaxed as I lay on the bed in my hotel-room and listened to his quiet voice. Once at ease he would suggest that I imagine facing a particular bowler and playing him at my best. I would conjure up different deliveries, and play them confidently. Jackson also offered techniques for relaxation which involved breathing,

Eight working and one watching before play on the first day of the second Test. The weather was overcast, the pitch well-covered with grass. Peter Loader, the ex-England fast bowler who, like Tony Lock, has lived in Perth for many years, advised us to put Australia in; he had given similar advice before the state match a week before, which I had not followed after Botham reported to me that he was swinging a new ball in the nets. That decision had probably been wrong, even though, as it happened, our first innings score of 144 was comfortably the highest score in the match. For the Test, we decided to follow Loader's advice; the next question was whether to pick a fourth seam-bowler or a second spinner – Lever or Edmonds. We four selectors spent a long time trying to settle this matter, and we did not finally resolve it until just before the toss. L to R: Willis, Barrington, Insole and Brearley. Bob's and my informal gear are evidence of our having just finished the pre-match exercises, which Insole Often joined, in a pair of wonderful 40s shorts. But we could not persuade Ken to run round the field.

A cartoonist's view of me that appeared in the *Guardian* on January 6, just before the fourth Test (cartoon by John Minnion).

physically 'ticking-off' different muscles, and mentally summoning up an image of a place that had happy associations. The theory is, I believe, that confidence is reinforced by the inner rehearsals because, under hypnosis, the mind works at a level too deep for doubt to interfere. Sadly, my knowledge of the theory is imperfect since, when Dudley Doust went to Arthur Jackson's house to research the subject in greater detail, under the effects of a glass of wine, a warm sun and a gentle voice he drifted into a trance! What I do know is that I was helped, especially by my two sessions immediately before the fourth Test.

On the afternoon of Friday January 5th, 1979, as I sat in my hotel room with its splendid view and thought about the match that was to begin in the morning, I knew that my main problems were not technical. The most important things were to avoid peering anxiously for the ball as if I might not see it at all and tightening up so much that a long innings would mean worn-down molars. I could laugh quite happily when Tony Greig, who had called in for tea, remarked as he looked out of the window, 'You know, this is the same room that Mike Denness had in 1975.' With Arthur Jackson's help, next morning I even won the toss.

CHAPTER 9

Sydney: Fourth Test. Back from nowhere

THROUGHOUT MY CAREER as a Test cricketer, I have never played in a match that was close at the end. The Centenary Test, which we lost by 45 runs, and the Jubilee Test at Lord's the following summer, when Australia were six wickets down and playing for a draw, were both evenly balanced for a long while, but neither drew excruciatingly close at the finish. The same applies to the fourth Test at Sydney. Still, the match was unique; and what will always set it apart was that our victory was the most remarkable comeback I have ever experienced in Test cricket.

There were, as usual, only three days between stumps at Melbourne and the toss at Sydney, a tight schedule when one considers the physical and mental exhaustion of Test cricket. The fact that the two came in the same week also meant that there was no chance to give match practice to those on the sidelines.

At our selection meeting we raised one main question: how could we strengthen the batting? There was no reason to change the bowlers. Willis had been below his best at Melbourne, but had bowled magnificently at Brisbane and Perth: there was no question of his not being selected. Besides, no-one could replace him as spearhead of the attack. Emburey had done all we could ask of him, as indeed had Hendrick. Miller and Botham were invaluable as in-form all-rounders. But how could we strengthen the batting? I had already made sure that the other selectors thought I was worth my place. Boycott, Gower and Randall were certainties. So the possibilities were for Radley or Tolchard to come in in place of Gooch or Taylor. But Gooch had played really well at Melbourne.

Should we consider changing wicketkeeper? We all dropped the idea as soon as it was voiced. Taylor's groin was now much improved; he was a superb craftsman, and might be especially valuable if, as we expected, the pitch took spin. Could we leave out a bowler to let Tolchard in? No – on a turning pitch we would need two spinners, and I could not conceive going into a Test match with only two seam bowlers. So, like Australia, we were unchanged.

At the team meeting we again talked about Hogg and the need to get forward to him. Boycott made the point that it was hard to rediscover one's rhythm of playing forward when the nets were so bad. We were again shocked at the state of the nets at Sydney, but, after my salutary experience in the Melbourne nets, we used old balls and had no-one bowl flat out. By contrast, poor John Maclean was struck full in the eye by a ball from Hurst, which apparently flew from a length. The net pitches had not been properly prepared; they had a thin crust on top, and the ball 'exploded' if it hit the surface with sufficient force. This injury, with its subsequent effect on Maclean's Test career, may have been a by-product of the surfeit of cricket played at the ground now that World Series Cricket were regularly using it. The news was that Maclean was likely to play.

At our meeting we also discussed the Australian opening batsmen. It is an advantage for the batting side to have a left-hander and right-hander in together, as the bowlers must constantly alter their angle. Moreover, when they were not actually running each other out, Wood and Darling kept changing the strike by taking so many singles.

However, many of their singles were so risky that we decided against taking special steps against them, except perhaps to bowl slightly wider of the off-stump, so that at least they would not be able to score so freely on the leg-side. Wood's run pattern was clear: he scored mostly to leg. I added that Hughes, Darling and Border had all, from time to time, played at very wide deliveries. I also thought our off-spinners might consider bowling wide of the off-stump to their left-handers. The danger of this method is that the ball has to be only fractionally short to give the batsman room to square cut, late cut, or force off the back foot. The advantage is that you can dictate which side of the wicket he has to play to.

Next morning, we found that much of the grass

Flesh and beer on the Hill. These girls must have had a touch of the coquette and/or the masochist to brave the catcalls and other missiles that must have come their way to and from their places. The scoreboard which, like all the others we saw, makes the board at Lord's look as homespun as a notched stick, shows that Australia are poised for a massive lead.

had been taken off the pitch. There was some dampness, and a likelihood of uneven bounce early on, as the grass was patchy. Barrington's pen-knife did not go in far, which indicated that the damp was superficial; this examination also revealed that when tiny pieces of earth were eased out of the pitch they crumbled easily between the fingers. We were sure the pitch would take spin later, so I was pleased, as well as surprised, to win the toss. It proved to be the only time in the series that I did so. We chose to bat.

Australian crowds are not, these days, notable for their subtlety or wit, their stock insult (concealing, dare I surmise, their own underlying fear?) alleging that 'all Pommies are poofs'. All the same, one wag from the Hill, after I had played a few balls from Dymock, shouted, 'Brearley, you make Denness look like Bradman!' For 55 minutes we played confidently; Dymock had been the most dangerous bowler, nearly having me LBW, and forcing Boycott to play and miss more than once. Hogg was below his best, his chest heaving with asthma, and was replaced after only three overs. It was Hurst, whom we perhaps had underrated as he lay in Hogg's shadow, who broke through, having Boycott caught at slip after a series of bouncers (he had been out in a similar fashion on the same ground against NSW), and having Randall brilliantly caught from a hook at backward short-leg by Wood for 0. We were 18-2.

Our more solid start had been quickly shattered, and before lunch I had been bowled by a superb ball from Hogg, and Gower caught behind off Hurst, trying to take his gloves underneath the lifting ball. 51-4. The pitch had given some assistance, as expected, and Hurst had taken full advantage. Throughout our innings he came in with a lively rhythm and bowled at a more hostile pace and length than previously. His confidence had been slow to mature; now that he felt himself to be a good bowler, in control of what he was trying to do, he was more willing to let himself go. All four batsmen dismissed before lunch either fell shortly after a spate of short-pitched balls or, in Randall's case, to a bouncer.

Midway through the afternoon, with the temperature well up in the 90s, Maclean had to leave the field. In the dressing-room he lay soaking wet on the table, his eye grossly swollen, and his arms clamped so rigidly round his chest that they could not be prised loose. In the same session, Hogg, too, was off the field with breathing problems. By this time the pitch was docile, and Hurst and Dymock were past their best. Unfortunately we had no specialist batsmen left, apart from Botham, to take advantage of this situation. Gooch had got out wantonly, pulling a rank long-hop to deep square leg where Toohey took a brilliant catch, and Miller had been caught at the wicket off Hurst. Wickets continued to fall, and at one time we were 98-8. Botham had played steadily and well; now he took command, driving and pulling with great power. Willis, obdurate again, helped him put on 43 runs. At last Hogg, working up pace, had Botham caught by Yallop, 'keeping in place of Maclean, for 59. The innings was soon over for a meagre 152, Hurst having taken 5-28. It was a fine all-round performance by Australia. Yallop kept respectably, even to the awkward Higgs; all four bowlers were accurate and probing; and for once everything went right in the field, some brilliant catches being taken.

When we took the field at four o'clock we started with a stroke of luck. Wood dragged an innocuous ball from Willis on to his stumps, with the score at one. We then bowled without fire or accuracy. Willis was ill; he could find no energy. I let him bowl an over too long before insisting that he went off. Botham was perhaps tired from his innings: he bowled too short. Darling in particular and Hughes hooked and drove with freedom: at close of play the score was a confident 60-1.

We had reached a critical point in the tour. I remembered the other Cambridge and Middlesex player who captained England in Australia, G. O. Allen, and what happened to that side: 2-0 up, they lost 3-2. The pitch was now easy for batsmen, but would turn later. The signs were there, for Higgs had already made some balls turn disturbingly. We could well have to field for two days before starting our second innings a long way behind. We came off the field dispirited. As soon as he had a beer in his hand, Hendrick sought me out to suggest that we had a meeting, then and there, to make the seriousness of our position crystal clear, and to inculcate a new resolve. We clustered together for this meeting – as we were to do for the frequent subsequent ones – in a small inner room inside the changing area. Sweaty clothes and towels hung down from lines; we had to lift

them up to be able to see each other.

Hendo said we should go back to basics, to square one. We had played that day like a second-rate county side. Taylor added that we had to concentrate every ball. We agreed to return to orthodoxy in the field, to aim at line and length – since the ball was not swinging or seaming, and the pitch was not fast. Boycott said that from his positions on the field (long-leg and mid-on) the bowlers looked to be bowling too short. He was aware, however, that the main problems lay with the batting. He for one would be glad if the bowlers or anyone else could point out what he was doing wrong.

The importance of the meeting was not so much its content as its resolve and fervour. We decided to repeat it at least once a day, sometimes once a session. Hendrick's role was interesting; he is often content to stay in the background, contributing the occasional piece of good sense or mordant wit. I think that one factor that led him to take a leading role at Sydney was his form with the ball, which made him feel so strongly: 'Here is my chance. We must not let it go.'

We repeated the talk, briefly, at ten to eleven next morning. Darling played well, though we did make his job harder on the second day. Hughes needed more luck, twice chopping balls from Willis and Botham just past the leg stump. However, both men survived until lunch, when the score was 126-1. We remained worried about Willis's health. I had visited him the previous evening; he had gone back to the hotel early and slept. Thomas had thought at first that he was suffering from mild sunstroke, which his hour-long innings without a hat may have produced. This diagnosis, already doubtful to Willis, since he reckoned his mop of hair was enough to ward off the sun even in the Sahara, was made less likely next day, when his weakness continued. I put him on after lunch, having told him: 'Have one more try: if you still feel weak, go off at once and back to bed.' The first ball of the session was to Hughes; it was medium pace, of fullish length, and Hughes, launching himself at it, was well caught at shoulder height by Emburey at mid-off. He had scored 48, exactly as he had in his second innings at Melbourne. 'That's the way I do it,' said Willis, wrily. But the mysterious virus did not relent; after two overs he did not object when I told him he should go back to the hotel. For much of the morning I had had Emburey bowling into the breeze (slight though it was), and kept a seamer going from the pavilion end. It was hard work.

Darling broke out with three pulled fours in two overs from Emburey off balls only marginally short. Despite exchanging his white helmet for an Australian cap he was now wilting in the heat, visibly struggling to get back his breath after each run. Miller came on for Emburey. Then Hendrick showed signs of distress, going pale and feeling sick. A second substitute, Edmonds, had to come on. Darling tried to drive Miller, edged, and Botham, fielding in Hendrick's place at backward short leg, caught a fine low catch. Botham had just bowled a spell of five or six overs, and was due for a rest. Now Toohey took a single, and was at the far end. I asked Ian if he could manage just one more over. I need not have asked. Fifth ball, Toohey, trying to force, edged straight to Gooch at second slip. 179-4.

At this point, with Yallop and Border, the two best players of spin in the side, at the wicket, Willis and Hendrick were off the field, and Botham was weary: we were never so depleted of bowlers as at this time. A pressman later asked me about my tactics and bowling changes during this innings: as I said, tactics are easy when casualties remove choice. Miller and Emburey bowled well, and every two or three overs one would turn quickly. Border might have been stumped in the last over before tea, but the ball bounced chest high and Taylor could not gather it cleanly.

The new ball was due shortly after tea, and I had been worried that Hendrick, if he was fit enough, would not be back in time to be allowed to bowl. We signalled frantically to the dressing-room, where, we discovered later, they were frantically trying to revive him in the shower. I said he could stand in the outfield, if necessary, but he must be on the field if possible. He did return before tea, and felt better. I decided that the way to squeeze the maximum numbers of overs out of Botham and Hendrick was to give Hendo four overs with the wind, take Botham off after two, replace him with Gooch, and then have Botham to replace Hendrick. Soon Hendrick had Yallop, who had again played excellently, brilliantly caught at slip by the ubiquitous Botham. Gooch now bowled five tidy and useful overs, almost having Maclean caught at slip.

We rounded off a tremendous day's effort with two late wickets. Australia had slumped, in the four hours between lunch and close of play, from 126-1 to 248-7.

The only criticism I could make of Border's batting in this match concerned his approach while the tail were in with him. Next morning he reached a fine 50, but did not try to take the initiative. Although the last three wickets lasted for 1½ hours, they added only 44 runs and were all out for 294, a lead of 142. We would have to play remarkably well to save the match.

Later, when the result was known, I was held to be a hero for our tactical approach to this innings. That accolade was absurd. Anyone could know that a side starting the third innings of a match 142 runs behind on a pitch increasingly helping spinners would have to score a lot of runs, and/or bat for a long time, to save, let alone win the match. Anyone, too, could tell that if this side did score over 300, they would have a chance of winning the match with their spinners. The problem was not knowing what to do, but doing it. And when Boycott was LBW to the first ball of the innings our chances of doing it looked slim.

As Boycott walked forlornly back to the pavilion, I am told that a member of the Australian Board of Control, watching the match, said, 'That is the final nail in Mr Packer's coffin.' I suppose he meant that Boycott alone might have stood in the way of the series being levelled by Australia. He was doubly wrong, for we saved it without Boycott; and as Mr Packer was not ailing let alone inside a coffin, the temporary surge of support for the official Test team that would have accompanied another win for Australia would have been only a minor irritant, a gadfly on the pachyderm's back.

It was very hot; one vivid memory I have of Sydney is of the Australians in the white-hot field red-faced under their floppy hats. Fortunately for them, and for Randall, the next day was to be a rest day. Randall's innings will be described from different points of view in the next chapter. What most struck me about it was his single-mindedness and restraint. Everyone knew, of course, that we had to bat for a long time, preferably for twelve hours. But we also knew that runs were invaluable: my view was that each player had to sort out the equation for himself. Randall played one off-drive for four, in the second over of the innings: an

'adrenalin shot'. The previous ball he had been perilously close to LBW to Dymock. After that, I cannot remember him playing a single drive for four, except from a full-toss. The reason was that the pitch was slow, and the ball would occasionally 'stop' or 'hold up', that is, disturb the surface as it landed and, instead of skidding through, would come through much slower; a batsman who drove at a ball that was not a full half-volley might spoon the ball up in the air. And playing a long innings is a matter of rhythm: it is hard for a batsman to alter the pattern he creates.

Dymock, as usual, bowled several testing overs with the new ball. Half an hour after lunch, Randall hooked him resoundingly for four. As we met in the middle of the pitch, I said, 'Tremendous shot, Arkle. Keep going.' I was irritated to read in the *Australian* next morning that, according to Henry Blofeld, apparently gifted with long-distance lip-reading, I had at that moment told Randall to cut out such 'perilous' strokes. This restrictive parental role had been attributed to me, again falsely, during out stand of 85 in the second innings of the Centenary Test, when Randall started to attack Lillee.

In fact, during this stand at Sydney, Randall was if anything the main advocate of caution. At one point he thought I was driving too freely at Higgs's leg breaks. ('Come on, skip, a bit loose. We've got to be here at t'close.') I enjoyed the tussle with Higgs enormously. The leg spinner's art appeals to me, both as a means of attack that I would like as captain to have at my disposal, and as an opponent. Both as captain and as batsman, I enjoy the range of possibilities that their freakish and difficult art opens up. Just consider the number of deliveries; leg-break and googly – both of which spin different amounts – top-spinner and flipper. The flipper is a strange ball bowled without spin but with a hand action that looks similar to the batsman to that used for spinning the ball. It seems to keep coming, to land much further up than the batsman at first thinks. A leg-spinner also naturally drifts the ball in to the batsman in the air. All this takes some controlling by the bowler, but it opens up a variety of attacking possibilities. Now, when Higgs came on after an hour or so, his field was amazingly defensive for a side in so commanding a position. Only one man, at slip, was in an attacking position. We could cease to worry about a bat-pad catch, or about edging or gloving a googly on the leg-side. For an hour Yallop persisted with this field, and only in the last over before tea, when the score was 74-1, did he put pressure on us with close fielders. At the end of this over I left my helmet and gloves to dry on the pitch; as I walked off, I turned and saw Wood give a gratuitous little kick to the headless helmet.

We had every encouragement from the rest of the side at tea. After the break we continued as before. Yallop and Higgs had obviously decided to attack more, and were more likely to get us out as a result. I cover-drove Higgs for three, but I carelessly ran one short: two runs only. That annoyed me. Randall continued, irrepressibly, to fidget and to talk to himself, taunting the bowlers, as he had taunted Lillee two years before. I prefer not to antagonize bowlers needlessly; but I get vicarious pleasure from Randall's antics.

Border came on. He is little more than a useful change bowler, but we both felt that it was dangerous on this pitch to drive him. I did not expect him to get me out playing defensively, but at 111 he pitched a ball on middle-and-leg; it turned past my defensive shot, and hit the off-stump. I thought it must have hit a pebble. Seeing the action replay, I realized that I turned my bat on the ball, to play it down on the leg-side, rather than keeping the full face of the bat down the pitch: I think I was afraid of a bat-pad chance to short-leg. Yallop's more attacking field had paid off. Gooch and Randall survived until the close when the score was 133-2. We were just nine runs behind, in precisely the same position Australia had been in at that Nottingham Test in 1977. The odds, still on Australia, had closed.

The temperature next day reached 115° but, mercifully, it was the rest day, and even the habitual beachcombers in the team restricted their sunbathing. Randall, Willis, Lever and I visited Arthur Jackson, not for treatment but for barbecued steaks and a swim in his pool.

On the fourth morning Thomas delivered a gloomy medical report. Gower, who had caught Willis's virus and stayed in bed through rest day, was ill with a high temperature. Willis was still wobbly, Hendrick was drained, and Botham had a splitting headache. It was a piquant situation, at least in news terms, but Insole and I decided not to mention it to the press, even off the record. At this delicate moment in the match, with Australia also weakening in the sun, such reports could only encourage the opposition. Australia kept up their efforts in the field, but Gooch was missed twice in the slips. He had batted almost two hours for his 22 when he was caught off pad and bat at silly mid-off: 169-3. Gower, who had come late to the ground, looked paler than ever, his light-blue eyes giving that strange impression both of innocence and decadence. Ill or not, he played the most fluently of all our players, suddenly making batting look ridiculously easy. Somebody said, 'Look at Lu-Lu: he's got 14 already. He's only been in five minutes, *and* he's sick!'

Yallop did not take the new ball until the 85th over, some time after lunch. I thought he had been right to wait, so as to have Higgs bowl at Gower when he first came in, and to give the fast bowlers the respite of the lunch break, though I would have taken it straight after lunch. The timing of this decision is often difficult: a captain fears that the second new ball will go more sweetly off the bat and lead to a flow of runs. As it happened, Hogg tried to bounce Randall, who hooked him for two consecutive fours to reach his hundred. Two balls later another bouncer was similarly despatched. It was a remarkably gritty century.

Finally, though Hogg and the other bowlers regained their cool against Randall. I can remember few other bouncers bowled at him since the first few overs. Hogg was near the end of his new-ball spell when Gower edged a widish ball to Maclean who had recovered, and who took the catch comfortably. The tantalizing readjustments of balance in the game continued. We were 237-4, only 95 runs ahead. Botham came in. He decided to try at all costs to stay in, and batted 1½ hours for six.

Afterwards, in the dimly-lit inner dressing-room, he and I discussed his method after he got out. It was hard to know whether it was the right one in the circumstances. Occupation of the crease was invaluable, but a quick 30 might have been equally

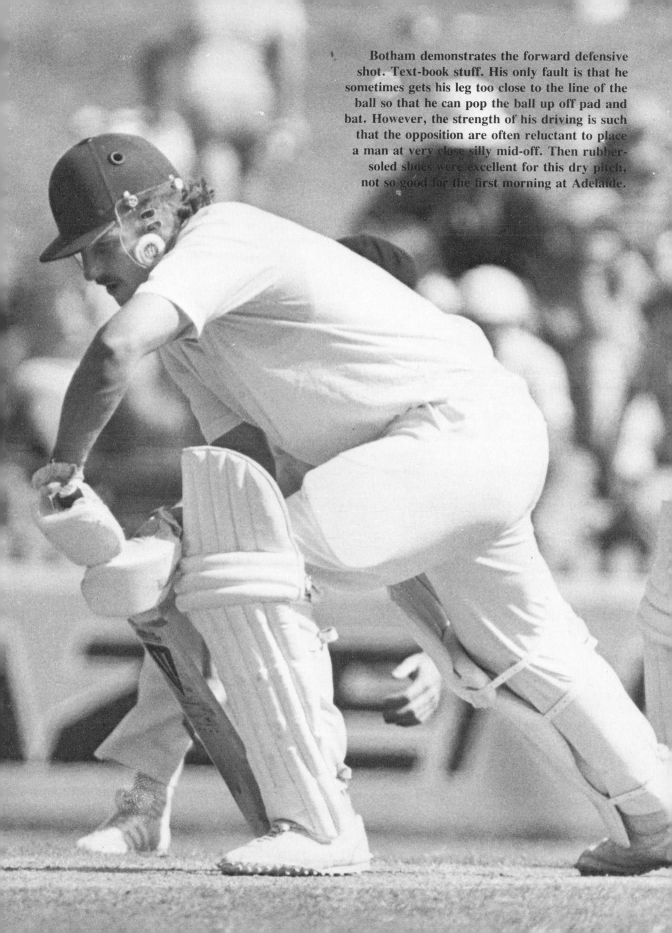

Botham demonstrates the forward defensive shot. Text-book stuff. His only fault is that he sometimes gets his leg too close to the line of the ball so that he can pop the ball up off pad and bat. However, the strength of his driving is such that the opposition are often reluctant to place a man at very close silly mid-off. Then rubber-soled shoes were excellent for this dry pitch, not so good for the first morning at Adelaide.

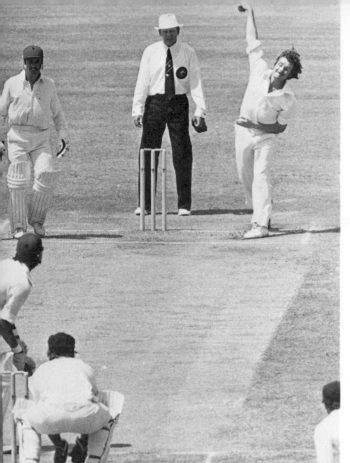

Jim Higgs bowling at Miller during our second innings; the non-striker is Taylor. He has a fine action, his arm high for a leg-spinner. In this innings he bowled 59.6 eight ball overs. His analysis of 5–148 could, with luck, have been 7–70. Leg-spinners are often humourous – they need to be these days, like flower-sellers, rag-and-bone men, and boot-blacks. Jim, when asked how he marks the beginning of his run-up, says he usually gets a mouldy old comb from the umpire. It is sad, for cricket, that Higgs cannot bat better, for then the leg-spinner might have been seen in the World Cup, and would be irreplaceable in the Test team.

useful. Yet Botham's six, so out of character, showed admirable restraint. We stayed in that inner room for a while, discussing what we would do after cricket. Guy could not countenance an office job, which certainly would be out of character. He hopes to take his pilot's licence and start an air passenger service. We also puzzled over a sign on a shower door: PLEASE REMOVE ALL CLOTHES BEFORE ENTERING SHOWERS. Why shouldn't you remove your clothes? Who wouldn't, and for what reason? Furthermore, if you didn't why should the Sydney Cricket Ground authorities really care? What would be the punishment? We then talked of Yallop's criticism of us – of me – in the previous day's press. He said, 'I am very surprised at England's strategy. I always attack, no matter what the situation. Right from the start it was obvious that England were more interested in saving the game than going out for victory.' It was at this time that Botham coined a nickname for the Australian captain. From then on we called him, 'Banzai!' – the cry of a Japanese Kamikazi pilot and would imitate his war-cry, 'Attack-attack-attack!'

Meanwhile, Randall's epic effort had ended. He even apologized for not staying there until the close, which at last came with England 304-6, a lead of 162. The match was poised absorbingly.

On the final day I asked Willis and Barrington to look at the pitch with me. I said, 'Look, supposing we bat really well this morning and get 220 or 230 ahead by lunchtime, should we declare?' Barrington thought that 200 would be enough, but that he would tell the players to hit out rather than declare. Willis too took a cautious line.

I now had two views, three including Randall's. Arkle had said the pitch was still very good (his modesty perhaps preventing him from thinking he could have batted so long if it were not) and he felt we were still in grave danger of defeat. I wanted to weigh several opinions before forming a policy about what position we would need to reach before declaring, or hitting out towards a declaration. If I had been a detached cricket-lover, I should have hoped that England would play some shots, declare and set Australia, say, 220 to win in over four hours. However, as captain I found it hard to countenance a declaration that would court defeat after such a recovery. To have declared and lost would seem worse than never having declared at all; I would have felt I had undone all our toil. On the other hand, if I was over-cautious, time could run out with eight or nine Australian wickets down. We were 2-1 ahead in the series. I knew that I would err on the side of caution. In the event, the decision was taken out of my hands. We were all out 45 minutes before lunch.

The target was 205 in 205 minutes plus fifteen overs. Any result was possible. After the now routine meeting, we went out on the field and

Willis bowled two overs. He was obviously not himself. He looked exhausted, so I told him to go off the field. The last over before lunch, the fifth of the innings, was bowled by Emburey. Two balls turned so sharply that, as we went off at the interval, Emburey turned to me and said, 'We'll win this match.'

For some time after lunch, however, we did not seem likely to do so. Emburey, conscious of his responsibility, was nervous and bowled short, his first three overs costing 19 runs. In his third over, Darling pulled a long hop savagely; the ball hit Botham on the helmet at short leg. Without the helmet he would have been hurt terribly. As we gathered round Botham I asked Lever, fielding as substitute, whether he thought we should change the bowling. He thought I should give Emburey another over, so that he might end on a higher note. I decided not to, for I was anxious to stop the flow of runs. Moreover, if he bowled another bad over, his confidence would have been further shattered.

Australia soon were 38-0. We needed a wicket. Hendrick was bowling with great precision and finally he was rewarded: Darling was well caught low down at second slip by Gooch who was there because Botham, still dizzy, had gone to mid-on. Hughes joined Wood, and six runs later we were presented with a predictable gift, a run-out. It involved Wood, of whom his State captain, Inverarity, told me, 'I have no trouble running with Wood. I judge every run for myself.' Hughes too had learned this rule. Wood hit the ball to cover off Miller, and Botham, at extra cover, ran round and grabbed it right-handed. Wood shouted 'yes', Hughes shouted 'no', and Wood kept running. He was out by almost the length of the pitch: 44-2. In the sun the pitch by now was slower and drier on top. The odd ball held up. Hendrick continued to bowl with pin-point accuracy, and when Yallop came in he bowled four balls all just outside the off stump. The fifth ball landed on the same length as the previous four but was bowled slightly slower. Yallop pushed at the ball and was caught and bowled. Australia were now 45-3. From that point they never looked like winning. Soon after Hendrick came off. He had bowled ten overs and taken two for 17; his bowling was the base from which the spinning operation could be launched.

Miller had confidently settled in at the other end.

Those eyes . . . Gower batting with a fever.

He rightly bowled quicker than he had done in earlier Tests, as the ball was turning sharply: he did not need to rely on flight. For Hughes, we had a six-three leg-side field, including two short legs and a long-on. After a couple of overs I suggested moving a seventh man to the leg-side, leaving short third man open. The advantages of such a move were that it packed the leg-side and encouraged a dangerous flirtation with the idea of scoring on the off-side, playing against the spin. Soon Hughes shaped to run the ball down behind square on the off-side: it spun quickly, took the inside edge as he adjusted his shot, and went via the pad to short square leg: 59-4. Toohey, also facing a seven-two leg-side field, was completely stuck, and when he tried to off-drive Miller he played over the ball and was bowled: 74-5.

Australians have a curious attitude to leg-side fields. They consider that it is always an unreasonably defensive tactic, and allow only five men on the leg-side in their domestic cricket. Once, captaining MCC against Greg Chappell's side at

Lord's, I put seven men on the leg-side for Geoff Miller: Chappell threw his bat on the ground in disgust. I find it hard to understand their annoyance at this method of attack. In the second innings of the fourth Test it would have been absurd to have fielders loitering on the off-side with nothing to do. The seven-two field on this pitch was an attacking field, and with it we took wickets quickly. Yet even then, after we took ten wickets in the space of two and a half hours, there were complaints in a radio interview that this field-placing was somehow unfair.

Border came in, to put up a resolute, skilful last-ditch fight. He played some splendid drives, especially on the off-side, and was particularly quick to get back and pull anything at all short. He hit six fours with that shot. On the difficult pitch, Miller and Emburey were bowling superbly, but rarely looked like getting him out, and he finished the match having scored 105 runs without being out. No-one else, however, was at all comfortable. Emburey had come back after Hendrick's fine spell to make an all off-spin combination. Although ideally one would wish one's spin attack to contain both types of spin, our two off-break bowlers complemented each other. Emburey, with his long, high arm action, starting off from down by his right calf, makes the ball bounce, which was why I usually brought him on before Miller while the ball was still hard. Someone described him as a slow-bowling Thomson. He has a good 'arm' ball, and it is difficult to come down the pitch to him. Miller, with his new approach, flighted the ball more, and invited the batsmen to make mistakes while attacking. He also helped Emburey by constant encouragement before and during this Test, and by pooling their knowledge of the spinner's art.

They used this knowledge to telling effect. After Miller yet again had Maclean caught close in, Emburey took the last four wickets. Hogg was caught at short-leg, Dymock dragged one on, Higgs was LBW, and Hurst had a whack and was bowled. We had won by 93 runs with 57 minutes to spare. After the tour, I heard a tape of Christopher Martin-Jenkins's commentary on the last half-hour. I could feel the romance of these early morning broadcasts from 'down under', and appreciate afresh the fact that this was 'the best comeback from nowhere that I have ever played in'.

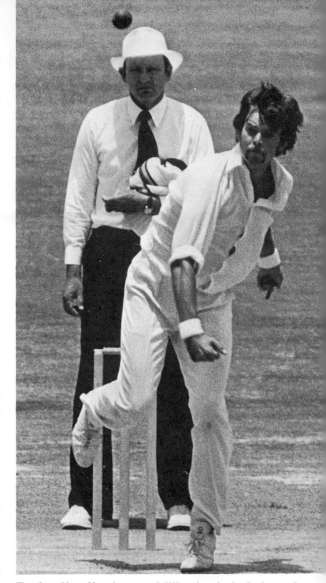

England's off-spinners. Miller is nicely balanced, while the picture of Emburey shows his Thommo-like action. Later in the series, Miller was asked by an Australian batsman to remove his sweat-bands while bowling; a reasonable request, after I had told Hogg I might be distracted and have to complain if he bowled with them on.

CHAPTER 10

Rags to Riches

The batting highlight of the fourth Test, indeed the highlight of the series, was Derek Randall's Man of the Match 150 in the second innings. Afterwards Dudley Doust spoke with all the bowlers Randall faced, the Australian captain, Randall's batting partner's, Randall himself, other members of the touring party, and, together with ball-by-ball records provided by Bill Frindall, reconstructed a memorable marathon.

ON THE MORNING of the third day of the fourth Test Derek Randall woke after ten hours' sleep, refreshed but uneasy. One thought had nagged deep in his mind throughout the night. Rags, you're going in to bat today, he thought, and you've got to get some runs. He swung his legs out of bed, gazed a moment at his dozing room-mate, Phil Edmonds, then got up and picked his way through a litter of clothes to the window.

The sun was already beating down. Sydney with the great Harbour Bridge and the glistening white fins of the Opera House lay below him. He was not impressed, his own idea of a fine view being one of green fields and a few trees and perhaps an English church spire in the distance. Still, the sky was blue and unblemished, much as it had been on the previous day, and this suggested a long, hot day for batting. The prospect lifted his spirits, and he broke into song. 'Oh, what a beautiful morning,' he hummed, '. . . I've got a beautiful feeling, everything's going my way.' He rubbed the palms of his hands together. 'Come on, Rags,' he said. 'Got to get some runs.'

Randall lives in a world of his own, peopled principally by himself, Rags. His team-mates call

him 'Arkle', after the racehorse, for his speed about the field, but, to himself, Randall, now 27, has been Rags ever since his ragamuffin days as a schoolboy in Retford, Nottinghamshire. It was there, as a little boy, that he developed his skill in pulling a ball. His companions, bowling, would dig in short balls and Randall, the tiniest of them all, would smash away at the lifting balls. His unlikely hero was the tall and elegant Tom Graveney, whose picture hung on his bedroom wall. His dream was to play for the Ashes in Australia.

Now the Ashes were in danger. England had lost at Melbourne, where their comfortable two-game lead was whittled to one, and in this fourth game Australia had moved into a 96-run lead with three of their wickets still standing in their first innings. The thought of returning to Nottingham, to his wife and son, to his mother, with the Ashes gone, subdued Randall. Instead of moving about in his usual effervescent, bird-like manner, he consciously restrained himself. He dressed slowly.

The telephone rang. It was Barrington on his morning ring-round. '9.15 in reception,' he said. 'Don't be late.' Randall went down to the hotel coffee shop where he took his customary breakfast of fruit, poached eggs and bacon, haunted by memories of his innings two days earlier. He had got out, second ball, caught for a duck at backward square leg off Hurst, hooking. Second ball and *hooking*. Randall recalled the lecture he had received from Insole that evening. The England manager had sought him out after stumps and, driving back to the hotel with him, had impressed two points upon Randall: if England were in trouble, as clearly they now were, it was his responsibility to stay in. It was his *responsibility* to have a long look at the bowlers and get the pace of the wicket before he started hooking. At Perth, Insole continued, Randall had been out fifth ball, senselessly mis-hooking Hogg. 'Another thing,' Insole later recalled telling Randall, 'you simply have *got* to learn to play your innings in segments. You have got to be there at lunch. You have got to be there at tea. You have got to be there at close.'

Randall had listened, half chastened. The bit about batting in segments was good advice, he agreed. But he was in two minds about restraining himself from hooking early in an innings. 'I've got to get a couple of good shots early on for my confidence,' he said. 'That's the way I play.' 'Well, in that case, and in these circumstances,' Insole had replied, 'maybe you had better give some serious thought to the way you play.' The lecture was over but, two mornings later, it was in Randall's mind.

By the time he arrived at the Sydney ground – about 10.30 – the temperature had climbed into the 90s, and Randall decided that although he was due for a full practice he would try to conserve his energy. The surfaces of the nets were so poor that England took their practice in the middle of the Sydney Cricket Ground's second field, in proper batting order. Randall faced only about forty balls, around half his usual number and, mindful of his first innings misadventure, he concentrated on rolling his wrists, getting each ball quickly on to the ground. Chris Old simulated the Australian seamers for him, Ken Barrington stood in for the spinners and John Lever took the role of the hostile Hogg, sharpening Randall's alertness with a few savage bumpers. By the end he was satisfied. He was also satisfied with the look of his bat. He uses a 2lb 7oz off-the-rack Gunn and Moore, with an extra wrapping of rubber round the handle. Glancing at it, feeling the smooth grains, he drew comfort from the fact that it was spotless: the evening before he had spent several minutes in the England dressing room sanding off the red ball-marks. The rest of his gear was similarly spick-and-span. The pavilion attendant had whitened his pads and boots while Randall himself had made certain his six pairs of flannels and shirts and twelve pairs of socks were all clean. His hotel room may be in shambles – the curtains drawn, bed rumpled, clothes and food trays strewn about, shaving gear cluttering the washbasin – but he comes immaculate to the crease. 'It is important that your gear is neat and tidy,' he says. 'It puts you in the frame of mind to *play* neat and tidy.'

In the dressing room Randall took a cold shower to cool his blood before changing into his fielding flannels – which, again, are trim and well-cut. His fielding boots are sturdy and bear long studs. He wore the second of the two caps allotted him for the tour: the first had been stolen by a fan the week before at Melbourne. At 11 o'clock the England side took the field. It took over 1½ hours to remove the last three wickets. Australia's innings finally closed at 294, 142 runs ahead of England.

England were left with eight minutes' batting before lunch. Randall took his second cold shower of the day and changed into batting gear: flannels, which to accommodate his thigh pad are looser than his fielding flannels; boots – lighter, and with shorter studs than his fielding boots; a box; and then his gloves – something out of the ordinary, for Randall is the only England batsman who wears inner gloves: the same as a wicketkeeper's inner gloves, but without the padding. Randall uses them to absorb sweat. Further, the first two fingers of his right batting glove have extra padding, despite which his right forefinger is often sore.

The one piece of gear Randall will *not* wear is a batting helmet. 'I've been hit on the head three times, once badly by Colin Croft,' he says. 'But I still won't wear a batting helmet. I haven't found one that is safe. They've all got a steel bolt just at your temple, and if the ball hits that the bolt will go straight through your head.'

Boycott and Brearley went out to open England's second innings, Randall settling in a corner of the dressing room, uncharacteristically solemn. He sipped a cup of tea. Before he had finished it a roar went round the ground: Boycott had been trapped for nought, first ball, LBW – once again to Hogg. Silence fell over the dressing room, interrupted by curses. Randall rose to his feet, swivelled his hips, swung his arms round his waist, then strode across the dressing room. Suddenly he shook his fist at the ceiling. 'Come on, Rags,' he shouted. 'Come on, England!'

He made his way down the pavilion steps, hardly looking up when he passed Boycott, who as usual remarked 'Good luck.' Randall nodded gratefully, then passed through the picket gate on to the field. He does not immediately cut an imposing figure.

He is small for a cricketer, standing 5ft. 8½in. tall and weighing 11½ stone. In contrast, his feet are enormous, size 11, and this lends a loping air to his entrance which soon becomes pure theatre. He windmills his bat full-circle round his side, then sweeps it forward in flowing cover drives. It is not just bravado: he feels this is his last chance to loosen up before receiving the dangerous first balls of an innings. It burns off nervousness, and enhances an image: here comes David to slay Goliath.

Thus began what was to be a tense, sweltering 582-minute battle between Randall and the Australians. His first minor skirmish was a personal one, with Yallop.

The Australian captain has no time for Randall, who he feels violates the spirit of the game. For example, Randall is cool towards the Australians: unlike Gower, Hendrick and especially Old and Botham, he does not join the Aussies for a dressing-room drink after a match. 'When in Rome,' Yallop will say, 'do as the Romans do.'

The Australian is irritated at Randall's constant fussing and jabbering at the crease. 'He's a clown – and that's putting it mildly. He sounds like an idiot, always talking to himself. A lot of people and players think his talk helps him concentrate in his batting. I disagree. I think if you can suggest a few questions for him to think about he will lose his concentration.' Accordingly Yallop was eager to fire off an opening psychological salvo. As Randall approached the middle Yallop beckoned to Graeme Wood and together they examined the pitch closely, picking at the wicket just short of a length. For almost a minute they conferred in hushed, conspiratorial tones then, their tactical mission accomplished, they resumed their places.

Randall saw what they were at and was not taken

This is not a stroke for the coaching manual, nor, Randall decided, was it one to be risked in England's present predicament. There is no name for the stroke. Randall occasionally played it to a ball outside the off-stump, well up but not half-volley length. He puts his left foot forward a short distance, then swings through with his right leg and right side, hitting the ball wide of mid-on. As Higgs said, 'He's inconsistent: if you twice bowl the same ball to Randall, he'll play the two in totally different ways.'

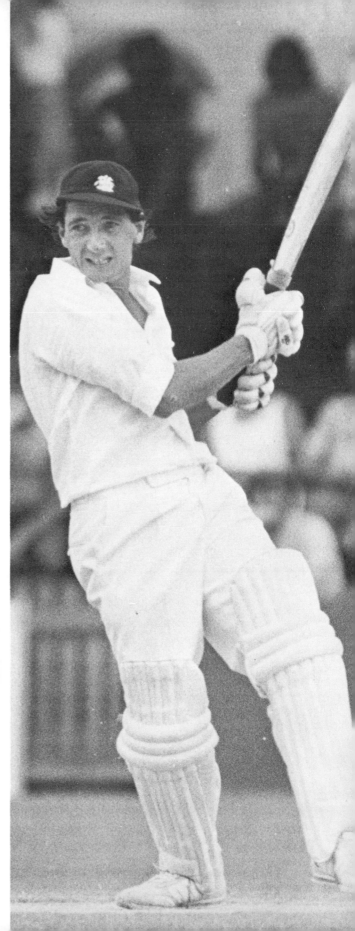

in. He knew that they were trying to suggest that the top surface of the wicket was breaking up for the spinners, but he could see plainly that it was still in fairly firm shape and wasn't worried. Nonetheless, he slowly paced down the wicket, he too now staring at the brown soil – but for a very different reason. Whatever Yallop might have thought, this was no counter-ploy: Randall's wicket-staring served a purpose. He had been in a darkened dressing room and he wanted his eyes to grow accustomed to the colour of the wicket – a tip learnt from Barrington during the 1976-77 tour of India. Yallop's antics allowed him precious extra time to acclimatize himself. Similarly, he turned to gaze down the wicket to the sight screen, so that his eyes might become used to the white glare of the screen.

Next he took guard. He scratched his right boot across the ground, loosening the hard-packed soil. Jabbing down his bat, he called to the umpire, Bailhache, 'Two legs, please, Robin.' By chance it came right, spot on, the face of his bat square to the line between middle and leg stumps. Bailhache signalled as much, and Randall was happy. A simple act had worked perfectly, first look and neat as a notch, and he found it remarkably comforting. Eagerly he knocked in his mark with the toe of his bat, deriving palpable pleasure from the feeling of it in the soil, then began talking to himself – softly at first but gathering in volume and venom according to the problems and pressures at hand. The monologue was maddening to the opposition, and it continued almost unabated for the nine hours and forty-two minutes that Randall spent at the crease. In part it would run:

> 'Come on, Rags. Get stuck in. Don't take any chances. Get forward, get *forward*. Get behind the ball. Take your time, slow and easy. You *idiot*, Rags. Come on, come *on*.
> Come on, England.'

If he makes a mistake or his concentration starts to flag, he will punch himself in the chest with his right fist. 'Wake up, Rags, concentrate. *Concentrate*, you idiot!' He especially pesters himself at the opening of an innings, an anxiety that dates back to the summer of 1974 when he 'made five ducks on the trot'.

Hogg still had seven balls left after his first, a looseler, had claimed Boycott's wicket. It was

Hogg's thirtieth wicket of the series. Twice he had got Randall, that time half-hooking at Perth and later LBW at Melbourne. Without doubt Hogg was Australia's discovery of the series, and appeared en route to a wicket-taking record (by comparison England's leading wicket-taker at the time was Willis with 15). At this early stage of an innings, however, his pace struck no terror in the England player. 'Hoggy always takes a few overs to loosen up,' is Randall's view. 'He's not Dennis Lillee. Lillee loosens up in the dressing room and comes out full of venom from the start.'

Like Lillee, however, Hogg is cast in the accepted emotional mould of the fast bowler: moody and temperamental. A fidgety batsman such as Randall, muttering a stream of incomprehensible gibberish, upsets him. Randall was not unaware of this. Indeed, he had managed to bait the tempestuous Hogg the first time he saw him. It was during the England-South Australia State match. Randall did not play, but after Hogg reaped a crop of first innings wickets, Randall muttered to him, 'Don't worry, Hoggy. You'll get your chance at me in future.' Hogg, for all his wrath, is a mild and innocent man, and he was puzzled by Randall's remark. It seemed ambiguous to him but, somehow, intentionally annoying. So did Randall's foot-shuffling. 'The very first time I bowled at Randall was in the First Test at Brisbane and he put me off a fair bit,' Hogg explained. 'When I come in I always watch the batsman or his bat, not the stumps, and Randall is always moving across before I bowl.' After three Tests Hogg now reckoned the way to bowl to Randall was a good length off stump or to bounce him, middle stump, up round the forehead, and hope for a top edge.

This tactic raised problems, Hogg realised. He couldn't properly bounce a ball at Sydney. 'They've got no life in the wickets. You can't get any pace or cut. You can't get the ball to lift at this place,' he says with disgust. That Hogg finds these wickets dead is not the only reason he loathes playing cricket at Sydney. What wind there is prevails from the Randwick End, which would be fine, bowling with the wind at his back, but such advantage is nullified by the fact that the run-up from the Randwick End is slightly uphill. Then, during the first England innings, Hogg had fielded at fine leg at the Paddington End where the air was

so hot and stuffy he suffered his worst attack of asthma in the series.

Finally, he was disappointed at his side's reply of 294 runs to England's first innings total of 152. He suffers the paranoia common among fast bowlers: his batsmen had let him down. 'We had England on toast,' he says, 'and then we screwed up our innings.' All these obstacles and setbacks, together with the pounding heat, left him in a poor frame of mind. 'Some days you feel like bowling and some days you don't; I didn't on that day.'

Randall could see Hogg's listlessness in the slump of his shoulders but, with only five minutes until lunch, it was a dangerous time to be slack. As Hogg walked back to his mark, Yallop turned on the screws. He crowded his fielders round the bat, and began to chant 'Come on, Aussies, come on!' It simply struck Randall as ironic: an Establishment player such as Yallop was singing a pop song that had been specially composed to promote Packer's cricket.

Hogg turned, heaved a sigh and came in off a fullish run, feet splayed. Randall shuffled across the crease but the ball came through slowly, outside the off stump, and he let it go. The next ball was equally benign and Randall pushed forward and took an easy single. He was off the mark.

He was now at the non-striker's end and, as

The apprehensive look of a man in the dock expecting an unfavourable verdict and the mandatory sentence. Counsel for the prosecution are convinced of his guilt, but Judge French gave Randall the benefit of the doubt. So much for our little joke that we were playing 'French' cricket – we were out if the ball hit us on the legs! Notice how Randall has quickly shoved his left leg outside the line of the leg-stump. Dymock is bowling, Maclean behind the wicket.

Hogg ran past to bowl at Brearley, Randall frowned conspicuously at the bowler's hand. He spoke to the umpire. Would he take a look at Hogg's right forefinger? Was it wrapped in tape? Bob Taylor had raised this suspicion to the team near the end of the first innings and, at the opening of the second innings, only moments before, Brearley had observed Hogg's finger and been satisfied that it was only discoloured. At Randall's request, however, Hogg's finger was examined. The fast bowler's eyes blazed. 'It's stuff for my blisters,' he cried out. Indeed, his finger was covered by a mild astringent, potassium permangate, which is used quite legally to dry blisters. But Randall had won another skirmish: so much so that Hogg stepped over to him and gave him a firm little slap on the jaw.

'What's that on your fingers, Hoggy?'

Later in the over Brearley scored a two and a single, and Randall then played a bad delivery – a half volley off leg stump – towards mid-wicket for two runs. He took off his cap to mop his brow: already the heat was oppressive. He was pleased, however, for not only had he survived the first over but he had scored three runs off four balls. He had also annoyed Hogg. He glanced at the pavilion clock. Less than a minute remained before 1 o'clock: still time for one more over.

Geoff Dymock was to bowl it from the Paddington End. A shy man with a wry smile, Dymock is 33 and first faced Randall on Australia's tour of England in 1977. On that tour the Englishman's habit of shuffling across his crease had been even more distracting to Dymock than it was to be to Hogg. In England, confused, Dymock had soon lost his line, then his length. In the current series, played on Australia's faster pitches, Randall's shuffling was even more pronounced, but Dymock had come to terms with it. Forget his feet, the left-hander reminded himself, with luck I'll get him LBW: he is vulnerable to the inswinger. And an inswinger was the first ball he bowled.

On target, the ball nipped into the Englishman and the next moment thudded against Randall's pad, just below the knee. Dymock was up in the air, arms thrown to the sky. To his dying day he will swear that the ball was on line for middle stump. Randall stood frozen to the spot, feeling sick and frightened. To himself, he thought: 'That's out.' But Umpire Dick French didn't move and Randall breathed a sigh of relief. A moment later he was cursing himself. 'Rags,' he muttered, 'you've got to get stuck in. You've got to get forward, get *forward*.'

Dymock tried the same ball again. This time, however, it was over-pitched, didn't move, and Randall, still frightened but now furious with himself, hit it firmly through the covers for four. He did not even bother to run. He was still fidgeting, though, and in the course of the next four balls he played and missed again. Dymock had beaten him twice in an over, and it was with relief that Randall went to lunch. England were 11 for the loss of one wicket, with Randall 7 and Brearley 4.

The temperature was approaching 100°F. As sweat ran down his face and gathered behind his knees Randall walked, pads flapping, towards the pavilion. At the boundary, he shed his wet inner gloves and his batting gloves and left them to dry in the sun. In the dressing room he took yet another cold shower and changed clothes for the third time. For the third time his non-playing team-mates, Chris Old, Roger Tolchard and Clive Radley, who served him well through the innings, carried the heavy wet clothing out of the dressing room, down some back stairs and to the boiler-room behind the stands. Randall eats very little during an innings – at most cheese, salad, ice cream and several cups of tea. He lay awhile on a bench and forty minutes later was back in the middle.

His battle with Hogg now began in earnest. The Australian enjoys a one-against-one combat as much as the next fast bowler. For example, through the series he was so eager to take the wicket of Ian Botham, his off-the-field companion, that he often fell down at the end of a delivery. After it had happened a couple of times Botham affected a ritual response. 'Come on, Hoggy, get up,' he would say piteously. 'I know you think I'm great, but there's no need to go down on your knees to me.'

Hogg found this amusing, even endearing. But there was nothing amusing about Randall's antics. He was a badger, always provoking, always baiting him. In the first over after lunch, Hogg was still toiling in frustration from the up-hill Randwick End. He was bowling at Brearley and, in his fourth delivery, stepped over the crease. No-ball. As he turned to make his way back to his mark he found Randall prodding the line with the toe of his bat. Hogg was livid. 'Stop scratching round where my foot lands!' he shouted. 'I'm not scratching round,' Randall replied, 'I'm showing the umpire where your foot landed.' Hogg swore. 'I don't go where a

PHOTOGRAPHS: MELBOURNE *AGE*

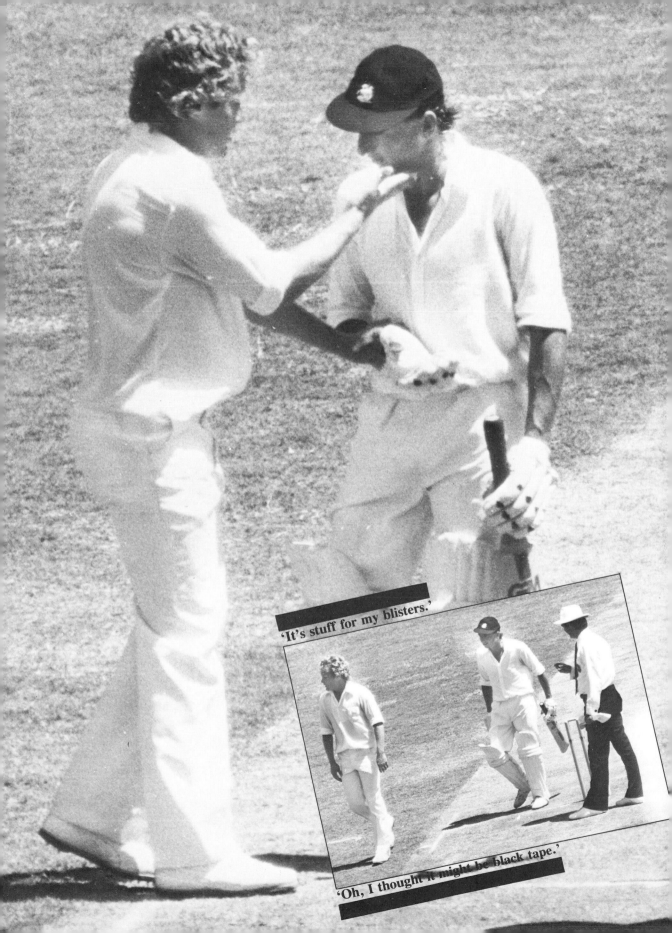

'It's stuff for my blisters.'

'Oh, I thought it might be black tape.'

batsman stands and start fiddling round.' He looked at the umpire. There ensued a brief discussion about whether Randall was digging at the spot where Hogg's foot was landing. Hogg became visibly upset. 'I like to keep an eye on where I land,' he said later. 'If it's all dug up I can crook an ankle or a heel.'

The next ball Hogg again stepped over the crease and Brearley dispatched the ball past cover point for two. Hogg immediately vented his frustrations. On his way back to his mark he indeed 'fiddled round' where Randall stood, stomping his boot into the ground, pawing it like a bull. A single two balls later gave Randall the strike. On the second ball Hogg again landed over the crease, and Randall played the no-ball neatly wide of deep third man for four. The Australian replied with a bouncer, slightly outside the off stump, which Randall let go. Hogg rushed in again, neck flung forward with the fury of a farmyard goose. An outstretched arm from Umpire Bailhache – another no-ball. It arrived wide, outside the off stump, and with regret Randall had to let it go by. 'Come on, England,' he muttered to himself. 'We've got Hoggy going now.' The final ball of the over came through harmlessly. For Hogg, shoulders slumped, pace and rhythm gone, it had been a calamitous beginning to the afternoon session. He had bowled twelve deliveries that over, four of them no-balls. Off two of these runs had been scored and, in all, nine runs had been put on by the Englishmen. The clock read 1.49. After three overs, England were 20 for one, with Randall on 11 and Brearley on 7. Both batsmen were well set.

Hogg, after consulting Yallop, decided he had had enough of bowling uphill and first Hurst, then Dymock, took over from the Randwick End. In the next two overs Randall twice played the same noteworthy shot. He angled the face of his bat, and by letting the ball come on he deflected scoring shots between slips and gully. Dymock, on the receiving end, calls Randall's stroke an 'English shot'. He finds it 'peculiar to English players. I don't know why.' Randall does. 'It's a "one-day" shot,' he says. 'It's not necessarily a good shot because you're playing it with half the bat, but it's a way of accumulating runs if you're not worried about wickets. And at that stage I felt confident and able to do it.'

After thirteen overs England had increased their total to 49 runs, with Randall on 28 and Brearley on 17. Drinks came on, and the two English batsmen mingled with the Australians. Randall drank a glass of Accolade, a glucose drink, and taking a second glass moved over to Hogg. 'Come on, Hoggy, show me your finger,' he taunted. Hogg glowered. 'I wouldn't show you my backside,' he answered. Randall chuckled. 'I see your backside every time you bowl.' Hogg puzzled over the ambiguity and swore. 'Randall annoys me a lot,' he said nearly a month later, still angry. 'He's always trying to get my goat. He's always saying something stupid.'

Randall batted without incident for the next hour. He is much at ease batting with Brearley. He finds his captain an excellent judge of a run, which is reassuring, and an unruffled player who can put a partner at ease. 'The only problem with The Captain', he will say, using Brearley's title with a nice blend of cheek and deference, 'is that when the crowd gets noisy I have to ask him to shout a bit louder.'

As Insole had suggested, Randall by now was playing his innings in sections: it was a rare display of discipline. Brearley, who was a partner during Randall's Centenary Test 174, is amused by the precision of Randall's thinking when he is in this mood. 'Come on, don't give it away,' Randall had urged at Melbourne. 'In only *five* minutes' time it will be only fifteen minutes until tea.' In his mind, the only way England might save the match – at no stage in his batting marathon did he believe England might win it – was to bat for a long while, perhaps for two days. He therefore chose to play slowly, using up as much time as possible without arousing the ire of the umpires.

One time-consuming ploy, used at this stage and throughout the innings, was to ask the umpire as often as possible for fly-repellent, even though the flies were not bothering him. Randall found that the cream repellent carried by French was the more useful in this respect: it took longer to apply than the spray from Bailhache's aerosol can. In the hour between drinks and tea he scored only three runs, all cautious singles, off the thirty balls he received. At tea England were 74, with Randall 37 and Brearley 33.

As they left the field Randall again drifted over towards the Australians. He singled out Dymock. 'You were hard done by,' he said. 'You had me plumb LBW on your first ball before lunch.' It took a moment to sink into Dymock – 'You don't expect someone to say that sort of thing,' he remarked later – and his friend Hurst overheard and shrugged. 'That's some consolation,' he said to his team-mate and the subject was dropped. During tea, Randall took his fourth cold shower and changed into his fourth set of clothing. He drank several cups of tea and ate none of the small cakes and sandwiches.

Back in the middle Randall enjoyed a respite. At 4.40 Yallop brought on Allan Border, the left arm slow bowler from New South Wales – not thought by England, or indeed by himself, to be a major Test problem. 'I'm the sort of bowler I like to bat against,' he says disarmingly. Border's idea was to bowl tight to Randall in the hope that the Englishman, basically an on-side player, would try to score to leg and make a mistake against the spin. Randall was not tempted, even by several half-vollies. Border felt Randall should have been more attacking, but the Englishman, by now very tired, was content with the occasional single.

The next milestone came at 5.13: Brearley's 50. Five balls later Randall swept the leg-spinner Jim Higgs for two to reach his own half-century. It had taken him 207 minutes and contained just four boundaries. So preoccupied had he been with spending time at the crease, craning round to look at the clock on the pavilion, that his 50 came as a surprise. Staring up at the scoreboard he also noticed the England score: 109. The dreaded Nelson was coming up and, indeed, a single by Randall and one by Brearley brought England exactly to 111.

'Nelson', according to legend, derives from a coarse old schoolboy joke. Question: what sailor does 111 stand for? Answer: Nelson – because he had one eye, one arm and one arsehole. Anyway, Nelson is England's superstitious sticking point (Australia's is 87, or thirteen short of 100), and the batsman on that number is doomed to get out. The legend does allow for one antidote which can nullify Nelson: all the team-mates of a player on Nelson must lift their feet off the ground.

The bowling had changed ends. On 'Nelson' Brearley faced Border. Back in the dressing room Willis commanded the other England players to pick their feet off the floor. Randall himself is not superstitious but it crossed his mind that in the

Hogg in agony: 'Trust you to get a nick on it when you'd have been plumb LBW.'

third Test at Melbourne he had been out, LBW, for 13: just to stay on the safe side, he gave little skips in the air as Border bowled to the England captain. It did no good. On the fifth ball of the over Border bowled Brearley with a sharply turning ball. He had scored 53 runs and left England at 111 for two.

Graham Gooch was the next man in. Randall met him in the middle and, with only forty minutes until stumps, he urged caution. 'We've got to stay in until the end.' As though to demonstrate this prudence, twenty minutes later Randall received a full toss, head-high, from Higgs. He later remembered the shot vividly. 'Most times I would have put it away for four, but I was so concerned with not losing my wicket I became over-cautious and played softly down to the man at square for a single. If I had gone for it I might have hit it straight down his throat.' As it was, Randall and Gooch kept the scoreboard ticking over, adding eleven runs in the next half hour. Then, in the final ten minutes, against Hogg and Border, Randall scored off a pair of loose balls, a three and a single. 'They got sloppy,' he said later. 'They thought I was already in the shower.' At stumps England were 133 for the loss of two wickets, and Randall, on 65, was still at the crease.

He was exhausted. Back in the dressing room he peeled off his sodden gear and slumped on to a bench. Insole came up and offered his hand.

Randall took it without a word: he had answered the call for caution. Stopping for neither a shower nor tea, he travelled back to his hotel and went straight to his room. There he soaked in a hot bath, drank two pots of tea and half-heartedly watched television as he waited for room service to send up his dinner. He dined alone on onion soup, steak and chips, strawberries and ice cream. Soon he was fast asleep. Near dawn, he began to snore, great saw-stroke snores that woke his room-mate, Edmonds, who reached over and thumped him in the ribs. Randall came half-awake, cursing. 'Leave me alone,' he muttered, 'got to get some runs,' and with that he went back to sleep.

The next day was Rest Day – no cricket – and Randall woke late. He thought of home and, with a pang of loneliness, of his wife speaking over the telephone of the snow falling over Nottinghamshire. He longed to go home and sit for a fortnight doing nothing. He thought of pigs. On his departure in October his wife had bought two of them to keep herself company. A few weeks later she bought four more and, worse still, both she and their infant son Simon had grown fond of the animals. Which put an end to the idea of pork. Then there was the matter of transportation. Randall had thought he might be able to carry the pigs in the back of the car but Ian Botham, who knew something about such things, said that was a poor idea: the pigs would eat up the back seat. Anyway, Randall concluded, Liz was coming out in a month. There would be time to discuss the pigs then.

Randall spent the afternoon and early evening with Brearley, Willis, Hendrick and Lever at the suburban home of Dr Arthur Jackson, the hypnotherapist. Randall was in fine form, clowning, riding the children's chute into the swimming pool, feasting on the barbecued steaks. Unlike Brearley and Willis, he would have nothing to do with hypnotherapy. 'None of that stuff for me.' Randall was in bed, resting, by the time his room-mate Edmonds returned from the beach in the evening.

On the fourth day of the Test the weather was even more humid – two drinks intervals, not one, were authorised per session for that day. When Randall got to the ground the temperature had already climbed over 100° and he decided not to go into the nets. Unusually, he signed no autographs. The six changes of shirts, flannels and socks were again out waiting for him.

The Australians opened with Hogg, Hurst and then Dymock – whom Randall did not relish facing again – from the Paddington End. Hogg toiled from the Randwick End.

Higgs is a right-arm leg-spinner from Victoria, and, since England rarely face leg-spinners, he can be awkward. Yet he now bowled the odd full toss, and spun the ball too much. But he was also bowling into the rough outside the off stump, so Randall had to play him with caution. He glanced at the scoreboard – the overs ticked by, 55, 56, 57 – and he longed for the return of Hogg.

Higgs laboured on. He went round the wicket, bowled outside leg stump, with a man at mid-wicket, a backward square leg on the fence, a short fine leg. He bowled around Randall's legs, trying to entice him to sweep. If he tries to hit it with any power, thought Higgs, he's going to be in trouble: I've got to get him to hit across a spinning ball. Randall fixed his mind on the task in hand: block and run for singles on the leg-side. Stay put at the crease. He thought of Barrington's cautionary aphorism: 'When it's going for you, book in for a bed and breakfast.'

At 11.50 England were 146, with Randall 73 and Gooch 10. It was then that an accident occurred in the stands which shattered Randall's concentration. Higgs was bowling at Gooch. Randall was at the non-striker's end when suddenly a cameraman toppled from his perch beyond the sight screen in the Bradman Stand. The man, who had passed out in the heat, landed on his head and shoulders on a concrete passageway. Randall, genuinely upset by the accident, appealed for the game to be stopped while the man was carried out of the ground. Yallop protested, claiming that once again Randall was stalling for time. That Randall had indeed been shaken by the incident was attested to by the next seven balls, when he twice played and missed, groping at deliveries from the pace bowler Hurst.

The final ball of that over was a crucial one. Randall was flustered; Hurst knew it, and moved in for the kill. He had reached the conclusion, after three Tests, that unless he could get a ball to rise above face-level to Randall there was no point in bouncing him. The Englishman could shuffle across his crease and hook for four any bouncer that didn't get up. Yet there was Randall, still chattering to himself, shifting from one foot to the other, a

Shortly before reaching his hundred.

bundle of nerves. He decided to bounce him.

Hurst pounded in, and delivered the ball with that singular slingy action of his. But it didn't get up, and only reached Randall about waist-high. Rolling his wrists, he hit it with ease through square leg for four. Hurst stood, hands on hips, cursing. He had had Randall on the ropes and now, after just this one shot, the irksome little Englishman looked back on top, his taste for the fight renewed. The shot also took England to 150, and Randall to 77.

The new ball was due next over, the 65th, but

Yallop persevered with the old, soon bringing on both spinners, Higgs and Border, to work a protracted spell in tandem for the first time in the innings. In the first over Higgs dismissed Gooch, well caught at silly mid-off by Wood, for 22. It was 12.32, England were 169 for three wickets, with Randall on 83.

Gower now came in, ill and with a high temperature. The England team recognize Gower as a virtuoso batsman, not to be tampered with, and, meeting him in the middle of the pitch, Randall did not this time urge caution. Yallop soon had his bowlers coming round the wicket to the left-hander, and constantly shifted his fieldsmen against him. At one stage Randall even gave the Australian captain some help, correcting Yallop and motioning a fieldsman still further along at fine leg. It was an act of pure mischief, and immediately the Australian captain complained to the umpire.

At lunch England were 191, Randall 87 and Gower 18. Randall showered again, again changed his clothing and ate nothing. He drank 'stacks of tea'. He had been batting for a day, had received 314 balls and was both nervous and exhausted.

The afternoon began slowly, and at 2.06, just before the 85th over, Yallop finally took the new ball. When Hogg returned next over he had enjoyed a 160-minute, 28-over rest. He was fresh, or as fresh as one could hope in a cauldron of 105°. Hogg's plan was plain. Randall was on 95, on the threshold of his century, but jittery. Hogg could hear him urging himself on: 'Come on, Rags. Keep forward. Don't throw it away.' Hogg reckoned the little son-of-a-bitch was ripe for yet another bouncer.

The Australian came thundering in, past Gower. The first ball dug in short. Randall was across his crease like a cat. He was up on his toes, too; and hooked it square to the boundary. Randall was 99. Hitching up his box, he jabbed anxiously at the ground: the shot hadn't come sweetly off the bat and he nearly had got a top edge. Next ball, another bouncer. Randall middled this one, hitting it finer, and this, too, galloped untouched to the boundary. 103: he had reached his century. He had also, he learned later, earned himself a place in the record books for having scored the slowest century – 411 minutes – in the long history of the 324 Tests which at that time had been played between England and Australia.

The fans poured out. One man even brought his girlfriend to shake Randall's hand. Gower came down the wicket to congratulate his team-mate. Yallop came across. 'Seeing you've done so well, Derek,' he said, thrusting in the needle, 'are you going to have a drink with us after the game?' Randall for once was lost for words. Then, 'Sure, I'll have a drink with you. But not until after we've won this Test match.' Perhaps for the first time the idea of victory seemed not wholly absurd.

Hogg meanwhile was wearing his anger badly. Randall glanced over his shoulder around the corner looking for the men moving at square-leg and fine leg. He reckoned correctly that he was in for another Hogg bouncer. It came two balls later, slow and more a long-hop than a bouncer. Randall later remembered the satisfaction of 'rolling my wrists on that one': it went for four, as much a pull as a hook. Three fours in one over. The clown was in the ascendant.

Drinks came on at the end of the over and Randall asked one of the umpires for a long dose of fly-spray; again more for a rest than for the flies. It was 2.20. England were 226, with Randall on 107 and Gower on 31.

In the next two hours – through a second drinks interval and tea – Randall struggled: his exhaustion was beginning to tell. In scoring twenty runs off seventy balls he was dropped by Hughes at slip at 113, dropped at the wicket by Maclean at 118 and finally at slip by Yallop at 124: Randall realized he had been lulled by the headiness of his century. 'Get back on top, Rags,' he said angrily.

The ailing Gower played his usual glorious strokes, flared and died in less than two hours, caught behind the wicket at 34. Botham came in, and spoke to Randall of the need to stay together until the close. Randall began to pummel his chest, trying to beat concentration back into his body. He was to score two more fours. The first was a tiring all-run affair after Darling misfielded at mid-wicket. The second came later, off Higgs. Higgs, in his forty-fourth over of the innings, chose to bowl one ball round the wicket at Randall. The change gave Randall a chance for another favourite ploy. Immediately he signalled for the sight-screen to be moved. Then he resignalled and resignalled again. 'If you're fussy about it – a few inches left, then a few inches right – you can waste a whole extra half minute.'

He was keen to waste time, not only for himself, but for England. They were down towards their tail. Botham, who had shown uncharacteristic restraint in scoring only six singles in ninety minutes, had lost his wicket for 6. Miller had come on with a message from the dressing room. 'We can win this game,' Miller reported as they met in the middle. Randall tried not to listen. 'No way,' he said. 'Stay in, don't give it away. Maybe we can save it.' At 149 he survived a confident LBW appeal, trying to drive a delivery from Hogg. A moment later he scratched a single for his 150. The milestone came after 578 minutes, and Randall lifted his bat in acknowledgement. Two overs and four minutes later he was out. A delivery from Hogg kept low and cut back, and then everything happened in a blur. Hogg leapt, swirled and shouted. The fieldsmen were up. And up, too, went French's arm. Randall had been trapped LBW. He lingered at the crease as the fact caught up with him, certain that in some replay in his mind the ball would miss leg stump. Randall's batting partners sometimes have to tell the reluctant Englishman to walk, but this time he moved off unbidden. As he left the field he thought: 'There's only a half-hour left. If we lose a couple more wickets the Aussies will be back on top in the morning.' He banged his bat against his pad in annoyance.

Randall's innings had spanned three days, and in that time England's score had been taken from 0 to 292. He had scored thirteen 4s, five 3s, fifteen 2s and fifty-one singles. Jim Higgs later put the innings in perspective. 'It wasn't really a memorable innings, because there weren't many memorable shots. But it was the innings that won England the Ashes.' Of the ball that got him out Hogg said graciously: 'He just missed it. He was as tired as I was.'

Randall once again spent little time in the dressing room, and that evening he met an old friend from Nottingham in the hotel bar. There, over a few beers, they discussed the day's play. They spoke of the new bowler Nottinghamshire had acquired and, ordering a couple more beers, they considered the club's prospects for the forthcoming season. The subject turned to football, and many beers later they had solved the problems of Nottingham Forest. It was near midnight when Randall, truly relaxed, slipped off to bed, happy in the thought that if the tail-enders got stuck in and kept batting English might yet save the Ashes.

CHAPTER 11

Packer's Cigars

ONE MORNING, SOON after we arrived in Australia, I was batting in the nets when David Hookes, the Australian Packer player, came out to the Adelaide ground. Hookes said 'Hullo' shyly from the corner of the nets as though he did not want to come out into the sunlight. I asked him how he was and said, 'Shall we be seeing you a bit?' When I looked up again he was gone. It was a most peculiar encounter. Adelaide was Hookes's home ground, the place where he had scored four centuries in five State innings, just before being selected for the Centenary Test – his first appearance for Australia.

The next time I saw him was about four weeks later on television, though I never spoke to him again. That first night match was being broadcast from Sydney, shortly before the first Test, and was an extraordinary evening. The ground was filled almost to capacity with 45,000 people. The players were introduced one by one and came rushing on to the field like prize-fighters into a ring. What struck me as the game progressed was that, while most of the batsmen wore helmets, there were no bouncers in the evening session at all and only one or two in the whole day. Although Colin Croft and Joel Garner bowled extremely well, they were not intimidating the batsmen. Some people felt this brought an artificiality into the game, although, of course, restricted run-ups in the John Player League have the same effect. In fact, in some ways cricket might be a better, if different, game without bouncers. It was a grafting match, in which the Australians dismissed the West Indians for 128 and ended up winners by five wickets.

The game was interesting to the connoisseur, but must have been dull to the majority of the spectators, however much they enjoyed the result. I also had mixed feelings about the television coverage. Channel 9 had given this match blanket advance publicity. The previous week they had covered the Australian Open Golf Championship, and every half hour or so they would break into the golf with an advertisement for the forthcoming WSC game. 'Channel 9 presents the best in golf by showing you Jack Nicklaus,' was the thrust of the station-break commercials. 'Can you afford to miss the best in cricket – which starts next week at the Sydney Cricket Ground?' The players appeared in advertisements constantly, Greig for cereals and irons, Hookes for air-conditioning, Daniel for MacDonald's hamburgers. The WSC Australians' theme-song, 'Come on, Aussies, come on' was repeated with relentless regularity.

The camera coverage of this and other matches was excellent. Violent, skilful and controversial moments were lingered over and repeated from many angles. There was one faintly disorienting feature of their technique: cameras behind the bowlers at each end meant that the watcher could not feel himself to be at any special point on the ground, and had no sense of the relationship between the play itself, the stands and the boundaries.

There were artificialities. Whenever a West Indian hit a four or took a wicket, the cameras switched to what looked like a rent-a-calypso section of the crowd – always it seemed to the same group of black faces. Advertisements occurred as often as between every over; indeed, this probably explains why World Series Cricket switched from eight- to six-ball overs.

The multi-national commentators (Fred Trueman; the Australians Richie Benaud, Keith Stackpole, and Bill Lawry; and the West Indian Tony Cozier) were glowing in their praise of the cricket, sometimes crushing in their condemnation of an umpire's decision. We were repeatedly told that we had just seen the best stroke, the best ball, the best piece of fielding ever. Hyperbole and false excitement became commonplace.

I was keen to see World Series Cricket under the lights for myself. After the fourth Test, the team went to Newcastle to play Northern New South Wales in a three-day match. I was originally to have rested during this match, and gone on to Tasmania with the team. Bob Willis was still unwell, so we changed plans; he rested during the Newcastle game, and led the team in Tasmania; I came back from Newcastle for a few days in Sydney. On 17 January, the World Series Australians were playing the West Indians in Sydney, in another 50-over match. This game would decide whether the West Indians or the World XI would play the Australians in the finals of the International Cup. The match also had interest as the first in which coloured uniforms were to be worn.

I asked Doug Insole if he had any worries over such a visit. He felt we should avoid offending our hosts and clear the visit with Bob Parish, chairman of the Austalian Cricket Board. Parish did not object. Australia was a free country, he said: I could go where I pleased. I went with Dudley, and as we approached the crowded ground in the darkening evening the sudden explosions of whistles and cheers reminded him of a crowd at an American baseball game. Indeed, to a cricket-loving time-traveller from the 1950s this night cricket would have seemed a different game. There were the six enormous floodlights ('Packer's cigars' as they became known) each 240 feet in height; white ball, black sight-screens, brightly-coloured clothes. The batsmen, in strawberry mousse (the West Indians), were embattled in a sea of yellow fielders (the Australians), with the two umpires in blue. The large crowd were young, noisy, loud-mouthed and happy. The odd streaker bounced across the field from the Hill. When the players came on to the field and were announced over the loudspeakers, they were greeted with roars and boos. Each time a non-Australian bats-

Big Brothers. One way of presenting the Captains; World Series Posters of Greig, Lloyd and Ian Chappell at the Sydney cricket ground.

man was dismissed the crowd went wild; the fielders hugged each other. All the bowling was fast or medium-fast. The fielding was dynamic.

From the back of the Noble stand, raised little above ground level, I could follow the white ball all the way. When Gordon Greenidge cut the third ball of Lillee's first over and was caught in the gully I never lost sight of it. At this distance, even in daylight, it would have been hard to pick up a red ball against the background of the crowd. So, from the spectator's point of view, the white ball was definitely an improvement. For the players it presents some problems, though they are not insurmountable. It gets dirty, especially on a pitch which is not very grassy. When the ball becomes brown or grey, as it sometimes does even early in a match, it is difficult for the players, especially the wicketkeeper and the slips. The obvious solution to the problem is to keep cleaning the ball. However, the umpires tried to do this with flannels and whitening substances but neither worked. Nor have the black sight screens. The WSC organizers have even considered spraying the pitch green so that the white ball would always be visible against a darker background, but the worry here is that the green would come off on the ball, and one could not be cleaning it after every delivery. Greg Chappell has suggested that the batsman, rather than the bowler, could call for a new ball whenever the old one became dirty, but this idea raises any number of tactical questions: would a batsman want to ask for a new ball knowing it would help the fast bowlers? If the dirty ball was so hard to see that batsmen frequently asked for a new ball, would slow bowlers be cut out of the game even more decisively? Rodney Marsh told me that at night, and certainly at dusk, it was difficult for the wicketkeeper and the slips to see a white ball, however new, against the batsman's white shirt, flannels and pads: the innovation of coloured clothes had at least this intrinsic rationale.

The spectators also gained. For instance, at one point Lillie bowled to Richard Austin. The ball hit him above the pad and ran back down the pitch. There was a loud appeal for LBW but, meanwhile, the batsmen, Austin and Lawrence Rowe, started running for a short single. Lillie stifled his appeal, dashed forward, picked up the ball, hurled it at the batsman's end and hit the stumps. There was an appeal for a run-out but Rowe was given not out. By then the ball had ricocheted past Marsh who turned and set off after it towards fine leg. All the fielders were converging, while Austin was still running for his life towards the bowler's end. He had no idea what was happening at the other end, where Rowe was running back down the wicket shouting to attract Austin's attention to come back for another run. As a piece of cricket it was a mess, but, with the yellow and strawberry colours, the game was made the more dramatic, because one could see who was on which side.

What one could not see, in the vastness of the Sydney Cricket Ground, was who precisely was who. I knew nearly all the players personally and might reasonably have been expected to have recognized them by their physical mannerisms but, from my place in the stands, I could not always do so. Why did Packer not go one stage further and put numbers on their backs? We later asked Packer about the coloured uniforms and about possibly numbering the players. Packer sounded genuinely uncertain and said that if the colours were wrong, the fans would say so; perhaps WSC might even sponsor a newspaper survey about the uniforms before the final colours were decided upon. When Dudley suggested that baseball players, after all, weren't particularly dehumanized by numbers on their backs, Packer's reaction was sharp. 'Look,' he snapped, 'if we *wanted* numbers on the backs of our players, we would have *put* numbers on the backs of our players.' But I do not want to ridicule the efforts made to get the best possible viewing for both spectators and players. In fact I admire them.

One player who needed no identification was Pascoe, who bowled several bouncers. From the games I saw, World Series Cricket oscillated between restraint and violence. In some matches it was hard not to think that a modicum of restraint had been agreed upon between the teams, and it was suggested that the batsmen were unable to 'pick up' the bouncer in night cricket. On the other hand, other matches became fierce battles, out of which great batsmen emerged battered and shaking, though some of the more serious injuries were prevented by the helmets. Tony Lewis reported on the 'heady elation of war, humour underlayed with fear'. He wrote in the *Sunday Telegraph* that 'Barry Richards jokes, and says that World Series Cricket will soon be played only by fast bowlers and batsmen in armour. No fieldsmen will be necessary because the batsmen will be unable to run in their protective clothing . . . Everyone evades the question about signing a new contract after the third season.'

This particular match was spoilt by rain, and by the curious uncertainty as to its result. The rain had started to fall in the break between innings (i.e. between 6 and 7. The hours of play were 2.30-6; 7-10.30). It stopped later, and there were several inspections of the pitch. The crowd grew restless. Eventually we were told that Andrew Caro, WSC managing director, had ordered the covers to be removed and the game to resume.

The Australians had scored 149 off their 50 overs, so the revised target for the West Indians was to be three runs an over. There was time for 16 overs only, so 48 runs were enough to win. After nine overs the West Indians were 48 for 4. The players thought the game was over. So did the spectators, who ran on to the field. But the umpires said no, they must bat the full sixteen overs or there would be no result; the match would be a draw. The crowd was eventually cleared from the field. The match was restarted. At 10.25 it began to rain again. Only twelve overs had been bowled. So, at the end of the match nobody knew the result. 'Windies Win!' one newspaper reported in headlines the following morning while a rival paper claimed, 'It's a Draw.' The John Player League has suffered similar confusions – every new form of a game has teething troubles – but the uncertainty about the rules was bad publicity for World Series Cricket. The eventual outcome was the sensible one: a win for the West Indians.

Next morning, 18 January, a letter addressed to me was delivered by hand to my Sydney hotel. Under the letterhead of the Office of the Chairman of Australian Consolidated Press Limited, it read:

Dear Mike,

On behalf of World Series Cricket I would like to put to you a challenge that we sincerely hope you are able to accept on behalf of your touring English cricket team. We wish to give you the opportunity to play a challenge match against Ian Chappell's Australians. The match would be played over the full five-day period of a traditional Test match, and World Series Cricket will put up a $50,000 purse for the winning players. We do not intend this to be a money-making venture for World Series Cricket and for that reason we propose that the total gate from such a match would go to the winners' backers. If Ian Chappell's Australians win the match, all the gate money will be donated to charities nominated by the team. If the English team win the match then the gate money is the M.C.C.'s, to use as they wish.

World Series Cricket is prepared to re-arrange its Australian schedule to allow the match to be held any time prior to the Australians' departure for the West Indies on 17 February.

We feel sure that you and your team would relish the opportunity to play Australia's top cricketers. The cricketing public would turn up in huge numbers to see such an encounter.

We would accept whatever playing conditions are acceptable to you and of course would be very happy to use the red ball instead of the World Series Cricket white ball.

We strongly urge you to give this proposal from us your very earnest consideration and we hope that our challenge can be taken up.

Yours sincerely,
Kerry Packer

The more I studied this unexpected missive, the more puzzled I became. Was there, behind it, a Machiavellian hand? Or was it sent innocently in the hope that the England players would jump at the challenge? It was hard to avoid the more cynical interpretation. For, whatever my response, Packer could put it to his own use. I went over the implications of the letter.

First, Packer was throwing down the gauntlet and would triumph if I – or we, since Doug Insole had also been sent a copy – did not pick it up. We could be seen to be backing away from a battle. Second, in the unlikely event that I might imply that the match, however impracticable, had merit, he might use the reply to show that I approved of his form of cricket. Third, any detailed reply from me, for or against the idea, could conceivably be used as a wedge between me and the Test and County Cricket Board, who after all were my employers, or even the International Cricket Council. Fourth, in the event that we should accept the challenge – well, World Series Cricket would have taken a giant step towards legitimacy. Implicitly they would have been welcomed into the family of cricket.

It is hard to believe that Packer genuinely thought the match a possibility. He knew that we were the official representatives of English cricket, playing in Australia as guests of the Australian Cricket Board. World Series Cricket was in direct conflict with these official bodies. Packer's own words when negotiations had broken down in 1977 were: 'Let the devil take the hindmost.' He knew that our tour schedule was solid between then and the end of the tour on 17 February. He could not have believed that I would be in a position to open negotiations for such a match.

His true motives were revealed more clearly less than twelve hours after I read the letter. Packer released the contents of his letter ('Dear Mike': it was a personal letter) to the Press, radio and television. The story was splashed into print. The Sydney *Daily Mirror*, sympathetic to Packer's cause, filled its back page with the news. 'Packer's $50,000 Challenge!' it reported; 'WSC Aussies versus Brearley's Poms.' On another page an editorial proclaimed, in part: 'If this proposed match is played it will settle a raging controversy that will continue for years otherwise: Can Brearley's team stand up to the WSC Australians?' The *Mirror*, moreover, announced they would give a motorcar to the Man of the Match.

Packer's instinct for publicity is finely developed, and such a brazen challenge doubtless delighted millions of his countrymen. Australians are not noted as good losers, after all, and here was a chance at last to avenge the Ashes. In the same paper Richie Benaud, one of Packer's leading lieutenants, was writing as though the match was signed, sealed and about to be delivered to the public. Yet the WS players themselves were taken by surprise by the news.

Benaud suggested the odds. Australia would be 10-9, he felt, with England 9-4. He picked teams, cocking a snook at the Australian Board by naming Jeff Thomson in the Australian XI. He evaluated each of the opposing players on tables of ten points, did his sums, and out of a possible 120 gave England 98 and the WSC Australians 100. In other papers, composite teams of WSC and traditional players were picked. I was asked to comment but, before doing so, I felt I must reply to Packer's letter. I consulted Doug Insole by telephone (he was now in Hobart with the team) and then wrote my letter:

Dear Kerry,

Thank you for your letter of 18 January.

I think you will appreciate that any matches we play on this tour have to be arranged with the Test and County Cricket Board. However, it is pretty clear, don't you think, that they, as I do, would regard your invitation as quite impracticable? We are involved with Test matches and one-day Internationals right up to 17 February, which also happens to be the date on which we leave Australia.

Yours sincerely,
Mike Brearley

In a couple of days all the air hissed out of Packer's trial balloon. The challenge was forgotten, and perhaps the amiable but misunderstanding Rodney Marsh's comment can stand as an epilogue to the episode. 'Kerry made a mistake,' he told us later over a beer. 'He shouldn't have put $50,000 on the table. He should have put $500,000.'

Rodney was underestimating his boss. In our last week in Australia a huge offer came – by way of Greig – to sign a group of English players, including the entire Test team, for World Series Cricket. The approach began after Miller, Radley and Gooch, having dined out early in the week of the sixth Test in Sydney, called at Greig's house for coffee. John Snow was there and, in the course of the evening, Greig mentioned the offer. Packer wanted the whole England party, plus other unspecified English players, to bring the total to twenty. Financially, the offer was staggering: each player would receive from $A 60,000 to $A 80,000 a year for four years. At about $A ¼ m £150,000) a man the money was incredible, perhaps literally so. There was one condition. Packer wanted the whole group as one package: everyone or no one.

Greig repeated the offer a couple of days later to Phil Edmonds, who bumped into him at Watson's Bay, one of Sydney's beaches. He invited Edmonds and his wife to a barbecue at his home on the rest day of the final Test match. Indeed, earlier in the tour he had mentioned the barbecue to us. The whole team was invited but, as the day approached, we decided as a group to decline the invitation. We were chary that the occasion, however hospitable, might turn into a recruiting party.

CHAPTER 12

Adelaide: Fifth Test. 'Come on, Derbys!'

AT ADELAIDE, WITH the Ashes retained, we told ourselves firmly that the series had still to be won. For their part, the Australians' spirits were low, so much so that they brought in a local football coach, a 'motivator', as the local press called him, who was reported to have spoken firmly to the team and to have shown them a motivational film. Before the match they also called in Alan Davidson as an advisor – only he was soon generously offering advice to both sides. At one point, Davidson was giving Lever tips about his action, suggesting that he should throw his right arm higher immediately before he bowled, while Barrington, in another net, was demonstrating to Wood why he was mis-timing his drives, and how he should turn his wrists when picking up his bat. Meanwhile, Taylor was renewing his acquaintance with Australia's new wicketkeeper, Kevin Wright of Western Australia.

Wright is young, 22, and keen to learn. Before the State match at Perth he had come up to Taylor, who had been rested for that game, and asked Bob to watch him and give him advice. Taylor told him he was taking to many catches one handed, and should try to get his feet and body behind the line of the ball. He wasn't anticipating quickly enough where the ball was going, especially down the leg-side. Also, Taylor thought Wright was getting up from his stance too soon to the medium-paced bowlers and spinners. Finally, he mentioned something that I, too, had noticed: that Wright was standing too far back to the faster bowlers. It was a perceptive report, and may have helped Wright become an Australian discovery of the season.

The decision to pick Wright was sound, but I felt sorry for Maclean. He was ungainly for a top-class wicketkeeper, and he would have fared much better with the bat if he had tried to attack the spinners; but he had a good pair of hands and had missed little in his four Tests. The Australian selectors were constantly in the same dilemma, brought about by the dearth of all-rounders: how to combine a well-balanced bowling attack with reasonable depth of batting. They would probably have won the fourth Test if Yardley had been selected: now they brought him in, together with Carlson, the all-rounder who had been twelfth man for the first two Tests. These two replaced Toohey and Dymock, both of whom we were glad to see out of the side.

The batsmen on both sides came to Adelaide hoping for a change in the pitches. We were not overjoyed with what we saw, a strip that was flat and hard, but covered thickly with grass. As Boycott said, when I asked his opinion an hour before the start of the match, 'It's not the sort of pitch you'd queue up to bat on.' But he, like the selectors, thought that we should bat first if we won the toss. There was not a cloud in the sky, and there were slight cracks in the pitch which might open up later. I found it hard to decide. Eventually the selectors agreed to keep the same team, with Lever again the unlucky man to be left out of the twelve. I told John this, and he said that in the circumstances he thought we had made the right decision in picking Emburey rather than him.

Television cameras had previously not been allowed on the pitch for the toss. For the current series, however, it was felt that, in the face of Packer, this moment of intimacy would heighten the drama of the occasion. I felt that the questions

Hurst bowling at Adelaide. He became more relaxed and more aggressive as the series went on. Though he was in the shadow of Hogg, he had a remarkably successful series taking more wickets (25) than any English bowler. He bowls close to the stumps, so that he should have a better chance of LBWs than Hogg – though I am not certain that this difference was always taken into account enough. Also, as Randall said, when the ball was older, he would often bowl a most awkward line, just outside the off-stump, while Hogg bowled so straight that it was easier to 'line him up'.

put to us were pointless, not because they were stupid, but because the captains were not likely to share their true thoughts with the world at large. When we were asked what we thought of the Adelaide pitch, I said, 'Let's wait and see what happens.' Yallop, for his part, said it looked 'beautiful', which usually implies 'beautiful for batting'. He then won the toss, and promptly put us in to bat.

We had yet another wretched start. There was plenty of bounce in the pitch, and some movement. Hurst and Hogg bowled well. Carlson took a marvellous diving catch at fourth slip, and after an hour we were 27-5, when Miller joined Botham. Miller played some useful knocks during the series, not least this 31. He was lucky to be dropped when 2, hooking a dangerous bouncer from the otherwise medium-paced Carlson. But he also hooked the quicker bowlers, with success, while as usual he collected runs off his legs. Surprisingly he was the dominant partner in his stand of 53 with Botham, but, with the score at 80, he fell LBW to Hogg. Botham now started to attack. He enjoys duels, indeed he provokes them. Over the series his contests with Hogg, whoever was batting, had become increasingly friendly, but no less fierce. He had shown restraint earlier in the innings, ducking under several bouncers and grinning at the bowler. Now he began to play more aggressively, hooking Hogg for four and driving him through extra-cover. At one point, when Botham was at the non-striker's end, Hogg muttered conspiratorially: 'You're beginning to play too well; it may be time for me to come off.' Botham had had a similar duel with Richard Hadlee of New Zealand; in each case hostility mellowed into friendly rivalry. In each case, too, Botham had the trump card, for he is both the better and the braver batsman.

At 113, Taylor was run out in tragi-comic fashion going for a fourth run. He said 'no', saw that Botham was on his way, halted, hesitated, then finally started to run. Hogg threw the ball to the wicketkeeper's end – he was at deep fine leg – so that Wright had to roll the ball down the wicket to Yardley, who just beat the diving batsman. I was reminded of when, as a child, I had heard amid the radio crackle that Arthur McIntyre had been run out going for a fourth run at Brisbane in 1951. Hutton and Compton had been kept back in the hope that the pitch would have eased by the next day. Similarly, we were afraid the pitch might have eased next day, and that we would be bowling.

Botham was finally dismissed by Higgs, for the fourth time in the series, for 74. He was in fact caught and stumped off the same ball: we told him it was typical of him to be twice dismissed for only once out. Willis, relieved of the responsibility of keeping an end going for a recognized batsman, played some amazing off-side slogs, including a six over cover off Hurst. A similar stroke off Hogg gained height but not length, and when Darling, tearing in from deep cover, caught the ball Willis was out for 24, England for 169, and Hogg had broken Arthur Mailey's record of wickets in a series against England. Willis was Hogg's 37th victim, a fantastic achievement for a man playing in his first Test series.

Although we had been dismissed relatively cheaply, we thought that the pitch would still help the bowlers. We were right. In Willis's first over he beat Darling twice. Then Darling shaped, adventurously, to cut. The ball came back from the off sharply, and struck him in the midriff. He collapsed in a heap. From my position at first slip, I had no idea for several seconds that he might be seriously hurt. In fact my first thought was that he was lucky to have escaped falling on his wicket. To O'Connell and Emburey, though, his condition looked desperate, if not critical. Max tried to breathe air into his mouth. John, who had been instructed in first-aid at Middlesex, laid him on his back and struck him firmly on the chest. Gasping and retching Darling started to breathe again. By now, the physiotherapists were on the pitch, followed a moment later by a doctor. Darling was soon carried off on a stretcher. The experts told us afterwards that he had been severely winded; but

whether the accident could have been fatal or not I never knew. Whatever the truth, it reinforced the wisdom of the Middlesex players' agitating for constant medical presence during all matches.

Such an incident can also be unnerving to a fast bowler. Willis was not one of those who rushed to the aid of the fallen batsman. The previous summer, in the much-discussed incident in which he hit the Pakistani Qasim in the mouth, he walked away. This response may appear callous, but is far from it. Bob was distressed by the Qasim and Darling incidents, but to retain his threat as a fast bowler he had to remain detached from such emotions. The Darling incident nonetheless did upset him, so that he immediately lost his bowling rhythm. However, Hendrick now dismissed Hughes, well-caught by Emburey, diving forward in the gully. Shortly after, Yallop, who had been uneasy about Hendrick's probing line around·off-stump, started to let the ball go; then, worried that it might be too close to leave, jabbed at it hurriedly. He succeeded only in edging the ball into his wicket. Hendrick had now taken his wicket four times in seven innings.

After three overs I brought Botham on in place of Willis. I had told him that on this pitch I wanted him to bowl fast; I promised him that he would only bowl in short spells. He was to be a strike bowler now whereas, for instance, on the slower pitch at Sydney, I had been forced to use him for longer spells and as a stock bowler. Now he struck quickly, unsettling Border and Carlson with bouncers, then having them caught behind off balls of fuller length, for 11 and 0 respectively.

At this point Australia were 24-4, with Darling off the field. We might have gone through all their main batting that evening had Botham not dropped Wood off Willis and then Yardley off Hendrick in the last hour. Even the best close fielders are fallible, and I regard Botham as second only to Greig amongst slip fielders with whom I have played. In the dressing-room Hendrick said to Botham, 'You stood up too early for that catch off Yardley.' Botham replied, 'I didn't see the ball,' as if that was all there was to it. Hendrick came back hotly, 'Listen to what I say: if you don't see it clearly, stay down. Catches off me don't go through at head-height.' Hendo was stressing a matter of method, but Botham seemed unwilling to understand his point of view.

Another example of Ian's instinctive but brief mulishness had taken place that same day, at lunch, when he was one of the not out batsmen. It concerned his boots. On many Australian pitches we found that, for batting, spikeless shoes gained the best grip while spiked boots felt uncomfortable on the hard pitches. Spikes had to be sharper than in England to go into the surface. That morning, however, I noticed that Botham was having to slide to stop after making a run because of the lush grass. At lunch, I said, 'You need spikes. If you're sent back in these, you'll end up flat on your back in the middle of the wicket.' His first response was that he was perfectly safe as he was. We said no more, but after lunch he wore his spiked boots. Similarly, he had listened to Hendrick. Soon the pair of them, the best of pheasant-shooting friends on holiday in England, had made up their tiff and were drinking beer, replacing the fluid they had lost under the Adelaide sun. Though Botham sometimes initially seems reluctant to listen, he does take a point.

Yardley, however, was still there in the morning. He poses problems for a fielding captain. He has a good eye and sense of timing, and is a high-quality off-side hitter. The ball flies through and over the slips and gullies at varying paces and heights. We tried a third man behind fourth slip: Yardley edged it over first slip. We had the third man fine: he slashed square. We had two third men: he edged gently through the empty third slip position at comfortable catching height. I was relieved when Botham bowled him early the next morning. Darling, bravely, returned, wearing a chest-protector. He opened his account with a charac-teristic pull for four off Hendrick. Then he hooked Botham high and square for six; we did not mind this, as we had two men back for the shot. Soon after, Botham bowled another bouncer, slightly more on the leg-side, and Willis caught a fine catch at long-leg, circling like a spider under the ball.

We also had some unusual fields for Wood, and a long and interesting tussle with him. Before the match, discussing Wood, Boycott said, 'We some-times bowl three or four balls wide of the off stump, which Woods lets go. Then we get bored, bowl a ball around middle-and-leg, Wood slips it to mid-wicket for two, and the pressure is off.' Botham in particular would get bored in this way. By the fifth Test we were prepared to be more

Below: Darling sinks to his knees after being struck below the heart. Wood looks on apprehensively. Right: Next day Darling returned and was soon, bravely, playing his hooks and pulls. He is one of the best hookers I have seen; he is in position for the shot early, with his right foot back and across, pointing down the pitch, a movement that must make it more difficult for him to play the fuller length ball outside the off-stump. He is one of the few players who has both feet off the ground just after hitting the ball.

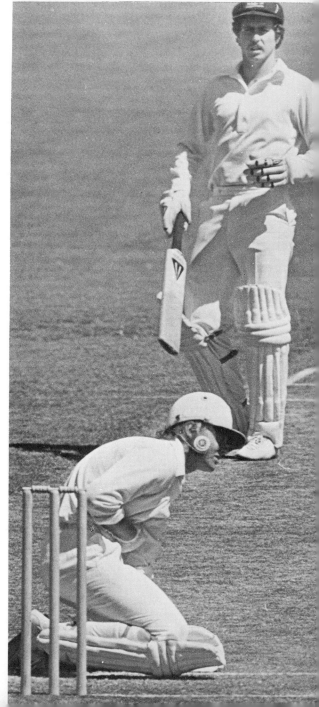

relentless in our tactics. We cut off Wood's chop shot through gully by having a backward point. Further, to deny Wood his method of pulling the ball to mid-wicket, I put a man halfway to the mid-wicket boundary, where he often lofts the ball. It was Emburey, though, building up pressure by his accuracy, who dismissed him. We knew that the shot Wood was most likely to use to break out against the off-spinners was the sweep, and if Emburey could keep the ball on the off stump his sweep would have to go almost square. Everything worked: Emburey pinned Wood down and kept his line, the Australian swept – and the ball went straight to Randall, whom we had placed twenty yards closer and twenty yards squarer than usual. Wood was out for 35.

Despite a useful debut of 29 by Wright, and a last-wicket stand of 31 by Higgs and Hurst, Australia were dismissed for 164, and we had

The two 'keepers in action. Taylor steers the ball away behind point, while Wright is open-mouthed in admiration. Taylor could theoretically be stumped, for his toe is only on the line, not over it, as the laws require.

gained a first innings lead of five runs.

It was now mid-afternoon on only the second day. The pitch was at its best, and the weather getting hotter. Our bowlers had brought us back into the match; but we were yet to hear from their bowlers. Hurst bowled even better than he had at Sydney, and by lunchtime on the third day we were struggling. This was, I think, our worst batting performance of the series. I played back instead of forward to Carlson and was LBW for 9. Then a strange skirmish took place between Randall and Hurst. Randall hooked Hurst for four; next ball, he hooked again and, cruising the easy single, ran in a wide curve to the other end. Hurst snapped at him, 'Just because you've hit a four you've no need to do a lap of honour.' It was just the type of puzzling, aggressive remark that Randall had used with such unsettling effect during his long innings at Sydney. Now the boot was on the other foot and Derek was perplexed. 'I was thinking "lap of honour?"' he said afterwards, 'what does he mean by "lap of honour"?' An over later he tried to pull Hurst again and skied an easy catch to mid-wicket. He said afterwards that he knew that Hurst had two men back for the hook, and that he should only

have played the shot if he was certain he could play the ball down, yet he felt rattled and hooked instinctively. Hurst also had the last word. Rushing down the wicket, he shouted at Randall, 'You want a bloody lap of honour for that one? Shove off!' In the pavilion Insole wondered whether Hurst wasn't 'over-motivated' by the football coach.

Boycott, meanwhile, had been looking his old, impregnable self. We could see from the dressing room, which is square with the pitch at Adelaide, that he was moving his feet better; he was more positive in moving both forward and back. One of Geoff's mottoes has always been: 'Be positive in defence as well as in attack.' And though he still was not as fluent as he could be, I was confident that he would get a huge score. He ended the day with 40 not out; Gooch, though hit several times by short balls from Hurst, survived; we closed at 82-2.

That overnight score soon became 97-3, when Gooch, playing loosely forward, was bowled between bat and pad by Carlson early next morning, and 106-4 when Boycott fell to a fine piece of bowling by Hurst. At Brisbane I had put Edmonds at silly-point when Yallop faced Willis. At Perth, and thereafter, Yallop had done the same for Boycott, standing there himself. His purpose, he said later, was to 'stare out' Boycott, as though generations of frustrated fielders had not already failed in staring and glaring out the Yorkshireman. I should have thought a better argument for Yallop's position would have been that, by leaving open the gully area, which is one of Boycott's favourite run-scoring directions, he might entice Boycott into playing a forcing shot to a lifting or wider ball. On 49, perhaps looking for a single, Boycott tried to force Hurst square on the off-side; the ball lifted, and Hughes caught a fine catch at first slip. Perhaps Yallop's tactic paid off, but perhaps, again, for the wrong reason. Geoff was unlucky; he made few errors in 3½ hours at the wicket.

The rot continued. Botham, who looked in towering form, was deceived by a slower ball, and Gower played a reckless pull against Higgs three minutes before lunch, and suddenly we were 132-6. As at Sydney, the rat was in the dog's mouth: could it wriggle out again?

Yallop's main worry this time was Hogg. His star bowler was complaining of a sore leg and had gone through his overs without enthusiasm. That Hogg

Wright attempts to stump Taylor off Yardley's bowling, during the long stand at Adelaide. Wright's feet have moved far from the line of the leg-stump, so that he has a long way to bring the ball back.

should again bowl with pace, Yallop realized, was central to thwarting our recovery. At one point Hogg left the field, apparently without talking to his captain: Yallop sprinted after him. For one delivery Australia had only ten men on the ground while Yallop was in the dressing-room with Hogg. The problem was crippling Australia, for Hurst had already bowled unchanged for an hour and a half before lunch. The new ball would be due in another half hour. Yallop decided to put Hurst on – risk 'busting the bowler' – in the hope that one more wicket might mean our total collapse.

In fact, Taylor and Miller scored 30 runs in 25 minutes, and when the tired Hurst and a dispirited Hogg took the new ball both main guns were spiked. It is hard to know whether I would have handled that situation differently. I think that I would have tried someone else for a few overs, to give Hurst at least some respite before the new

Rest Day of Adelaide Test, with Willis and my parents in the wine-growing Barossa Valley.

ball. Yallop could have bowled Yardley or Carlson with Higgs. But the Australians were stretched, as we had been at Sydney, by injury and fatigue: there was no obvious strategy.

I have never seen Taylor play so well. He moved down the pitch to the spinners, played well back and forward to the quick bowlers. Later we asked him why he had been able to play so much better in this innings. 'I don't really know,' he said. 'I'd batted many times with Geoff Miller, and we said to each other "Come on, Derbys," as well as England. There's been something missing, obviously, in my batting; I should have the concentration for batting in a Test, being a wicketkeeper. I think on tour it's easier to play a long innings, because at home all four county competitions involve limited overs, and I'm not naturally a stroke-maker. I'm a grafter, and certainly I grew in confidence having stayed at the wicket a while. But I can't really put my finger on why I played better . . . unless my wife had something to do with it. She'd just arrived in Adelaide.'

Miller stayed with Taylor until they had more than doubled the score, before getting out for 64. Emburey helped add another 69: but then, with the score at 336-7, Taylor, on 97, faced Hogg. It was the last delivery before lunch on the fourth day. It was down the leg-side, a harmless-looking ball; Taylor glanced, the ball went fine, and Wright took the catch.

Bob had never scored a century. Emburey had never made a fifty, and we were beginning to hope this milestone at least might be reached when he was yorked for 42 by Hogg. In a few weeks his confidence as a cricketer had blossomed. In his previous three Test innings he had fallen to Higgs.

First, he had tried to defend, but pushing forward too firmly at the ball had been caught at short-leg. Then, in a desperate attempt to attack, he had been caught at cover off a wild mis-hit; in the first innings at Adelaide, he had been bowled trying a stand-up sweep shot. We arranged that he should go into the nets to face Barrington's leg-breaks with the particular aim of gaining the confidence to play the good-length ball defensively by keeping his grip loose and allowing the ball to come to him. His 42 was a result of these sessions in the nets.

Our innings finally closed at 360, so that Australia needed 366 to win in about nine hours; it was not an impossible target on the now excellent pitch. Darling started aggressively, but with the score at 31 moved too far across to Botham and was bowled behind his legs. Five runs later Botham was involved, indirectly, in the next dismissal, that of Wood. It was the fourth time Wood had been involved in a run-out. He drove Botham firmly to mid-on, and called for a run. Hughes responded immediately, but Boycott, with only one stump to aim at, hit it. Wood was well out, but looked disgruntled about having been forced wide by Botham who was watching the ball as he ended his follow-through. Wood had then collided with Bailhache as he dived for the crease. To my mind, there was never a run there.

After tea, with Australia resuming at 44-2, Willis had further trouble with his rhythm. Much of the trouble lay in his run-up: each time he found any fire in his action, his foot was well over the line. Bailhache was helpful, indicating how close he was each ball; but in one over alone there were four no-balls. I came from slip to mid-off to keep in touch with him. He was by now showing his distress; he was wincing in his follow-through, and as he trudged back the vast distance to his mark his head was drooping. 'It will come right,' I kept saying. 'Keep your head up. Walk with a spring in your step.' Miller, too, who was often near to Willis at mid-on or mid-off, kept saying: 'Don't look down as you approach the wicket, Goose. Watch the batsman as usual.' Willis was to recall Hendrick and Botham in the slips both punching their hands to encourage him. At the end of an over, as he 'meandered' (Bob's word) down towards fine-leg, Taylor would run up to him and reassure him: 'Much better, much better. It's coming right.' Bob, lifted by this help, said afterwards, 'That is the strength of this team.'

Meanwhile Hughes and Yallop played them-selves in soundly, the only discomfort being Yallop's against Botham, who again bowled with fire. They played the spinners with circumspection, and without much risk. Between tea and stumps Australia scored only 38 off 27 overs, but, more important, they had not lost a wicket. The innings of each side had so far followed similar patterns; oddly enough, their score at the close was 82-2, the same as ours at the end of the second day.

On the last day they needed 284 to win. We felt our position was the stronger at this stage, but that Hughes and Yallop were capable of creating a situation from which Australia could win. And they started as if they intended to go all out to do so. I began with the spinners, thinking that, as they were most likely to make the ball do something off this placid pitch, our best chance of an early wicket lay in letting them bowl with close fielders, before the batsmen had played themselves in. However, after only the briefest look, both batsmen went on the attack, Yallop playing his characteristic shot over wide mid-on, and Hughes off-driving two hand-some fours. They scored 29 in 25 minutes. I quickly brought back Hendrick and Botham to stem the flow of runs.

Yallop, perhaps thinking of his mistake in the first innings, let the second ball of Hendrick's second over go: to his amazement it came back off the pitch and clean bowled him. Hendrick had now taken Yallop's wicket five times in eight Test innings. The score was 115-3.

Next over Hendrick struck again. 'Bowl wider at Hughes,' I said. He did. Hughes drove without getting on top of the ball, and was superbly caught by Gower at backward point: 120-4.

The heat was again intense, and there was no breeze. After four overs I took Hendrick off, and replaced him with Willis. He came in round the wicket at Border, and the first ball, quick and accurate, bowled him through the gate: 121-5. Three balls later, Yardley, driving, edged the ball straight to me at slip: 121-6. Just because he failed,

The beginning of Willis' return to form, second innings. His first ball, bowled from round the wicket to the left-handed Border, squeezed between bat and pad and hit the top of the off-stump.

Gower, who has just made a fine catch to dismiss Hughes in the second innings, is hugged by Botham. Hendrick, Gooch and Brearley are about to join in. I had more letters criticising us for the exuberance of our celebrations than for any other aspect of our cricket. My view is that the Englishman has, in the last 20 years, become less stiff-lipped, less embarrassed by displays of emotion; we are more intimate as people, more open and informal than a generation ago. On the whole, I approve of the change, and the obviously shared pleasure and enthusiasm at each other's success was a factor in our overall success.

Yardley was roundly criticized in the press for this shot: yet such shots are integral to his particular method. By now Willis was his old self. For some reason, everything had clicked into place, and he bowled two savage overs at Wright to remind us of what we had been missing since Perth. Willis is a magnificent fast bowler in this mood, cruising in with a fine rhythm, and extracting hostile bounce even from this gentle pitch and even with a ball 50 overs old.

We remembered that we too had lost four wickets before lunch, and had slumped to 132-6; but Australia had no Taylor, Miller or Emburey to save them, and though Botham was drained after a six-over spell, all our bowlers would be fresh after the interval. But even before lunch arrived Miller took two more wickets with perfectly flighted off-breaks, having Wright caught at short square-leg, and bowling Hogg through the gate. At 130-8, Australia had lost six wickets for 15 runs. After lunch the final ceremonies did not take long. Hendrick picked up a third wicket when he had Carlson caught at mid-wicket, and Willis bowled Hurst. At the prize-giving ceremony, Phil Ridings, Chairman of the Australian selectors, gave us generous praise for our performances on and off the field. Botham was named man of the match: we owed much to him, and much also to the "Derbys" trio.

We were relaxed and contented. We had won the series, and to have done so at Adelaide was all the more pleasing: for it was there, more than once, that an Australian had come up to us and, dropping his voice, had whispered, 'Well done.'

CHAPTER 13

A Bleeding Jaffa

Test wickets are the centres of play, and often the centres of controversy, and to learn more about them and how they are prepared Dudley Doust took a day off from the fifth Test at Adelaide to speak with Arthur Lance, who for a quarter century has been the curator at the Adelaide Oval.

THE ADELAIDE OVAL was given its name in 1872 by an English settler, a Surrey supporter, who longed for the sight of the Kennington Oval in London. His homesickness seems well placed now, for the ground, unmarked by gasometers, lies in the most English of settings. The spires of St. Peter's Cathedral rise beyond the scoreboard at the north end, the River Torrens curls lazily through the park below the south stands, and in the distance the range of Lofty Mountains might well be the Malvern Hills. Ken Barrington, who has travelled widely as both player and team official, ranks only Queen's Park at Port-of-Spain and Newlands in Capetown as equal in beauty to the Adelaide Oval.

Barrington also ranks Adelaide, given a good wicket, the best batting strip in the world – as well he might, for he scored 63, largely off pace bowling, and than an unbeaten 132, nicely handling the spinners, in a Test match there in 1963. Accordingly, after he ceremoniously thrust his pen-knife into the wicket on the first morning of the fifth Test he pronounced it a 'bleeding Jaffa'. In his language this is a citric reference meaning 'it looks good, tastes good and is ideal for eating.' On the tour Barrington was over-generous in distributing 'Jaffa' awards but this one came near to earning it: certainly after the first day, Adelaide proved to be the best Test pitch of the tour.

The ground has been spared the excessive ravaging wear of Packer cricket. It has also been blessed down the years with splendid, dedicated groundsmen, or 'curators' as they are called in Australia. The first one to pop up in cricket literature was Charlie Checkett, who early in the century shod his big chestnut horses in soft leather 'slippers' to avoid tearing up the ground as they went over it with rollers. Sir Pelham Warner, on the occasion of the 1911-12 England tour of Australia, held Checkett in the highest esteem and spoke of his pitch preparation in his account of the tour. He wrote:

> Checkett of the Adelaide Oval is probably the most famous groundsman in Australia. Three or four days before a match he floods the pitch that is to be. When the turf is at a certain temperature – somewhere between 70 degrees and 80 degrees and of a gluey nature – he puts a roller on for a few minutes, after which he cuts the grass with a scythe, it being impossible to set the blades of a mowing machine low enough. Then the heavy roller is applied for two or three hours. When the ground begins to dry up and to crack, the roller is used again at intervals of every two hours. Before a match the pitch is at night covered with a heavy tarpaulin, which makes it 'sweat' and keeps a glossy surface on it. On the day of the match the tarpaulin is removed, and the result is a wicket that has practically no grass on it. The pitch, indeed, is like concrete. The ball seldom if ever gets up higher than the top of the stumps, if anything it is inclined to keep a little low . . .

The pitch for years retained its concrete hardness. Harold Larwood remembers his first visit to the Oval in 1928 and in his home in Sydney he spoke of that match, his first against South Australia. 'I wore the shoes I wore in England, ones with spikes hammered into the soles,' he said, 'The wicket was so smooth and hard it shone back at you like sun off macadam. Pretty soon I started to slip. I had nought for about 80 and I was blaming the footholes. Then the captain came up and took a look at my shoes. All my spikes were gone – broken clean off on that iron wicket.' In fact, Larwood had 1 for 92 and 0 for 60 in that match. He thereafter screwed sturdy studs into his boots and in 1932-33 was bowling his Bodyline bouncers at the Oval. 'The wicket was a beauty but it had no pace,' he recalled, and took great pride in the fact that only by bowling 'hellishly quick' did he achieve his lethal lift in that match. This time he took 3 for 55 and 4 for 71.

The current curator, Arthur Lance, came to the Oval in 1953, and the first Test wicket he prepared was for the forthcoming Ashes match against Len Hutton's Englishmen. Lance, then in his mid-30s, was anxious to present a perfect wicket. There were three bare patches of grass on it, however, though luckily they were outside the off-stump. 'I dug up "plugs" of earth from the outfield,' he recalled, 'and put them in the bare patches.' As the match progressed, the wicked dried out and, as with human tissues, the wicket rejected the 'foreign' plugs. Lance recalled the incident and shuddered. 'The plugs *shrunk*. You could wobble them. I was a very fortunate young man that on the last day no ball pitched on one of those plugs. Lord knows how it might have bounced.'

Lance, now 62, is the doyen of Australian Test curators, earning $A 230 (£138) a week gross, a handsome enough salary but one that carries heavy responsibilities: he oversees a staff of eleven men and looks after fourteen bowling greens, eight tennis courts, a cricket nets area and a second cricket pitch as well as the Oval. His house, tucked under the Hill at the south end of the Oval, is a tidy, cream-coloured bungalow for which he pays a peppercorn rent of $A 9 a week, including all facilities except telephone bills. The day I visited him a tiny tricycle stood in his back garden: his daughter, who as a child used to help her father tug tarpaulins over the wickets during sudden squalls of rain, now has a son who 'helps' his grandfather

drive 'Puffer', the three-ton diesel roller.

Lance is an orderly man – comb-strokes remain in his corn-coloured hair – and when he explains his job he begins at the beginning: which is a huge mound of black earth, perhaps 100 tons of it, covered by tarpaulins near his back garden. This is his supply of top-dressing for his wickets, his black gold: it looks rather like pithead slurry but in fact it is rich, black clay brought down from a particular gully of a stream in the Lofty Mountains, some six miles from Adelaide. The gully now has been digested into the hungry maw of Australian suburbia. In future the South Australian Cricket Association will have to fetch its clay from Mambray Creek, some 200 miles away. But with one ton per wicket per year for each of his eight wickets, Lance is supplied with enough choice clay to see out his days. 'It is beautiful clay,' he said. 'It sets hard and you can grow grass on it at the same time.'

The Oval is also used for Australian Rules football, and not until October, the Australian spring, does Lance get to work on his wickets. His basic wicket, dug out and laid long ago, was moulded from a 'dough' made from 50 per cent black clay and a mixture of sand, gravel and humus. It lies rock-hard about nine inches deep on a bed of metal and cinders, and each spring Lance tops it up with a shallow new mixture of the same basic dough and seeds of couch grass, a coarse broad-leafed grass (a dreaded weed in England) which sweeps in long roots across the wicket. He rolls his top dressing in, and every two or three years makes the wicket level with the help of a professional surveyor.

In mid-December, six weeks before the fifth Test was to begin, Arthur Lance began preparing for it. He picked the wicket, then banned play on it prior to the match. Next he saturated it, much as Checkett had done, cut slots in the bare areas and painstakingly shoved grass seedlings into the sodden soil. Then the rolling started. The wicket was first rolled with a 2-cwt roller which darkened and broke up the earth. As the wicket dried, so the curator increased the weight of the roller: 8 cwt, 2½ tons and finally the 3-ton, climb-aboard 'Puffer'. By this time, Lance was rolling meticulously. He not only rolled up and down the wicket but he rolled across it, moving only six inches further

Arthur Lance putting out the tarpaulin covers over the Adelaide square.

down the wicket each time, so that it was rolled cross-wise well over one hundred times. Lance is chary of over-rolling straight down the wicket. 'It is a hard job to get the rolling right,' he said, 'because if you roll cross-wise too heavily on a soft wicket you get ridges. On the other hand, if you just go up and down, up and down, it is even worse because you make the undulations deeper.'

Weather, such as the unusually dry winter of 1978 in Australia, can wreak havoc on pitch preparation, but on the whole Lance sets out an approximate timetable for his work. His preparation is achieved over six weeks, in three cycles of a fortnight. Three times he 'prepares for a week and then lets it go for a week'. If all goes well, the result is a compact wicket, with a uniform growth of grass. Lance, like most modern curators, lives in fear of a wicket drying out, breaking up dramatically before the final day of a match. Accordingly, when he scythes his wicket before a match he does not cut as close as they did in the days of Checkett. He admits this, but what he will not tolerate is the accusation during the present tour that he dampened the grass prior to the fifth Test match. 'The day before the match I put covers on the wicket to keep it from drying out,' he said defensively, 'but any "dampness" arose from the amount of sap in the leaves of the grass.' It was this sap and the sheer amount of grass that kept the wicket, said Brearley, from being an excellent one on the first day of play. On subsequent days Lance mowed it with a cut set at 3/16 of an inch. Stung by criticism, he offered a gentle rebuke to complaining captains. 'They should come along before a match and see the curator to get the details and the amount of preparation,' he said. 'They ought to learn when it was last watered and last played on. Given good weather, you know, once a wicket has been prepared it comes up better in its second preparation. It will be harder and that should interest a captain.'

The outfield preparation was much easier. A week before the match, Lance fertilized it, 'so that it would look nice and lush'. Three days before the Test match he cut and collected the grass and each morning thereafter cut it and let it lie on the field. During a match, the Australian Cricket Board stipulates, at least half the outfield must be cut, half rolled in the mornings. Here Lance prides himself on his thoroughness: he both cuts and rolls the entire field before each day's play. The procedure is not that simple. Adelaide is on Daylight Savings Time, and there is dew on the ground until about 9.15. Lance and his staff first dry the outfield by dragging the field with a 40-ft length of hessian suspended between two tractors. These tractors are then followed by a tractor dragging mowers which, in turn, is followed by another tractor dragging a 3-cwt roller. Lance claims the result is a fast outfield. In all, by the end of the match he was well pleased with his pitch. It had borne up under the thunder of five days of Test play, but now he looked with alarm at the next onslaught it was to suffer. It wasn't more cricket, or even Australian Rules football. 'We've got Rod Stewart coming in for a pop concert,' he said. 'Believe me, the last thing I want is that fellow jumping all over my wicket.'

Lance concluded the conversation with an epilogue to his story of the first Test pitch he ever prepared at the Oval. He said that only a few days ago a man had come to his bungalow carrying a parcel wrapped in an old newspaper. The man said it contained a souvenir he had got as a boy and over the past quarter century he had kept it locked in a safe. Opening it, he wondered if Lance recognized its contents. Arthur Lance did, like a shot. 'It was one of those dirt plugs I put in Hutton's wicket,' he told me with satisfaction. 'Still as black and hard as a block of iron.'

CHAPTER 14

Sydney: Sixth Test. Treading it in

ONE EVENING, SHORTLY after we had returned to Sydney, Harold Larwood told me a further story about Jardine. In 1933, when England came to Sydney for the last Test with the series standing at 3–1 in their favour, Larwood asked his captain if he could miss the match since the Ashes were won, he was tired and he had never in all his life watched a Test match as a spectator. The request was sternly rejected. 'We've got them down, Harold,' said Jardine, 'now we'll tread on them.' Likewise, our tour did not end with the winning of the series. For financial reasons, six Tests are now routine, rather than five, and in addition there are now the one-day international matches. We had a busy fortnight ahead, with several one-day games before the Sydney match. At least the Test would be over five days and not six; if the series had been equal or if there had been only one win between the sides, the last match would have been played over six days. We had objected to this rule on the grounds that a side that is one behind is given an extra day in which to draw level in a series, but the argument was now academic. Nevertheless, we would have to lift ourselves for a final assault.

David Bairstow helped to keep up the enthusiasm. We were appalled by Roger Tolchard's injury. without which he might well have forced his way into the Test team as a batsman. But if a breath of fresh air was needed to blow life into the party, Bairstow was the man to do it. The first impact of his arrival, however, had been on him rather than on us, when his arms collapsed under Thomas's weight in some dressing-room gymnastics, and his nose was broken – for the ninth time. His second impact had come when he fielded as substitute in

Tasmania; his first throw-in struck the umpire a painful blow on the thigh. Before the fifth Test we had picked him for a one-day International at Melbourne. I told him to treat the game like a county match; if he noticed anything, to let me know; just to be himself. He settled in at once, and

There was once an England fast bowler who used an ingenious ploy to waste time in a Test match in England. At tea he filled his pockets with bread and cake crumbs, which he leaked out at the end of his run-up. Soon swarms of squawking, fighting sea-gulls were milling around behind him. This tactic would not be popular with the opposition if there was, as both sides had in 1978-9, a reduced amount of prize money if the over rate did not reach a certain level. The target was 12½ eight ball overs per hour. We fell narrowly short but we did increase our rate by almost two overs an hour compared with 1974/5. In 1971, Stackpole hit a seagull while batting at Sydney. Willis carried off the injured bird to the treatment room. In the second innings, when Lawry was defending for hour after hour, someone shouted, 'Good on yer, Bill. Those seagulls aren't in too much danger now.'

contributed to our easy win. We bowled Australia out for 101, Hendrick taking 4 for 25, and won by seven wickets. The pitch had been bare and uneven, the rest of the square as black as a silted river-bed from which the water had recently receded.

The one-day series had been badly hit by the rain. The first match scheduled for Melbourne on Boxing Day, had been postponed after storms and floods, and the second, at Sydney just two days after the exhausting fourth Test, had been abandoned after only eight overs. So we agreed to rearrange these matches for the interlude between the fifth and sixth Tests. The first of these re-arranged matches took place on February 4th. On a dim, overcast day, we were put in to bat. The new ball – Hogg for once was missing, nursing his injuries – behaved alarmingly, and we played very well to score 212 for 6, Gower reaching a magnificent century by hitting the last ball of the innings between long-off and deep extra-cover for four. Perhaps we assumed too readily that this total would suffice. Certainly Hendrick was less lively than usual, and Botham was in a euphoric not to say other-worldly state over the birth the night before of a daughter to his wife Kathy. However that may be, Hughes, Toohey, Cosier and others hit with sense and power to give the crowd at Melbourne a second taste of victory as Australia won by four wickets with ten balls to spare.

I was annoyed to read in the papers next day a quote from Gary Cosier, that: 'for the first time England was under pressure and total confusion reigned. The bowlers were accusing Mike Brearley, and Brearley was accusing the bowlers.' We had refused to comment on the obvious breakdown of respect between Yallop and Hogg at various points in the series, out of a sense of solidarity with our fellow cricketers. Yet after their win in the third Test Yallop had hinted darkly: 'All is not cheese and kisses in the English camp,' a decorative phrase, but, as far as I knew, without a grain of metaphorical truth. Now Cosier was making capital out of a minor blow-up between Botham and me, about why he kept being hit on the off-side when at his request he had six men on the leg-side! Cricket teams, like families have tensions; there is nothing wrong with the occasional heated argument, provided that those involved have mutual respect. Hogg later asked me, in a puzzled voice,

how Willis had persuaded me that he was not well at Sydney and needed to be off the field; I told him that, on the contrary, Willis was reluctant to leave and I had to talk him into going off.

Our defeat at Melbourne meant that the one-day series was levelled at one-all, and a decider would be played three days later. Unfortunately, the practice we had arranged to be held under the lights at Sydney had to be cancelled, so we did not have the chance to try night cricket for ourselves. Once again, Australia won a vital toss, and put us in. This time Gower did not rescue us. We were all out for 94, and lost by six wickets. I scored 46: a welcome improvement on my recent record at the MCG, and indeed I felt more relaxed at the crease than for over a year. One rare event was Bairstow's being run-out while going for a sixth run. I drove Cosier wide of mid-on, to the furthest point on the ground. We ran five comfortably; when the relay of fielders at last got the ball in, it was thrown over the 'keeper's head. I called Bairstow for another run, but he had gone past the stumps at the 'keeper's end. He almost made it to the bowler's end, but his desperate dive did not quite beat Hughes's throw.

We left Melbourne and flew to Sydney for the final Test. Although we were 4–1 up in the series, our defeats in the one-day matches did not leave us in quite the agreeable position in which Jardine and his team had placed themselves. Perhaps the unpleasant taste of defeat did us no harm. I was particularly keen that we produced a win that was convincing throughout, rather than victories like

Yallop's characteristic shot, the lofted on-drive. He played this difficult stroke urgently against our off-spinners. The head stays still looking at the ball; and the arms go through with the freedom of a golf-swing. There is no tendency to 'drag' with the bottom hand. The position of Yallop's back leg makes it most unlikely that he could be bowled. This picture was taken at Melbourne, first day, when his partner was Wood, the umpire French. He played this stroke to even greater effect at Sydney in the sixth Test, as he had done a year before against India at Adelaide when making 121. The Indian spinners take a great pride in outwitting a batsman who plays what they consider to be a dangerous stroke such as this, and I am told it took them longer to put a man back at long-on for Prasanna.

those at Sydney and Adelaide that smacked of the escapologist's art. To concentrate attention on the matter in hand, we banned talk about home, remarks about Jumbos, and glances at aeroplanes.

Our various selectorial and other preparations were also directed at achieving the will to win that we had had at Brisbane. At the selection meeting, we quickly agreed on the same side for the fourth consecutive Test match. Willis suggested we go through our players one by one considering whether everyone was in the right frame of mind for the match. We were slightly worried about Randall, who was only too aware of his low scores at Adelaide and in the one-day Internationals; but we felt the return to Sydney would stimulate and encourage him. Hendrick and Botham would raise their game for a Test match. Gooch was the one player who was perhaps becoming fatalistic; he could be feeling that it was merely lack of competition that kept him in the side, for Tolchard had only just rejoined the party, his face still lopsided, and Radley had never had the chance to show his true ability. The manager said that he would like to talk to Graham, and remind him of his chance here, not only to salvage some pride in personal success on the tour, but also to stake a stronger claim for the future.

For our last pre-Test team meeting, we hardly discussed tactics or the opposition. We agreed that our task was, simply, to play at our best. I mentioned the lesson of Bangalore where two years before we had lost a Test after gaining an invincible 3–0 lead. Willis cited the help he had had at Adelaide. We agreed to continue with the regular dressing-room chats. The atmosphere then and at the dinner was calm and relaxed compared with Brisbane. Teams, like individuals, have to find the right blend of relaxation and concentration, and I felt that the signs were propitious.

On the morning of the match I was glad to wake up feeling much better after a day in bed suffering from the ill-effects of a second cholera injection I needed for the visit I planned to India after the tour. Willis and I looked at the pitch. Taking Arthur Lance's rebuke seriously, we asked the groundsman how he thought the pitch would play. 'It'll hold together all right,' he said. We found this hard to believe. The pitch was barer than for the fourth Test, with the extra drawback that at the Randwick End the marks of fast bowlers' follow-

throughs in that match were clearly visible on a length just outside the off-stump. Once again, the slight damp would give some help to bowlers before lunch, but it would be a good toss to win. Despite the indications that spinners would be helped, Border, who had played so well here in the fourth Test, was surprisingly named twelfth man; he was replaced by Toohey. Darling was also dropped in favour of Andrew Hilditch, who, along with the two umpires, was making his Test debut.

Over the whole season Yallop won the toss fifteen times out of seventeen. In six Tests, I won once; in all three one-day Internationals I called wrong, and in five State matches I won only once. In Tom Stoppard's play *Rosencrantz and Guildenstern Are Dead*, Guildenstern's paranoia is fed by the fact that a coin he spun came down heads on ninety consecutive occasions, and on all ninety he called tails. As he says, 'The equanimity of your average pitcher and tosser of coins depends upon a law, or let us say a probability, or at any rate a mathematically calculable chance that ensures that he will not upset himself by losing too much, nor upset his opponent by winning too often. This made for a kind of harmony and a kind of confidence. It related the fortuitous and the ordained into a reassuring union which we recognized as nature.' 'The world is out of joint,' as Hamlet said, in another play.

In our play, the fortuitous was beginning to seem unnaturally ordained, and I would by now have been surprised to call right. Willy-nilly, we took the field. We soon had another cause for complaint: vast vibrating cranes were at work building a new stand to replace the one whose recent demolition had further spoilt the charm of this lovely cricket ground. The one to go had been the third of a row of jaunty Victorian stands with green-painted ironwork. Its passing was regretted by environmentalists in Sydney, with good cause, as one of the city's main charms is its elegant architecture with elaborate iron tracery. The bombardment of Test cricket by the loud and the new was symbolized in this noisy activity over the boundary. Our complaint silenced the cranes (at some vast cost in Saturday overtime rates; strong and strike-happy unions are considered to be one of the main British contributions to Australia's present), and our bowling and fielding silenced the small crowd. (Only 8,000 came to see the first day's play, but the

paucity of the crowd is put into some sort of perspective when placed beside the average daily crowd for the Super-Tests, which was only 11,000.) After Wood took 13 off Willis's first over, Hilditch, the NSW captain, became the tenth run-out casualty for Australia when Gooch made a fine stop and flick from third slip. This was a dismissal through nervousness. At 19 Wood was brilliantly caught by Botham off Hendrick, and the heroes of the first Test, Yallop and Hughes, came together. Then Hughes had been the sounder; now he looked more vulnerable, and it was no injustice when in the last over before lunch Willis had him caught at slip off a fine delivery that moved away off the pitch.

After lunch a procession of batsmen came and went in conditions that were good for batting. Botham took two wickets and Emburey two, so that well before tea the score was 124 for 7.

Gooch, down the wicket, on-drives Yardley during his innings of 74. He is surprisingly quick on his feet for a heavy man, and plays spinners best when he looks to attack them. He had also changed in his manner on the field. His fielding sombrero topped with sleepy aptness the droopy moustaches; the swarthy look and lazy gait combined to suggest a racial stereotype, and earned him the name 'Zapata', or 'Zap' for short. I knew from personal experience that this exterior concealed an alert mind. What I impressed on Zap was that an air of indolence can be catching; that everyone on the field has a responsibility to motivate each other: that bowlers *need* to be encouraged, and that they like to see their fielders looking lively. Zap was now much more energetic in the field. It is impossible for one or two people to motivate a team; the habit has to be instilled in everyone.

Through all these disasters Yallop had played very well, apart from some near misses off Hendrick and occasionally Botham. Now he had carte blanche to attack, which he did with much unorthodox verve. Some of his strokeplay could without injustice be described as butchery; but it was high-quality butchery. If Botham bowled straight, he swung him over mid-wicket; if outside the off-stump, he cover-drove, or slashed. I brought Willis on to keep him quiet; he took 15 runs off a reasonably directed over. Against the spinners he was less free, but he did show examples of his ability to hit off-spinners without a hint of danger against the spin over mid-on. Only John Edrich shows the same consistency with this difficult shot.

Tactically, I was torn between the need, at this stage, to bowl spinners at Yallop and the desire to bowl faster bowlers at Hogg and Higgs, who between them helped their captain to add 74 runs, of which Yallop scored 56. We did restrict Yallop's run-rate after tea, particularly by the off-spinners' bowling just outside the off-stump with six men on the off-side. (The ball was already turning, and Hogg fell to Miller, caught at short-leg.) At last Yallop tried one heave too many against Botham, and was caught at square leg for 121. It had been a remarkable innings, which enabled Australia to reach 198. Yallop, like Denness in 1974/5, had had an onerous series as a captain, and it was the mark of a tough player that he could summon the drive to score this century, as Denness had done in 1975.

We went in and for the last forty minutes I again felt more relaxed at the crease. I was also dropped, for the only time in the series, at slip off Yardley. Apart from that, we were in little trouble, and the close of play score was 24 for 0. The whole side had responded marvellously with restored vigour.

Next day vigour continued. Boycott and Randall were out fairly cheaply, but Gooch and I added 69 before I was caught at cover off Higgs for 46. Gower played a carefree innings of 65, without the control of some of his earlier knocks. But the highlight of the day was undoubtedly Gooch's innings. He batted purposefully, moving down the wicket to attack both spinners, and looking to play his shots against the quick bowlers too. He was finally fourth out at 182, stumped off Higgs for 74. Botham and Gower were again together, and by tea-time had added 34

entertaining, if sometimes chancy runs, on the already deteriorating pitch.

Unfortunately, the humid weather, so oppressive to the fieldsmen, suddenly burst with a thunderstorm of tropical intensity. Lightning struck the elegant Ladies Stand, where I was sitting eating rich English fruit cake, but these elemental forces did no structural damage to the building. The field was quickly under water; within half an hour the sun was out again, the air crisp and fresh, and games that were a cross between cricket and aquaplaning were started on the outfield by spectators. However, the ground was too wet for serious play that evening.

Next morning our hopes of quick runs for a substantial lead were disappointed when Botham, as at Perth, holed out at mid-off to Yardley, and Gower was caught off a googly which bounced and turned. The score was 247 for 6, a lead of only 49. We needed more runs, however long they might take to score, and Taylor, with help from Miller and Willis, saw us beyond the 300-mark. We were finally dismissed for 308, one run short of our highest first-innings score of the series, at Perth.

When Australia went in to bat again Hilditch went early, caught low down by Taylor off Hendrick. He looked unhappy about the decision, but from my position at slip there seemed no doubt about the catch, although when I watched it on television that evening the ball appeared to have bounced. Bob is the last man I would suspect of claiming a wicket if he knew the ball had touched the ground. Neither on this occasion nor in our first innings when Boycott was caught very low at slip did I see the umpire at the bowler's end ask his colleague whether he thought the ball carried, though in each case the square leg umpire was close to the incident. It was a bonus on this pitch to take a wicket before the spinners came on, and after six overs they were operating at each end. Hughes went first, caught off a sharply-turning ball at backward short-leg. The score was 28-2.

Wood and Yallop played skilfully. For once, the left-handers had a slight advantage on the worn pitch in that the worst patch was outside their leg stump; that was at the Randwick End, where there were now cracks and craters, and the ball leaped and turned. Wood has always looked to hit the off-spinners to leg: after some time we sensed that he was itching to play the ball there, so for

The two forms of cricket last winter. *Above* a typical celebration at the fall of a wicket, second Test, Perth. *Inset* Part of traditional cricket's answer to Packer razzmatazz: a parachutist lands at Melbourne shortly before the third Test. *Below* Two photographs of Packer cricketers wearing coloured clothes for the first time: Sydney Cricket Ground, 17 January, 1979. Both pictures show Lillee (WSC Australians) bowling to Austin (WSC West Indians).

Miller has Maclean caught by Gooch at silly point for a duck at Perth during Australia's first innings. The first three times Maclean was dismissed in the series he fell to Miller. Of his seven dismissals in Tests six were to our off-spinners.

Miller we left mid-wicket quite open. Wood tried to on-drive, the ball turned, took the leading edge, and was well caught by Willis running out towards deep extra-cover from mid-off. Next over, Toohey and Carlson completed the trio of classic dismissals by Emburey, caught at short-leg, and 48-2 had become 48-5. In these conditions a batsman needed luck to stay in at the start, and afterwards much skill; yet the severe critics on the Hill turned upside down the large banner proclaiming 'THE PETER TOOHEY STAND'.

There was half-an-hour to go that evening, but any wild ideas we might have had about finishing the match within three days were thwarted by the two Ys, Yallop and Yardley. The former's technique was faultless; he judged the length well and played forward or back with a loose grip. Yardley's method was quite different, but even more effective. He moved down the pitch, especially to Emburey who was still bowling into the craters outside the off stump. If he reached the pitch of the ball Yardley drove hard, especially to the off; if not, he kicked the ball away. Sometimes, too, he stayed back and scored off the back foot.

Their partnership added 22 runs before stumps, and a further 12 in the morning, so that Australia, on 82 for 5, were only 28 runs behind. At last, Miller lured Yallop down the pitch; the ball took the edge, and was caught by Taylor, who also broke the wicket to make doubly sure. Yallop showed in this match a range of technique against the spinners that I have not seen anyone surpass.

We now felt confident of victory. However, the tail-enders were unusually stubborn, and Yardley unerringly resourceful. With Wright he took his side's total ahead of ours, but their lead was only four when Wright, trying to sweep Miller, was caught by Boycott at square-leg. Emburey took the wicket of Higgs, and Miller dismissed Hogg and Hurst to finish with 5 for 44, the first time he had taken five wickets in a Test innings. So England needed 34 runs to win, a total large enough to let the bowlers hope that they could improve their averages, but small enough to make it hard for the batsmen to do more than play themselves in; not, in short, a situation that opening batsmen relish.

We relished it even less when the umpires allowed Australia to bowl with an old ball. Just before they were due to go out they told me that Yallop wanted to start with an old ball. I said, 'I'm sorry, but I don't agree to that.' They said they would see Yallop again; and came back to tell me that they had decided to let him have his way. Insole and I were fuming inwardly; we said that if that were allowed any captain could bowl with an old ball with the string hanging down. We were sure that the Laws disallowed the old ball without the *mutual* consent of the captains, and we also knew from decades of first-class cricket that the umpires' ruling went against all precedent. However, you can do no more than protest, and try to relax enough to bat, so Boycott and I went out to face Yardley and Higgs.

The advantage of an old ball to the fielding side is that the spinners can grip it from the start. There is no chance for the openers to score a few runs and get their feet moving against the new ball. When we had scored 12, Insole discovered the passage in the Laws – Law 5 – which states categorically that 'Subject to agreement to the contrary either captain may demand a new ball at the start of each innings.' Insole's dilemma was: should he take the copy of the Laws on to the field and protest, or let us continue? He decided that he could not risk facing either Geoff or me if, having protested, the

Bairstow, who made a robust and important contribution to the tour in his five weeks with us, in typical pose.

PHIL MERCHANT

innings were re-started and one of us was out for nought against a new ball. In fact, I took a leaf out of Yardley's book; I decided that if I tried to play him from the crease I would be unlikely to survive against his lift and turn, so I went down the pitch to him and drove him. We were within three runs of victory when Boycott tried to force a short ball that turned, and hit an easy catch to cover-point. Randall had to face two balls from Higgs; as he reached the stumps he suddenly leapt back in consternation. Wood had put a rubber snake in the crease. Umpires have at varying times been asked to hold helmets, caps, and false teeth; snakes are not their commonest burden. The second ball of the next over, Yardley bowled around middle-and-leg and I lifted it over mid-wicket for four. We had won the sixth Test by nine wickets.

Bruce Yardley holds the disputed ball. Yardley was an enigma during the tour. At times, he looked a matchwinner with the ball, achieving exceptional bounce and turn, especially in the state match at Perth. We felt that he could well have won the fourth Test had he been picked; but in the sixth Test, on a pitch even more suited to spinners, he did not bowl a consistent length and line, and was much too expensive. Like Lance Gibbs, he preferred bowling over the wicket, and found the left-handed Gower difficult to bowl at. Unlike Miller and Emburey he does not bowl a drifter. Yardley is also a dangerous attacking batsman, but remains difficult to assess as an all-rounder.

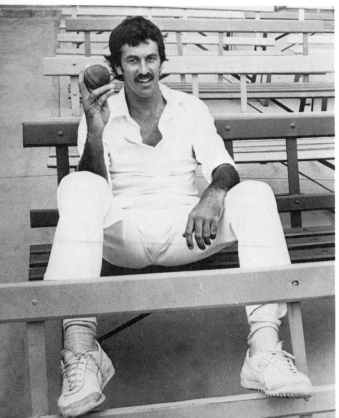

CHAPTER 15

The Games Players Play

THE UNIQUE FEATURE of England's tour of Australia in 1978/9 was that it had a constant competitor and companion in World Series Cricket. Inevitably I asked myself what I thought of this form of the game – and, indeed, what I felt about the more traditional forms of cricket.

Cricket has obviously changed considerably over the last thirty years. Even twenty years ago there would be silence during play except for ripples of applause. The game would be held up while a plane went over. Batsmen might refuse to continue while there was slow hand-clapping. One umpire, Alec Skelding, once went over to a section of the crowd and wagged his finger at them, even threatening to call the game off completely if they did not keep quiet. In the days when professionals appeared on scorecards with their initials after their names (days which ended in England only in 1962) an announcement once came over the loudspeaker at Lord's of a correction to the scorecard: 'For "F. J. Titmus" read "Titmus, F. J."' The emotions of crowd and players were understated: when Laker took 19 wickets in a Test match in 1956 he and his colleagues looked embarrassed at their success.

However, although cricket of that time offers a striking contrast to, say, Packer's limited-over night cricket, many modern developments are not peculiar to World Series Cricket. They reflect the social demands and changes of the times, as well as traditional cricket's efforts to make the product entertaining enough to survive. Just as Packer has introduced his own innovations, such as circles 30 yards from the stumps within which so many fielders must stand, in the John Player League bowlers' run-ups are restricted to 15 yards; and in all one-day cricket in England umpires are instructed to signal 'wide' for a delivery which is not technically a wide, in order to prevent players bowling deliberately wide as a defensive tactic.

World Series Cricket may have shifted the balance; but none of its innovations implies that its cricket is not 'fair dinkum', as the Australians would say. But are the other criticisms levelled at Packer's style of cricket more justified?

Take the criticism that results of his games had been decided beforehand. One respected writer was convinced half-way through the Australian season that he could predict results of the WSC games not on the basis of the relative strengths of the sides but by working out which result would better suit the WSC organization. He pointed to the pre-series build-up of the Australian team, including film of them in training, their pop-song, and flashes of the matches the previous season which showed the home team on top. He suggested that the West Indians did not pick their strongest team for the first night match at Sydney, and that their batsmen played even more recklessly than usual. According to this view, the WSC West Indians were like the Harlem Globetrotters, presenting a display of skills rather than contesting the game in earnest.

I do not agree with this view. The finals of the International Cup were arranged on a best-of-five basis on consecutive nights in Melbourne. After three matches, the West Indians (playing in the finals as a result of the midnight decision on January 17th) were leading 2-1. Clearly, WSC stood to gain if the Australians won this fourth match. That morning, the rest day of the Adelaide Test, several of the England side drove out for lunch in the Barossa Valley. One of the team offered me odds of 3-1 against the West Indians. I laid out A$10, Clive Lloyd's team won, and I collected A$30.

I tell this story both to show an example of the not infrequently-voiced cynicism about WSC, and to deny allegations of their lack of effort. Many critics in their haste to put their finger on what is wrong have jumped to a false conclusion. It seemed to me that not only did the West Indians have an immediate, short-term financial interest in winning that match at Melbourne, but also that all World Series cricketers have a long-term interest in proving that their cricket is truly competitive. They have an interest in creating unpredictable outcomes in general, so that, for example, the result of the fourth game in a series of five is not a foregone conclusion. I also knew most of the players involved, and I could not believe that they had lost their pride of performance, or their aggression. My impression of the little World Series Cricket that I saw supports this view.

Sporting authorities take a harsh view of those who 'fix' games, as the life-ban on Sheffield Wednesday players back in the Fifties testifies; and rightly so, for failing to try in a competitive game to which spectators are welcome is a cheat on the audience and on your fellow-players, unless it is, as in professional wrestling, so stylized and extreme that nobody is taken in; but so exaggerated an activity has ceased to be a sport and is more a form of drama or morality play. However, I saw no hint of any such dishonesty in WSC. Some of the cricket I saw looked uncomfortably fierce.

'Fixing' matches is one thing, but equally to the point is the general attitude of the participants in a game. I have often been asked whether cricket becomes 'merely a job', and whether professional cricketers play from love of the game. Have we lost all contact with the spontaneous play of children? After a thunderstorm during the sixth Test at Sydney, spectators came on to the ground and 'played cricket' – on the soaking grass they slid and gambolled and frolicked. Is this the true paradigm of cricket, or of play as contrasted with the grim struggle they had paid to watch?

I have always felt that a game, essentially, should be just as much a game whatever the audience. When 'Rabbit' Angstrom in John Updike's *Run Rabbit* stands watching some boys playing basket-

ball around a telephone pole with a blackboard bolted to it, the narrator says, 'His standing there makes the real boys feel strange. Eyeballs slide. They're doing this for themselves, not as a show for some adult walking around town in a double-breasted cocoa suit.' So: does the attitude of professional players mean, in effect, they have stopped playing a 'game' at all?

Logically, a game is complete without any spectators at all, unlike a play at the theatre, which name itself implies a spectacle. It is unduly puritanical, however, to feel that the only satisfactions of the game should come from within, and from earning the respect of one's peers, the other players, for there are many different kinds of satisfaction, just as there are many different kinds of game-playing.

When we reflect on the notion of play, the first examples to come to mind may be very different from organized sport. Sport's need for winners and the concern it breeds about results may seem undesirable and untypical of play itself. When a four-year-old plays with his cars he is untrammelled by complex rules imposed from outside. When he paints or draws he is enviably spontaneous. Children, of course, play games, and then rules become more prominent, as in hide-and-seek or snakes-and-ladders. Sometimes the framework of a game consists of the roles which constitute the game, as in cowboys-and-Indians, or doctors-and-nurses; but not all behaviour is consistent with being a cowboy or a nurse. There are restrictions on what is permissible within the game.

Fully-blown competitive games, by extension, have more severe restrictions and limitations. Individual wishes have to be denied in the face of rigid rules imposed from outside. Sportsmen, on the whole, are conservative in character; and their willingness to enter into activities organized and controlled from outside, with the accompanying rules and social pressures, may explain why sports-players tend to be less radical than, say, artists.

Something is lost when any game becomes institutionalized, and when it becomes a major part of an individual's life, whether or not he is paid to play. One gain, however, of the organization of games is the provision of a setting stable enough for sustained competition and the measuring of skills. Just as in science one requires stable conditions for tests to be made, so in cricket stability of rules and a stable administration are essential if Tests are to be played. There is an element of relentless plodding in a Test match, admirable in its way, but akin to repetition rather than to creativity. However, creativity in any field is seldom achieved without repetition or plodding. Within the laws of cricket, and within the limiting conditions of pitch, weather and time there is remarkable scope in the methods that can be employed to reach the goal of scoring more runs than the other side. So I would defend both WSC and the established game, seeing them both as justified forms of games playing, only with their own special laws and rewards.

A further criticism, levelled particularly at World Series Cricket, but also at the professional game in general, is whether playing for money does not in some special way necessarily imply the loss of the spirit of play. The question is asked because people feel that games are essentially aside from the practicalities of life. Like films, or art, they take us away from immediate demands: they have their own completeness. Thus games do not offer efficient means to an end — there are simpler ways of getting balls into holes than by using golf clubs. From a practical point of view, the restrictions are artificial. If a man wanted to get from the start of a 200m race to the end as quickly as possible to report that a bomb had been placed under the stand, he would not run round the edge of the track. Perhaps it is partly because they are often impractical that games resonate so deeply and mean so much. They seem to be unsullied by questions of profit and loss. This purity may be put another way: a move in a game is often understandable in terms of the goals of the game itself, not in terms of factors outside the game. And it may be felt that the purity is spoilt if the game is played for money. But the argument is flawed: moves within the game (pawn to QB3, short-leg to fourth slip etc.) may be explicable only within the game: but why enter into that particular system of rules and goals at all? The answer may be for love, for money, for exercise, for amusement, or for several reasons together. But money need not spoil the game, nor the attitude of its participants: if you do something for money it does not follow that you do it only, or primarily, for that reason.

A specific criticism made of the World Series players was that when they first signed for Packer they showed that they valued money more highly than playing for their country. They were accused of disloyalty; and the suggestion often was, what is the point of the game if money rather than national honour is the matter at stake? People are always more strong-minded in advocating that others be altruistic than in being it themselves. And Underwood and the others certainly did lose something by putting their Test careers in jeopardy. Underwood knows he has lost a lot. Early in the tour we happened to cross paths with the WSC players at the airport in Sydney. We were on our way to Brisbane for the first Test, while they were going to Perth. I found the meeting touching in a way, but for Derek it was awkward, even painful. Later he was reluctant to meet us, as it reminded him of the Test scene, and the team spirit that an England side can engender. So I do not feel that World Series players are disloyal, or concerned with wrong priorities: they have simply chosen one option among many. And on the question of motives, there is as much selfishness and bad temper in the club cricket I have played as in the professional game.

Another criticism of Packer's cricket has been 'Who will remember the results of WSC matches?' But what memories of sport do we value anyway? Most often we value images of players and individuals: the fearsome speed of Rodney Hogg, the artistry of Bishen Bedi, the grace of David Gower or the optimism and power of Ian Botham. Packer's cricket has produced its images, too. Also some Packer results may mean a lot; it is difficult to feel much about a World team whose squad consists improbably of five Englishmen, five Pakistanis and five South Africans, but here the English players are less fortunate than some of their colleagues in the other teams, who may well feel a national unity and team spirit akin to what is possible in Test teams.

I believe, then, that much of the condemnation of WSC is unfounded; but there are four particular criticisms that I cannot dismiss.

First, Mr. Packer's interests were originally, and presumably primarily, not in cricket but in televising cricket. Connected to this was the need to encourage sponsorship. Even outside WSC, of course, sponsorship and promotion have expanded greatly; but there is one crucial difference between traditional cricket and World Series Cricket: in the former no-one, *qua* cricketer, is employed by a sponsoring company, and any contribution made by a sponsor to the game is under the control of cricket's governing bodies. The question with WSC is: who is the master and who the servant?

The second disconcerting feature about WSC is the way it encourages mindless excitement, with its gladiatorial introductions, its pop songs and its frenzied public address system. They are like inconsistent parents of unruly children, working their charges up to a pitch of excitement yet still expecting them to keep their place at the dinner table. Ian Chappell was outraged by the behaviour of the fans at the January 17th match. his comments made front-page headlines: 'CRICKET GORILLAS: CHAPPELL SLAMS ROWDY WSC FANS.' He said in the story: 'If we arrest a few of these bloody gorillas and charge them it would soon stop. It's becoming a bloody disease.' There had been only 28 policemen assigned to the match to control 40,000 or more spectators. The potential for trouble was frightening.

Third, and more importantly, there is the danger that a private promoter may misuse his power in a way that sacrifices authenticity. In the one match that I saw, Caro usurped the umpire's role by ordering play to restart. No doubt in traditional cricket umpires have been 'got at', but such disregard for their independence is rare. A further incidence also involved Caro. The fourth game of the series at Melbourne (on which I had my bet) was approaching its close. The Australians looked unlikely to get in their full quota of overs before the finishing time, in which case the game would have to be decided on run-rate at that time. To avoid this, Packer told Caro on the 'phone that he wanted an extra quarter of an hour played. Caro felt he could not run out and deliver the message himself, so he asked the Australians' twelfth man to take it out for him. The twelfth man gave the message to Chappell, but not to the umpires or to Clive Lloyd who was batting. At 10.30 the umpires and batsmen left the field, the West Indians delighted that they had won. As a result, Caro resigned from his job, allegedly saying: 'Dear Kerry, he just can't emotionally, keep out of it.'

Even without incidents like these, the whole system is so closed that there is constantly a burden of proof on every branch of the organization to show that umpires and selectors are independent, that matches are played under proper conditions and with a genuine competitive attitude. The players do try; but the context in which they play makes the cricket open to questions that could not be raised when one country plays another at Test cricket. And the propaganda of the commentary box does not suggest that criticism and independence are positively encouraged.

This leads on to my fourth point – that World Series Cricket is separated from the rest of the game; yet it is parasitic upon it. Packer has signed up some 60 leading players and engaged them to play matches throughout the period in which most first-class cricket is played in all countries except England. These players have been trained within traditional cricket. WSC trains no-one, though they have done a little coaching in Australia. None of their revenue comes down to the rest of cricket.

The natural intermingling of top-class players with those on the next rung of the ladder is missing. WS cricketers play against other WS cricketers. They do not, between internationals, play in lower-grade cricket. The only regional cricket played in Australia by WSC were the exhibition matches between the left-over players in various towns in the outback. The intermingling that is missing has various values. It enables an up-and-coming player to test himself against the best, and perhaps show that he deserves to be promoted to their ranks. There is a permanent pool of players fully available for the highest class of cricket. It offers the public a regional competition where they can identify with local teams, and it allows the stars to recover form against less perpetually testing opposition.

Given these strictures, is there a way forward? I have always believed that there is room in the cricketing calendar for a bonanza, say a month or six weeks in which all manner of cricketing and promotional ideas could be tried out. Kerry Packer might well be the person to run such an event. All players could be available, and all players would be available for all Tests. Some of the money raised in such a competition would go to the cricketing countries. If the sides for these matches were selected by their own countries, all the fears and suspicions that I have discussed would drop away. It would be 'fair dinkum' cricket, even if its style was new, brash and commercial. At the time of writing cricket seemed to be moving this way, as Packer had won the rights to televise Test cricket in Australia; and that was the source of the original conflict.

CHAPTER 16

The Social Side

IN HIS GENEROUS speech after the fifth Test, Phil Ridings said that there was less between the teams than the results suggested. I agree, and would add that the Australians were unreasonably criticized for their defeat. The media's tendency to categorize people as either heroes or villains seems prominent in Australia, and home losers are given short shrift, though it was worse in Pakistan in 1967: when the national hockey team returned from a 4-1 defeat by India in the Asian Games, the entire defence had to apologize to the nation. In the 1978/9 series, Australia scored four centuries to England's two: an Australian took five wickets in an innings seven times to our two: and two of their bowlers each took more wickets than any of ours. Individually, they were a match for us; but under pressure they played as individuals, as they themselves acknowledged. They also pointed to the reason: too many young and inexperienced players had come together at the same time. Normally, players new to a Test team are slotted in between more experienced players, and their failures are less noticeable or drastic. It is a creditable reflection of the depth and resilience of Australian cricket that so many talented players have been unearthed so quickly.

The substandard pitches were also to Australia's disadvantage. Seasoned travellers like Alec Bedser, Barrington, Boycott and Willis were amazed at the amount of help these pitches gave the bowlers. England scored 2,665 runs for the loss of 104 wickets, an average per wicket of 25.62; Australia's 120 wickets fell for 2301 runs, an average of 19.17. The odds were always stacked against the batsmen, but particularly against the less experienced Australian players, who learned to bat on even surfaces where they could safely hit through the line of the ball. Moreover, their attack included two quick bowlers and a wrist spinner, whose special skills would have been relatively more crucial on hard, true pitches than the seam-bowling and finger-spin that predominated with us. These handicaps were, of course, increased unnecessarily by our opponents' ridiculous habit of running each other out. In six Tests there were ten Australian run-outs compared with only two on our side.

The main weakness in the home side lay in its lack of balance. To achieve an all-round bowling attack, they would have liked to include Hogg, Hurst, Dymock (or Lawson), Yardley and Higgs. But if you add to this combination Wright or Maclean, neither of whom can bat very well, the tail starts at number six, so they were forced either to weaken the seam bowling – by doing without the excellent new-ball bowler, Dymock (as they did in Tests 1, 5, and 6) – or weaken the spin attack, by omitting

Ken Barrington, the Colonel, shows his physique at Sydney.

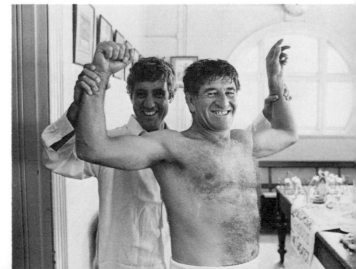

Higgs (as in Test 2) or Yardley (as they did in Tests 3 and, disastrously, 4). By contrast, our middle-order performed with increasing skill, thanks to Botham and the application of Miller and Taylor with the bat, so we were always able to field a full five-pronged attack.

One principle of selection that has always been typically Australian was the method of choosing a captain. They picked a side, and from that team named a captain. Ideally, of course, this method will produce the same results as the English method, which is to choose a captain and then pick a side. But the ideal is rare in life, and I think it is true to say that neither Yallop nor Brearley would have been the captains in this series if the methods of selection had been reversed. I am not being highly critical of Graham Yallop when I say that a man of Inverarity's perception and experience would have done the job better. Calculating this advantage against the likely loss in batting skill is a nice matter, on which fortunately I have no need to give an opinion. On one matter I was amazed: that Yallop at no stage of the series was co-opted on to the selection committee. Yet it is he who must have confidence in his players, and he who receives the blame if things go wrong. Incidentally, he later lost his job to Hughes. On our side, Gower, Randall, cool cat and hot cat, and Botham, our youngest and most attractive batsmen, scored most runs. We had five bowlers who could almost always be counted on to bowl accurately and well. And our fielding and wicketkeeping was of a high level. As the experienced Geoff Dymock said, 'England were a truly professional side, and kept their unity as a team.'

Much of the credit for this goes to the management of the team. Bernard Thomas's contribution has been chronicled above; as has been mentioned, he also takes responsibility for the room arrangements. Apart from Willis, Boycott, and myself, everyone has to share rooms on tour; surprisingly, most prefer it this way. We start the tour by putting youngsters with old-stagers. The room-list is changed every three weeks or so; on one occasion, we felt that two players were fanning each other's exuberance, and made the change a week earlier. The location of rooms can even make a difference to the 'feel' of a stay; in Brisbane we were placed on two adjoining floors, each of which had its rooms arranged in a square. People wandered in and out of rooms. It was more like a neighbourhood of terrace houses, with back doors welcomingly open, than the usual tower-blocks. At Sydney, on the contrary, the hotel had two towers unconnected except at ground level. On our first stay there, the manager's room and its adjoining team-room were on the 22nd floor of the east tower, while all the rest of the party were scattered up and down the west tower. The whole point of the team-room was nullified, especially as this hotel was also notable for the inefficiency of its lifts.

The role of assistant manager can be nebulous. 'The Colonel', as Ken Barrington has been known for at least twenty years, likes to have things clearly laid down. His first job was to make sure no-one overslept on match or travel mornings. The son of a sergeant-major in the British army, Ken awakes regularly at dawn – as I can witness, having shared a bungalow with him at Bahawalpur, Pakistan, where he provided cigarette smoke and strong tea at 6.30 precisely. For us all, day broke with Barrington, or at least with his voice over the telephone. He took care of another area of communication, putting notices up in dressing-rooms and team-rooms, a job he did with a flourish of handwriting. It was Ken's job to make sure that cricket laundry was collected from the dressing-room. Stock questions asked of the Colonel were: 'When's laundry collected?' and 'What time do we leave the hotel in the morning?' and he would always respond, with an initial trace of annoyance, that it was all on his notice, until he realized that he was again being teased. When Barrington went for drinks with the Board before lunch during matches he would justify himself with the remark that it was 'good P.R.' However, he never took this aspect of his job as seriously as a predecessor who, it is reported, would enrich the nervous silence of the Test dressing-room with his post-prandial snores.

Barrington's main area of responsibility was, of course, organizing practice, and I have spoken of his help here. Chris Old reckoned that the practice was better run than on any of his previous tours. In the latter stages, Ken would add spice to the more relaxed net session by claiming A$1 every time he got anyone out with his leg-breaks, a challenge which led to personal duels and heated arguments about edges, LBWs, and stumpings. He also enjoyed a flutter at trotting-meetings and on his regular golf rounds with Botham, Old and Tolchard.

I went with Ken on the 1964/5 MCC tour of South

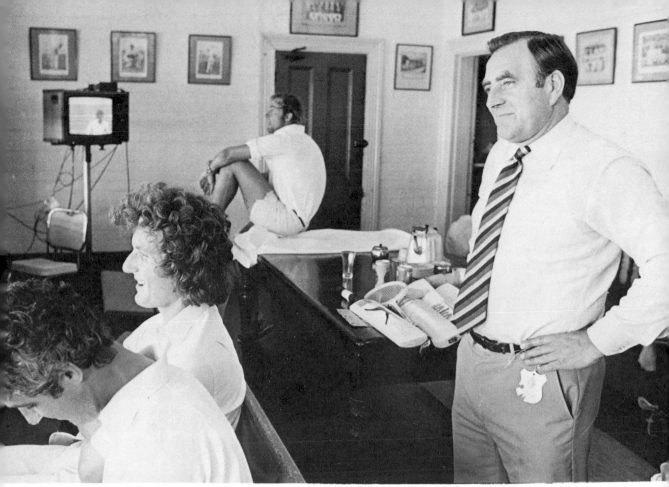

Africa, and can well remember his nervousness when waiting to go in to bat; he would sit chain-smoking, watching every ball but saying little. Tour managers also live every ball, but do not have the chance to do the job themselves. Their contribution in the dressing-room was vital, however, though the price was damage to their nails and nerves.

Despite the ordeals of the job, neither Barrington nor Doug Insole once fell into the tempting trap of insinuating even unintentionally that the game was better in their day. Another trap for those in authority is interfering too much; again I think the balance was right. A year before we had interfered with Randall's batting, trying to persuade him to cut out some streaky shots and get rid of his famous shuffle. But Randall has to fizz in his own peculiar way, and was, in Australia, rightly chary of advice. It matters even more to him than to others to play some crisp attacking shots early in an innings. So we never commented on the shuffle (except occasion-ally to query his apparent certainty that the ball to which he had been given LBW would have missed the leg stump), though there was the occasion where

On whom does the strain most tell? The manager looks careworn during the fourth Test, as Willis waits to go in. Willis was a regular and compulsive watcher during his hours off-duty. At Adelaide he and Hendrick would not allow those who had not been watching from the start to view the Taylor-Miller stand for fear that their luck would be changed. I also watched most of the time. Edmonds looks bored in front of the television, and is no doubt envious of the spin bowlers playing in the match. He and Lever were the reserve fielders for the last four Tests, and twice they had to rush back from the beach when their transistor announced another first-innings collapse by our batsmen. More generally, those who did not play in Test matches made a vital contribution to the team's success; the 'dawn patrol' arrived early to 'book' the practice pitch, they all helped in the menial dressing-room tasks and they kept morale high throughout. The table is typically littered, a squash racquet used by the non-players, bats to be signed, and the permanent tea-pot.

Doug talked to him at Sydney about hooking before playing himself in.

Off the field we had no curfews, nor did we have rules about drinking or diet. I once observed a hawk-eyed coach of an athletics team from Rhode Island University stridently reinforcing dietary instructions to his team as they passed along the self-service counter for lunch: 'Don't forget,' he roared, 'it's roast beef and *no* gravy.' Our supervision was less stringent, though I have been known to call together the Middlesex team to berate them for over-indulgence in the roast potatoes at lunch at Lord's. Similarly, we did advocate moderation in drink on this tour. Ian Botham told me he had decided to go 'on the wagon' just before Christmas. Two days later, on the flight from Adelaide to Melbourne on Christmas Eve, he asked me if he could break his abstinence for Christmas. I said 'No, with you, Botham, it's none or plenty.' He took this remark in good part, and stuck to orange-juice for several weeks.

As a team, we drank more orange-juice in the team-room than anything else. There were of course the regular beer-drinkers, and many of us enjoyed local wine. Spirits we hardly touched. Also readily available in the team-room was fresh and dried fruit, which the manager, squirrel-like, laid by in great stores. Australia's cosmopolitan cities and stereotyped modern hotels made the team-room even more important than, say, in India. For there, particularly in the smaller centres, we, like Victorian families, depended on each other for company and amusement; at Nagpur we enjoyed Willis's marvellous facility at charades, at Gavhati Randall's penchant for the microphone.

One occasion which did remind some of us of the sub-continent was the Christmas Day lunch. Christmas is desperately hard to deal with on tour. It falls in the middle of the most hectic cricket schedule, following soon after the second Test, and being followed by a one-day international and then two more Tests with hardly a break between them. It is half-way through the tour, so any honeymoon period is over. Homesickness is most likely to be felt then. Team festivities can be forced and liable to underline people's separation from their families rather than suppress it. However, thanks largely to the work of Mr. Miller, the Social Secretary, and his associates – Lever, Hendrick, Gower and Gooch – the Christmas lunch at the Hilton in Melbourne was

a memorable one. Miller and Hendrick, alias Arthur and Sam, Derbyshire miners, compèred the show, which included 'Blofeld' over the crackly radio, the miners' pub-talk and our variation on the 'Partridge in a Pear Tree', with contributions for the twenty days of Christmas from all present. We dressed up in clothes or roles whose name began with a designated letter, so that the manager was enabled to fulfil his desire to impersonate Chief Inspector Clouseau, and Willis an umpire, complete with white stick, stocking over face, loaded scales, and a badge proclaiming 'Fiery's Favourites'. Fiery is an old name for Boycott.

The lunch ended appropriately when we asked the Australian National Boys' choir, who had been singing carols in the lobby, to perform under the temporary direction of the choirmaster, Randall. It turned out that while the boys all wanted to be Test cricketers, Randall had always wanted to conduct choirs.

Doug Insole also showed a spark of talent in an unexpected direction. The manager has many roles on tour; a long-stop for discipline, a buffer, though not necessarily an old buffer, between the players

Hoggy at his most engaging and friendly – off the field. Of his manner on the field, however, he admitted, 'I've got a bad temper. You've got to have something to motivate you.' Despite all the early doubts, he bowled more overs in the series, 217.4, than anyone else. Most were delivered in short spells. 'Bowling bloody short spells is why I've been successful,' he said. 'Why bloody change? I know Yallop's had a dicy attack; but I'm not going to get results bowling long spells. I'd lose what juice I've got.' He added that in five short spells a fast bowler can get through 17 eight-ball overs in a day. 'I sometimes sensed that the captain wasn't going to take me off, so I bowled within myself and didn't get wickets.' Hogg made an interesting observation on the success of our team. He noted the reliability and tightness of our off-spinners, and pointed out that some of their success stemmed from the fact that few Australian batsmen swept well, so that our short-legs were rarely threatened physically. Enough has been said in the commentary of the book about his bowling. On the evidence of these few Tests, Hogg is to be rated amongst the best three or four fast bowlers in the world today.

and the press: an adviser on such things as contracts for club cricket in Australia for the following season. Now he assumed the mantle of Party Poet:

. . . Kenny gave the first report
He's assistant gaffer
Said 'Each track I've seen out here
Has been a bloody jaffa.'

Said Boyks 'I love the Christmas tree
I think it's very pretty
And those eight fairies on the top
Look like Yorkshire's Cricket Committee.'

'But there's bowlers waiting in the nets
And I should be there with 'em.
With any luck by New Year's Day
I'll have got back my rhythm.

. . . And then old Bobby Willis
To make his day complete
Has had two hundred Christmas cards
About his bloody feet

Bernard Thomas then spoke up
As ever, lithe and keen.
He said 'My latest breakthrough
Is a brand new sex routine.

'I really think I've cracked it –
Secured the final prize.
The ultimate in ecstasy
Combined with exercise.'

On the subject of sex, one of our first managerial jobs soon after the team had been picked, was to decide whether to impose any restrictions on wives coming to join their husbands. We knew that on previous tours there had been criticism that the unity of the team was affected by the number of wives and families present, that the Christmas party in 1974 had been enlivened by the presence of many children in paper hats, and that though this might have been in itself delightful it was not so easy for a man playing in a Test match to do himself justice if, in a small and strange room, his child cried all night, and if he had to organize crèches before going off to the nets. We also agreed that any player was entitled to have his woman with him, and that, provided the player was aware that his responsibilities to the rest of the team were not replaced by those to her, the presence of women often agreeably leavened the heavy dough of an all-male party. So we suggested

that players tried to arrange for their wives and girl-friends to come in the second half of the trip, when a solid team-spirit would already have been established. Kathy Botham, as has been said, was unable because of her pregnancy to fly after early December, so of course she came earlier, and the birth of Sarah on February 3rd became a team celebration. By the end of the tour thirteen out of the twenty in the party had had wives or girl-friends to visit, and there were no problems.

Insole and I also agreed to ban journalism by the players during the tour, since it is easy for a man to be lured into a controversial or stupid remark after a hard day's play. Boycott was excepted, since he already had a contract with a Sydney newspaper; Doug did press him to write fortnightly rather than weekly articles, and, as the TCCB contract lays down, Doug would vet the pieces. Boycott agreed with this.

We all needed respite from cricket on a busy tour. The number of days totally free of cricket, travel or official functions could be counted on one hand, though afternoons and evenings were often free. Some days stand out in my mind: picnics and walks in the Botanical Gardens of Melbourne and Sydney: the rest day of the Melbourne Test, spent with my girl-friend and my parents at the seaside home of a Melbourne family. I went swimming with my father, for the first time in perhaps twenty years; we were caught in an undertow, which recalled a time in my childhood when my father swam far out to sea to retrieve a beach ball, and the rest of the family watched appalled as his bobbing head grew smaller. The cinema also provided relaxation and a place where no phone rings.

Travelling involves many good-byes. Ansett airlines have looked after the MCC for many years, and one of their liaison officers, Les Teague, gave a party to mark his retirement. It was rumoured to be Alex Bannister's last tour, after 25 years as the *Daily Mail*'s Cricket Correspondent. He has always been one of England's staunchest supporters, and was moved to be given a little memento in the dressing-room during the last Test.

Another farewell put all cricketing matters in perspective. On the last afternoon of the Brisbane Test, the Secretary of the Queensland Cricket Association asked me if I would have a chat with a twelve-year-old boy called Patrick Byrne who had a hole in his heart. He was a delightful and independent cricket enthusiast, full of ideas about the game. I took him into the dressing-room to meet the players, where he told us there were a 'few things' wrong with his heart and how he had had surgery at various stages of his life. He said he was commissioned to write an account of the match for *World of Cricket*. His perceptive article appeared in the March issue, but Patrick never saw it in print. In January I received a letter from his parents: on 29th December he had died peacefully without pain, at the home of his grandparents.

Looking back, I find I forget the bad moments. There was, indeed, that sleepless night in Melbourne. The constant packing and unpacking becomes a bore. And there is my final, pet hatred about Australia – the ferocity of their handshakes. One perennial problem for a right-handed opening batsman is bruised fingers and joints in the right hand, and the major ordeal of my tour was standing in a reception-line next to the Mayor of Adelaide and shaking three hundred bear-like fists.

After the sixth Test only half the party flew straight home. Gooch went to Perth, to play more cricket. Gower, Edmonds, Thomas and Taylor went to Singapore. Boycott, Radley and Emburey stayed on in Australia, and Willis went to New Zealand. I had ten days in India, where the handshakes, like the culture, are more gentle.

Guy the Gorilla at the Christmas party.

APPENDIX OF STATISTICS
* denotes captain   † wicketkeeper

FIRST TEST MATCH

Played at Brisbane, December 1st, 2nd, 3rd, 5th, 6th.
England won by seven wickets. Toss: Australia.

Close of play scores:
1st day: England 60-2 (Randall 43, Taylor 2).
2nd day: England 257-8 (Miller 19, Old 17).
3rd day: Australia 157-3 (Yallop 74, Hughes 51).
4th day: England 16-0 (Boycott 9, Gooch 2).

AUSTRALIA

	1st Innings		2nd Innings	
G. M. Wood	c Taylor b Old	7	lbw b Old	19
G. J. Cosier	run out	1	b Willis	0
P. M. Toohey	b Willis	1	lbw b Botham	1
*G. N. Yallop	c Gooch b Willis	7	c and b Willis	102
K. J. Hughes	c Taylor b Botham	4	c Edmonds b Willis	129
T. J. Laughlin	c sub (J. K. Lever) b Willis	2	lbw b Old	5
†J. A. Maclean	not out	33	lbw b Miller	15
B. Yardley	c Taylor b Willis	17	c Brearley b Miller	16
R. M. Hogg	c Taylor b Botham	36	b Botham	16
A. G. Hurst	c Taylor b Botham	0	b Botham	0
J. D. Higgs	b Old	1	not out	0
Extras	(LB 1, NB 6)	7	(B 9, LB 5, NB 22)	36
Total		116		339

Fall of wickets: 1-2; 2-5; 3-14; 4-22; 5-24; 6-26; 7-53; 8-113; 9-113; 10-116.
           1-0; 2-2; 3-49; 4-219; 5-228; 6-121; 7-310; 8-339; 9-339; 10-339.

ENGLAND

	1st Innings		2nd Innings	
G. Boycott	c Hughes b Hogg	13	run out	16
G. A. Gooch	c Laughlin b Hogg	2	c Yardley b Hogg	2
D. W. Randall	c Laughlin b Hurst	75	not out	74
†R. W. Taylor	lbw b Hurst	20		
*J. M. Brearley	c Maclean b Hogg	6	(4) c Maclean b Yardley	13
D. I. Gower	c Maclean b Hurst	44	(5) not out	48
I. T. Botham	c Maclean b Hogg	49		
G. Miller	lbw b Hogg	27		
P. H. Edmonds	c Maclean b Hogg	1		
C. M. Old	not out	29		
R. G. D. Willis	c Maclean b Hurst	8		
Extras	(B 7, LB 4, NB 1)	12	(B 12, LB 3, NB 2)	17
Total		286	(3 wickets)	170

Fall of wickets: 1-2; 2-38; 3-111; 4-120; 5-120; 6-215; 7-219; 8-226; 9-266; 10-286.
           1-16; 2-37; 3-74.

ENGLAND: BOWLING

	1st Innings				2nd Innings			
	O	M	R	W	O	M	R	W
Willis	14	2	44	4	27.6	3	69	3
Old	9.7	1	24	2	17	1	60	2
Botham	12	1	40	3	26	5	95	3
Gooch	1	0	1	0				
Edmonds	1	1	0	0	12	1	27	0
Miller					34	12	52	2

AUSTRALIA: BOWLING

	1st Innings				2nd Innings			
	O	M	R	W	O	M	R	W
Hurst	27.4	6	93	4	10	4	17	0
Hogg	28	8	74	6	12.5	2	35	1
Laughlin	22	6	54	0	3	0	6	0
Yardley	7	1	34	0	13	1	41	1
Cosier	5	1	10	0	3	0	11	0
Higgs	6	2	9	0	12	1	43	0

Umpires: R. A. French and M. G. O'Connell. Man of the match: D. W. Randall.

SECOND TEST MATCH

Played at Perth, December 15th, 16th, 17th, 19th, 20th.
England won by 166 runs. Toss: Australia.

Close of play scores:
1st day: England 190-3 (Boycott 63, Gower 101).
2nd day: Australia 60-4 (Toohey 6).
3rd day: England 58-0 (Boycott 23, Gooch 26).
4th day: Australia 11-1 (Wood 2, Hughes 1).

ENGLAND

	1st Innings		2nd Innings		
G. Boycott	lbw b Hurst	77		lbw b Hogg	23
G. A. Gooch	c Maclean b Hogg	1		lbw b Hogg	43
D. W. Randall	c Wood b Hogg	0		c Cosier b Yardley	45
*J. M. Brearley	c Maclean b Dymock	17		c Maclean b Hogg	0
D. I. Gower	b Hogg	102		c Maclean b Hogg	12
I. T. Botham	lbw b Hurst	11		c Wood b Yardley	30
G. Miller	b Hogg	40		c Toohey b Yardley	25
†R. W. Taylor	c Hurst b Yardley	12	(9)	c Maclean b Hogg	2
J. K. Lever	c Cosier b Hurst	14	(8)	c Maclean b Hurst	10
R. G. D. Willis	c Yallop b Hogg	2		not out	3
M. Hendrick	not out	7		b Dymock	1
Extras	(B 6, LB 9, W 3, NB 8)	26		(LB 6, NB 8)	14
Total		309			208

Fall of wickets: 1-3; 2-3; 3-41; 4-199; 5-219; 6-224; 7-253; 8-295; 9-300; 10-309.
1-58; 2-93; 3-93; 4-135; 5-151; 6-176; 7-201; 8-201; 9-206; 10-208.

AUSTRALIA

	1st Innings			2nd Innings	
G. M. Wood	lbw b Lever	5		c Taylor b Lever	64
W. M. Darling	run out	25		c Boycott b Lever	5
K. J. Hughes	b Willis	16		c Gooch b Willis	12
*G. N. Yallop	b Willis	3		c Taylor b Hendrick	3
P. M. Toohey	not out	81		c Taylor b Hendrick	0
G. J. Cosier	c Gooch b Willis	4		lbw b Miller	47
†J. A. Maclean	c Gooch b Miller	0		c Brearley b Miller	1
B. Yardley	c Taylor b Hendrick	12		c Botham b Lever	7
R. M. Hogg	c Taylor b Willis	18		b Miller	0
G. Dymock	b Hendrick	11		not out	6
A. G. Hurst	c Taylor b Willis	5		b Lever	5
Extras	(LB 7, W 1, NB 2)	10		(LB 3, W 4, NB 4)	11
Total		190			161

Fall of wickets: 1-8; 2-34; 3-38; 4-60; 5-78; 6-79; 7-100; 8-128; 9-185; 10-190.

1-8; 2-36; 3-58; 4-58; 5-131; 6-143; 7-143; 8-147; 9-151; 10-161.

AUSTRALIA: BOWLING

	1st Innings				2nd Innings			
	O	M	R	W	O	M	R	W
Hogg	30.5	9	65	5	17	2	57	5
Dymock	34	4	72	1	16.3	2	53	1
Hurst	26	7	70	3	17	5	43	1
Yardley	23	1	62	1	16	1	41	3
Cosier	4	2	14	0				

ENGLAND: BOWLING

	1st Innings				2nd Innings			
Lever	7	0	20	1	8.1	2	28	4
Botham	11	2	46	0	11	1	54	0
Willis	18.5	5	44	5	12	1	36	1
Hendrick	14	1	39	2	8	3	11	2
Miller	16	6	31	1	7	4	21	3

Umpires: R. C. Bailhache and T. F. Brooks. Man of the match: R. M. Hogg.

THIRD TEST MATCH

Played at Melbourne, December 29th, 30th, January 1st, 2nd, 3rd.
Australia won by 103 runs. Toss: Australia.

Close of play scores:
1st day: Australia 243-4 (Wood 100, Border 25),
2nd day: England 107-8 (Miller 3, Willis 3).
3rd day: Australia 163-7 (Maclean 10, Dymock 3).
4th day: England 171-8 (Emburey 2).

AUSTRALIA

	1st Innings			2nd Innings	
G. M. Wood	c Emburey b Miller	100		b Botham	34
W. M. Darling	run out	33		c Randall b Miller	21
K. J. Hughes	c Taylor b Botham	0		c Gower b Botham	48
*G. N. Yallop	c Hendrick b Botham	41		c Taylor b Miller	16
P. M. Toohey	c Randall b Miller	32		c Botham b Emburey	20
A. R. Border	c Brearley b Hendrick	29		run out	0
†J. A. Maclean	b Botham	8		c Hendrick b Emburey	10
R. M. Hogg	c Randall b Miller	0		b Botham	1
G. Dymock	b Hendrick	0		c Brearley b Hendrick	6
A. G. Hurst	b Hendrick	0	(11)	not out	0
J. D. Higgs	not out	1	(10)	st Taylor b Emburey	0
Extras	(LB 8, NB 6)	14		(B 4, LB 6, NB 1)	11
Total		258			167

Fall of wickets: 1-65; 2-65; 3-126; 4-189; 5-247; 6-250; 7-250; 8-251; 9-252; 10-258.
1-55; 2-81; 3-101; 4-136; 5-136; 6-152; 7-157; 8-167; 9-167; 10-167.

ENGLAND

	1st Innings		2nd Innings	
G. Boycott	b Hogg	1	lbw b Hurst	38
*J. M. Brearley	lbw b Hogg	1	c Maclean b Dymock	0
D. W. Randall	lbw b Hurst	13	lbw b Hogg	2
G. A. Gooch	c Border b Dymock	25	lbw b Hogg	40
D. I. Gower	lbw b Dymock	29	lbw b Dymock	49
I. T. Botham	c Darling b Higgs	22	c Maclean b Higgs	10
G. Miller	b Hogg	7	c Hughes b Higgs	1
†R. W. Taylor	b Hogg	1	c Maclean b Hogg	5
J. E. Emburey	b Hogg	0	not out	7
R. G. D. Willis	c Darling b Dymock	19	c Yallop b Hogg	3
M. Hendrick	not out	6	b Hogg	0
Extras	(B 6, LB 4, NB 9)	19	(B 10, LB 7, W 1, NB 6)	24
Total		143		179

Fall of wickets: 1-2; 2-3; 3-40; 4-52; 5-81; 6-100; 7-101; 8-101; 9-120; 10-143.
1-1; 2-6; 3-71; 4-122; 5-163; 6-163; 7-167; 8-171; 9-179; 10-179.

Third Test Match, Melbourne, cont'd.

ENGLAND: BOWLING

	1st Innings				2nd Innings			
	O	M	R	W	O	M	R	W
Willis	13	2	47	0	7	0	21	0
Botham	20.1	4	68	3	15	4	41	3
Hendrick	23	3	50	3	14	4	25	1
Emburey	14	1	44	0	21.2	12	30	3
Miller	19	6	35	3	14	5	39	2

AUSTRALIA: BOWLING

	1st Innings				2nd Innings			
Hogg	17	7	30	5	17	5	36	5
Hurst	12	2	24	1	11	1	39	1
Dymock	15.6	4	38	3	18	4	37	2
Higgs	19	9	32	1	16	2	29	2
Border					5	0	14	0

Umpires: R. A. French and M. G. O'Connell. Man of the match: G. M. Wood.

FOURTH TEST MATCH

Played at Sydney, January 6th, 7th, 8th, 10th, 11th.
England won by 93 runs. Toss: England.

Close of play scores:
1st day: Australia 56-1 (Darling 35, Hughes 15).
2nd day: Australia 248-7 (Border 31, Dymock 0).
3rd day: England 133-2 (Randall 65, Gooch 6).
4th day: England 304-6 (Miller 16, Taylor 3).

ENGLAND

	1st Innings		2nd Innings	
G. Boycott	c Border b Hurst	8	lbw b Hogg	0
*J. M. Brearley	b Hogg	17	b Border	53
D. W. Randall	c Wood b Hurst	0	lbw b Hogg	150
G. A. Gooch	c Toohey b Higgs	18	c Wood b Higgs	22
D. I. Gower	c Maclean b Hurst	7	c Maclean b Hogg	34
I. T. Botham	c Yallop b Hogg	59	c Wood b Higgs	6
G. Miller	c Maclean b Hurst	4	lbw b Hogg	17
†R. W. Taylor	c Border b Higgs	10	not out	21
J. E. Emburey	c Wood b Higgs	0	c Darling b Higgs	14
R. G. D. Willis	not out	7	c Toohey b Higgs	0
M. Hendrick	b Hurst	10	c Toohey b Higgs	7
Extras	(B 1, LB 1, W 2, NB 8)	12	(B 5, LB 3, NB 14)	22
Total		152		346

Fall of wickets: 1-18; 2-18; 3-35; 4-51; 5-66; 6-70; 7-94; 8-98; 9-141; 10-152.
1-0; 2-111; 3-169; 4-237; 5-267; 7-307; 8-334; 9-334; 10-346.

AUSTRALIA

	1st Innings			2nd Innings	
G. M. Wood	b Willis	0		run out	27
W. M. Darling	c Botham b Miller	91		c Gooch b Hendrick	13
K. J. Hughes	c Emburey b Willis	48		c Emburey b Miller	15
*G. N. Yallop	c Botham b Hendrick	44		c and b Hendrick	1
P. M. Toohey	c Gooch b Botham	1		b Miller	5
A. R. Border	not out	60		not out	45
†J. A. Maclean	lbw b Emburey	12		c Botham b Miller	0
R. M. Hogg	run out	6	(9)	c Botham b Emburey	0
G. Dymock	b Botham	5	(8)	b Emburey	0
J. D. Higgs	c Botham b Hendrick	11		lbw b Emburey	3
A. G. Hurst	run out	0		b Emburey	0
Extras	(B 2, LB 3, NB 11)	16		(LB 1, NB 1)	2
Total		294			111

Fall of wickets: 1-1; 2-126; 3-178; 4-179; 5-210; 6-235; 7-245; 8-276; 9-290; 10-294.
   1-38; 2-44; 3-45; 4-59; 5-74; 6-76; 7-85; 8-85; 9-105; 10-111.

AUSTRALIA: BOWLING

	1st Innings				2nd Innings			
	O	M	R	W	O	M	R	W
Hogg	11	3	36	2	28	10	67	4
Dymock	13	1	34	0	17	4	35	0
Hurst	10.6	2	28	5	19	3	43	0
Higgs	18	4	42	3	59.6	15	148	5
Border					23	11	31	1

ENGLAND: BOWLING

	1st Innings				2nd Innings			
Willis	9	2	33	2	2	0	8	0
Botham	28	3	87	2				
Hendrick	24	4	50	2	10	3	17	2
Miller	13	2	37	1	20	7	38	3
Emburey	29	10	57	1	17.2	2	46	4
Gooch	5	1	14	0				

Umpires: R. C. Bailhache and R. A. French. Man of the match: D. W. Randall.

FIFTH TEST MATCH

Played at Adelaide, January 27th, 28th, 29th, 31st, February 1st.
England won by 205 runs. Toss: Australia.

Close of play scores:
1st day: Australia 69-4 (Wood 19, Yardley 28).
2nd day: England 82-2 (Boycott 38, Gooch 11).
3rd day: England 272-7 (Taylor 69, Emburey 0).
4th day: Australia 82-2 (Hughes 30, Yallop 16).

ENGLAND

	1st Innings		2nd Innings	
G. Boycott	c Wright b Hurst	6	c Hughes b Hurst	49
*J. M. Brearley	c Wright b Hogg	2	lbw b Carlson	9
D. W. Randall	c Carlson b Hurst	4	c Yardley b Hurst	15
G. A. Gooch	c Hughes b Hogg	1	b Carlson	18
D. I. Gower	lbw b Hurst	9	lbw b Higgs	21
I. T. Botham	c Wright b Higgs	74	c Yardley b Hurst	7
G. Miller	lbw b Hogg	31	c Wright b Hurst	64
†R. W. Taylor	run out	4	c Wright b Hogg	97
J. E. Emburey	b Higgs	4	b Hogg	42
R. G. D. Willis	c Darling b Hogg	24	c Wright b Hogg	12
M. Hendrick	not out	0	not out	3
Extras	(B 1, LB 4, W 3, NB 2)	10	(B 1, LB 16, W 2, NB 4)	23
Total		169		360

Fall of wickets: 1-10; 2-12; 3-16; 4-18; 5-27; 6-80; 7-113; 8-136; 9-147; 10-169.
1-31; 2-57; 3-97; 4-106; 5-130; 6-132; 7-267; 8-336; 9-347; 10-360.

AUSTRALIA

	1st Innings		2nd Innings	
W. M. Darling	c Willis b Botham	15	b Botham	18
G. M. Wood	c Randall b Emburey	35	run out	9
K. J. Hughes	c Emburey b Hendrick	4	c Gower b Hendrick	46
*G. N. Yallop	b Hendrick	0	b Hendrick	36
A. R. Border	c Taylor b Botham	11	b Willis	1
P. H. Carlson	c Taylor b Botham	0	c Gower b Hendrick	21
B. Yardley	b Botham	28	c Brearley b Willis	0
†K. J. Wright	lbw b Emburey	29	c Emburey b Miller	0
R. M. Hogg	b Willis	0	b Miller	2
J. D. Higgs	run out	16	not out	3
A. G. Hurst	not out	17	b Willis	13
Extras	(B 1, LB 3, NB 5)	9	(LB 1, NB 10)	11
Total		164		160

Fall of wickets: 1-5; 2-10; 3-22; 4-24; 5-72; 6-94; 7-114; 8-116; 9-133; 10-164.
1-31; 2-36; 3-115; 4-120; 5-121; 6-121; 7-124; 8-130; 9-147; 10-160.

AUSTRALIA: BOWLING

	1st Innings				2nd Innings			
	O	M	R	W	O	M	R	W
Hogg	10.4	1	26	4	27.6	7	59	3
Hurst	14	1	65	3	37	9	97	4
Carlson	9	1	34	0	27	8	41	2
Yardley	4	0	25	0	20	6	60	0
Higgs	3	1	9	2	28	4	75	1
Border					3	2	5	0

ENGLAND: BOWLING

	1st Innings				2nd Innings			
	O	M	R	W	O	M	R	W
Willis	11	1	55	1	12	3	41	3
Hendrick	19	1	45	2	14	6	19	3
Botham	11.4	0	42	4	14	4	37	1
Emburey	12	7	13	2	9	5	16	0
Miller					18	3	36	2

Umpires: R. C. Bailhache and M. G. O'Connell. Man of the match: I. T. Botham.

SIXTH TEST MATCH

Played at Sydney, February 10th, 11th, 12th, 14th.
England won by nine wickets. Toss: Australia.

Close of play scores:
1st day: England 24-0 (Boycott 6, Brearley 18).
2nd day: England 216-4 (Gower 47, Botham 17).
3rd day: Australia 70-5 (Yallop 13, Yardley 16).

AUSTRALIA

	1st Innings		2nd Innings	
G. M. Wood	c Botham b Hendrick	15	c Willis b Miller	29
A. M. J. Hilditch	run out	3	c Taylor b Hendrick	1
K. J. Hughes	c Botham b Willis	16	c Gooch b Emburey	7
*G. N. Yallop	c Gower b Botham	121	c Taylor b Miller	17
P. M. Toohey	c Taylor b Botham	8	c Gooch b Emburey	0
P. H. Carlson	c Gooch b Botham	2	c Botham be Emburey	0
B. Yardley	b Emburey	7	not out	61
†K. J. Wright	st Taylor b Emburey	3	c Boycott b Miller	5
R. M. Hogg	c Emburey b Miller	9	b Miller	7
J. D. Higgs	not out	9	c Botham b Emburey	2
A. G. Hurst	b Botham	0	c and b Miller	4
Extras	(LB 3, NB 2)	5	(B 3, LB 6, NB 1)	10
Total		198		143

Fall of wickets: 1-18; 2-19; 3-67; 4-101; 5-109; 6-116; 7-124; 8-159; 9-198; 10-198.
1-8; 2-28; 3-48; 4-48; 5-48; 6-82; 7-114; 8-130; 9-136; 10-143.

ENGLAND

	1st Innings			2nd Innings	
G. Boycott	c Hilditch b Hurst	19		c Hughes b Higgs	13
*J. M. Brearley	c Toohey b Higgs	46		not out	20
D. W. Randall	lbw b Hogg	7		not out	0
G. A. Gooch	st Wright b Higgs	74			
D. I. Gower	c Wright b Higgs	65			
I. T. Botham	c Carlson b Yardley	23			
G. Miller	lbw b Hurst	18			
†R. W. Taylor	not out	36			
J. E. Emburey	c Hilditch b Hurst	0			
R. G. D. Willis	b Higgs	10			
M. Hendrick	c and b Yardley	0			
Extras	(B 3, LB 5, NB 2)	10		(NB 2)	2
Total		308		(1 wicket)	35

Fall of wickets: 1-37; 2-46; 3-115; 4-182; 5-233; 6-247; 7-270; 8-280; 9-306; 10-308.
1-31.

ENGLAND: BOWLING

	1st Innings				2nd Innings			
	O	M	R	W	O	M	R	W
Willis	11	4	48	1	3	0	15	0
Hendrick	12	2	21	1	7	3	22	1
Botham	9.7	1	57	4				
Emburey	18	3	48	2	24	4	52	4
Miller	9	3	13	1	27.1	6	44	5
Boycott	1	0	6	0				

AUSTRALIA: BOWLING

	1st Innings				2nd Innings			
Hogg	18	6	42	1				
Hurst	20	4	58	3				
Yardley	25	2	105	2	5.2	0	21	0
Carlson	10	1	24	0				
Higgs	30	8	69	4	5	1	12	1

Umpires: A. R. Crafter and D. G. Weser. Man of the match: G. N. Yallop.

ONE-DAY INTERNATIONALS

At Melbourne, December 26th.
Match abandoned.

AUSTRALIA

(From) *G. N. Yallop, A. R. Border, P. H. Carlson, C. J. Cosier, W. M. Darling, G. Dymock, R. M. Hogg, K. J. Hughes, A. G. Hurst, †J. A. Maclean, P. M. Toohey, G. M. Wood.

ENGLAND

Team not announced.
Umpires: R. C. Bailhache and A. R. Crafter.

Played at Sydney, January 13th.
Match drawn. Toss: England.

AUSTRALIA

G. M. Wood	c Tolchard b Old	6
W. M. Darling	not out	7
K. J. Hughes	not out	0
Extras	(LB 4)	4
Total	(1 wicket, 7.2 overs)	17

*G. N. Yallop, P. M. Toohey, A. R. Border, G. J. Cosier, †J. A. Maclean, P. H. Carlson, G. Dymock and A. G. Hurst did not bat.

ENGLAND: BOWLING

	O	M	R	W
Lever	3	0	8	0
Old	3.2	1	5	1
Hendrick	1	1	0	0

Fall of wicket: 1-17.

ENGLAND

G. Boycott, *J. M. Brearley, D. W. Randall, G. A. Gooch, D. I. Gower, †R. W. Tolchard,
I. T. Botham, C. M. Old, P. H. Edmonds, J. K. Lever, M. Hendrick.
Umpires: A. R. Crafter and C. E. Harvey.

Played at Melbourne, January 24th.
England won by seven wickets. Toss: Australia.

AUSTRALIA

G. M. Wood	c Gower b Edmonds	28
A. M. J. Hilditch	c Bairstow b Botham	10
A. R. Border	c Willis b Hendrick	11
*G. N. Yallop	run out	9
K. J. Hughes	lbw b Hendrick	0
P. H. Carlson	c Randall b Willis	11
T. J. Laughlin	c Willis b Hendrick	6
†J. A. Maclean	c Edmonds b Botham	11
R. M. Hogg	c Botham b Hendrick	4
G. Dymock	c and b Botham	1
A. G. Hurst	not out	0
Extras	(B 4, LB 2, NB 4)	10
Total	(33.5 overs)	101

ENGLAND: BOWLING

	O	M	R	W
Willis	8	4	15	1
Lever	5	2	7	0
Hendrick	8	1	25	4
Botham	4.5	2	16	3
Edmonds	7	0	26	1
Gooch	1	0	2	0

Fall of wickets: 1-27; 2-52; 3-54; 4-55; 5-76; 6-78; 7-94; 8-99; 9-101; 10-101.

ENGLAND

G. Boycott	not out	39
*J. M. Brearley	b Hogg	0
D. W. Randall	c Yallop b Dymock	12
G. A. Gooch	b Carlson	23
D. I. Gower	not out	19
Extras	(LB 5, NB 4)	9
Total	(3 wickets, 28.2 overs)	102

I. T. Botham, P. H. Edmonds, † D. L. Bairstow, J. K. Lever, R. G. D. Willis and M. Hendrick did not bat.

AUSTRALIA: BOWLING

	O	M	R	W
Hogg	6	1	20	1
Dymock	6	1	16	1
Laughlin	5	1	13	0
Carlson	5	0	21	1
Hurst	5.2	1	14	0
Border	1	0	9	0

Fall of wickets: 1-7; 2-29; 3-69.

Umpires: A. R. Crafter and C. E. Harvey. Man of the match: M. Hendrick.

Played at Melbourne, February 4th.
Australia won by four wickets. Toss: Australia.

ENGLAND

G. Boycott	lbw b Laughlin	33
*J. M. Brearley	c Wright b Dymock	0
D. W. Randall	lbw b Dymock	4
G. A. Gooch	c Hurst b Carlson	19
D. I. Gower	not out	101
I. T. Botham	c Wood b Hurst	31
†D. L. Bairstow	run out	1
C. M. Old	not out	16
Extras	(B 3, LB 3, NB 1)	7
Total	(6 wickets, 40 overs)	212

J. K. Lever, R. G. D. Willis and M. Hendrick did not bat.

AUSTRALIA: BOWLING

	O	M	R	W
Hurst	8	1	36	1
Dymock	8	1	31	2
Carlson	8	1	27	1
Cosier	8	0	48	0
Laughlin	8	0	63	1

Fall of wickets: 1-0; 2-7; 3-50; 4-89; 5-153; 6-158.

AUSTRALIA

G. M. Wood	b Old	23
W. M. Darling	c Old b Willis	7
K. J. Hughes	c Boycott b Lever	50
G. N. Yallop	c Gower b Hendrick	31
P. M. Toohey	not out	54
G. J. Cosier	b Lever	28
P. H. Carlson	c Brearley b Lever	0
T. J. Laughlin	not out	15
Extras	(LB 6, NB 1)	7
Total	(6 wickets, 38.6 overs)	215

†K. J. Wright, G. Dymock and A. G. Hurst did not bat.

ENGLAND: BOWLING

	O	M	R	W
Willis	8	1	21	1
Lever	7	1	51	3
Hendrick	8	0	47	1
Old	8	1	31	1
Botham	7.6	0	58	0

Fall of wickets: 1-7; 2-55; 3-90; 4-145; 5-185; 6-185.
Umpires: R. C. Bailhache and D. G. Weser. Man of the match: D. I. Gower.

Played at Melbourne, February 7th.
Australia won by six wickets. Toss: Australia.

ENGLAND

G. Boycott	c Cosier b Dymock	2
*J. M. Brearley	c Wright b Cosier	46
D. W. Randall	c Hughes b Dymock	0
G. A. Gooch	c Hughes b Hurst	4
D. I. Gower	c Wood b Hurst	3
I. T. Botham	b Cosier	13
†D. L. Bairstow	run out	3
P. H. Edmonds	lbw b Laughlin	15
J. K. Lever	b Laughlin	1
R. G. D. Willis	c Wright b Cosier	2
M. Hendrick	not out	0
Extras	(LB 2, NB 3)	5
Total	(31.7 overs)	94

AUSTRALIA: BOWLING

	O	M	R	W
Hurst	5	3	7	2
Dymock	6	1	21	2
Carlson	8	2	22	0
Cosier	7	1	22	3
Laughlin	5.7	0	17	2

Fall of wickets: 1-10; 2-10; 3-17; 4-22; 5-42; 6-56; 7-91; 8-91; 9-94; 10-94.

AUSTRALIA

G. M. Wood	c Bairstow b Botham	30
W. M. Darling	c Brearley b Willis	14
K. J. Hughes	c Brearley b Willis	0
*G. N. Yallop	b Lever	25
P. M. Toohey	not out	16
G. J. Cosier	not out	8
Extras	(NB 2)	2
Total	(4 wickets, 21.5 overs)	95

P. H. Carlson, T. J. Laughlin, †K. J. Wright, G. Dymock and A. G. Hurst did not bat.

ENGLAND: BOWLING

	O	M	R	W
Willis	5	2	16	2
Hendrick	6	0	32	0
Botham	5.5	0	30	1
Lever	5	0	15	1

Fall of wickets: 1-29; 2-37; 3-54; 4-87.

Umpires: R. C. Bailhache and D. G. Weser. Man of the match: G. Dymock.

SOUTH AUSTRALIA

Played at Adelaide, November 3rd, 4th, 5th, 6th.
South Australia won by 32 runs. Toss: S. Australia.

SOUTH AUSTRALIA

	1st Innings		2nd Innings	
J. E. Nash	lbw b Miller	124	st Taylor b Miller	33
W. M. Darling	c Miller b Willis	17	c Edmonds b Old	1
I. R. McLean	c Taylor b Edmonds	30	c sub (D. W. Randall) b Miller	52
B. L. Causby	c Brearley b Miller	20	c and b Edmonds	4
J. N. Langley	st Taylor b Edmonds	1	st Taylor b Edmonds	0
*R. K. Blewett	c Taylor b Willis	22	b Edmonds	12
P. R. Sleep	c Taylor b Lever	45	c Taylor b Edmonds	3
†T. J. Robertson	c Taylor b Willis	2	b Edmonds	24
R. M. Hogg	b Lever	11	run out	16
G. R. Attenborough	lbw b Miller	19	run out	3
A. T. Sincock	not out	14	not out	1
Extras	(B 2, LB 2, NB 2)	6		
Total		311		149

Fall of wickets: 1-31; 2-133; 3-195; 4-196; 5-200; 6-245; 7-261; 8-272; 9-281; 10-311.
1-11; 2-55; 3-64; 4-64; 5-84; 6-90; 7-112; 8-144; 9-146; 10-149.

ENGLAND XI

	1st Innings		2nd Innings	
G. Boycott	lbw b Hogg	62	lbw b Hogg	6
G. A. Gooch	c Robertson b Hogg	4	b Sleep	23
C. T. Radley	hit wkt b Hogg	4	c Sleep b Sincock	3
D. I. Gower	lbw b Attenborough	73	c Blewett b Sincock	50
*J. M. Brearley	b Sincock	27	run out	25
G. Miller	c Langley b Hogg	0	lbw b Sincock	5
†R. W. Taylor	c Blewett b Sleep	6	c Langley b Attenborough	4
P. H. Edmonds	not out	38	c Robertson b Attenborough	0
J. K. Lever	c and b Sleep	1	b Hogg	28
C. M. Old	c Darling b Sleep	4	c McLean b Sleep	40
R. G. D. Willis	absent hurt	–	not out	0
Extras	(LB 5, NB 8)	13	(B 4, LB 1, NB 7)	12
Total		232		196

Fall of wickets: 1-9; 2-15; 3-148; 4-148; 5-149; 6-179; 7-215; 8-222; 9-232.
1-19; 2-22; 3-67; 4-100; 5-108; 6-117; 8-124; 9-192; 10-196.

ENGLAND XI: BOWLING

	1st Innings				2nd Innnings			
	O	M	R	W	O	M	R	W
Willis	11	1	61	3				
Lever	16	1	67	2	9	0	40	0
Old	18	2	78	0	5	1	20	1
Edmonds	21	5	53	2	21	3	52	5
Miller	18.4	5	41	3	16	2	37	2
Gooch	1	0	5	0				

SOUTH AUSTRALIA: BOWLING

	1st Innings				2nd Innings			
Hogg	12	2	43	4	12.4	1	39	2
Sincock	9	0	42	1	10	2	28	3
Attenborough	15	1	49	1	11	2	49	2
Sleep	17.5	3	72	3	12.5	1	49	2
Blewett	10	4	13	0	5	1	19	0

Umpires: R. A. French and M. G. O'Connell.

VICTORIA

Played at Melbourne, November 10th, 11th, 12th, 13th.
Match drawn. Toss: Victoria.

VICTORIA

	1st Innings			2nd Innings	
J. M. Wiener	c Edmonds b Lever	48		not out	16
P. A. Hibbert	c Tolchard b Old	6		not out	14
D. F. Whatmore	c Edmonds b Lever	27			
*G. N. Yallop	b Edmonds	10			
P. Melville	c Edmonds b Emburey	16			
J. K. Moss	c Emburey b Edmonds	73			
T. J. Laughlin	run out	37			
†I. L. Maddocks	c Radley b Edmonds	8			
I. W. Callen	c Tolchard b Emburey	8			
A. G. Hurst	b Emburey	1			
J. D. Higgs	not out	1			
Extras	(LB 15, NB 4)	19		(NB 3)	3
Total		254		(no wicket)	33

Fall of wickets: 1-11; 2-84; 3-93; 4-113; 5-129; 6-213; 7-239; 8-244; 9-249; 10-254.

ENGLAND XI

	1st Innings	
*J. M. Brearley	not out	116
G. A. Gooch	lbw b Hurst	3
D. W. Randall	b Wiener	63
D. I. Gower	c and b Wiener	13
C. T. Radley	c and b Higgs	22
†R. W. Tolchard	c Whatmore b Higgs	0
P. H. Edmonds	c Melville b Higgs	5
C. M. Old	c Maddocks b Hurst	4
J. E. Emburey	c Higgs b Laughlin	5
J. K. Lever	did not bat	
M. Hendrick		
Extras	(LB 3, W 2, NB 5)	10
Total	(8 wickets declared)	241

Fall of wickets: 1-7; 2-121; 3-145; 4-195; 5-199; 6-207; 7-225; 8-241.

ENGLAND XI: BOWLING

	1st Innings				2nd Innings			
	O	M	R	W	O	M	R	W
Old	17	5	44	1				
Lever	18	3	52	2	4	1	3	0
Hendrick	11	2	29	0				
Edmonds	22	6	48	3	2	0	3	0
Emburey	26.5	5	56	3	5	0	11	0
Gooch	2	0	6	0				
Randall					2	0	9	0
Radley					1	0	4	0

VICTORIA: BOWLING

	1st Innings			
Hurst	17	4	44	2
Callen	16	4	44	0
Higgs	39	8	82	3
Laughlin	15.7	5	24	1
Wiener	13	3	31	2
Yallop	2	0	6	0

Umpires: R. C. Bailhache and K. J. Carmody.

NEW SOUTH WALES

Played at Sydney, November 17th, 18th, 19th, 20th.
England XI won by ten wickets. Toss: England XI.

ENGLAND XI

	1st Innings		2nd Innings	
G. Boycott	c Border b Lawson	14	not out	4
G. A. Gooch	c Rixon b Border	66	not out	0
D. W. Randall	c Hughes b Clews	110		
C. T. Radley	c Hughes b Border	13		
D. I. Gower	b Hourn	26		
G. Miller	st Rixon b Hourn	5		
I. T. Botham	c Toohey b Clews	56		
†R. W. Taylor	c Hilditch b Lawson	9		
J. E. Emburey	c Johnston b Lawson	0		
*R. G. D. Willis	not out	21		
M. Hendrick	b Border	20		
Extras	(B 17, LB 6, W 2, NB 9)	34		
Total		374	(no wicket)	4

Fall of wickets: 1-20; 2-145; 3-173; 4-250; 5-252; 6-276; 7-305; 8-313; 9-336; 10-374.

NEW SOUTH WALES

	1st Innings		2nd Innings	
J. Dyson	c Boycott b Miller	67	c Gooch b Willis	6
*A. M. J. Hilditch	c Taylor b Willis	4	b Botham	93
P. M. Toohey	c Gower b Hendrick	23	c Gooch b Botham	20
A. R. Border	c Taylor b Miller	11	c Taylor b Botham	12
D. A. H. Johnston	c Hendrick b Miller	16	c Gooch b Botham	3
G. C. Hughes	c Hendrick b Miller	27	b Emburey	11
M. L. Clews	st Taylor b Emburey	1	run out	5
†S. J. Rixon	c Hendrick b Miller	10	c Botham b Emburey	24
G. G. Watson	c Boycott b Emburey	2	not out	14
G. F. Lawson	not out	0	c Miller b Willis	7
D. W. Hourn	c Emburey b Miller	0	b Botham	0
Extras	(LB 1, NB 3)	4	(B 6, LB 4, W 1, NB 4)	15
Total		165		210

Fall of wickets: 1-5; 2-47; 3-65; 4-107; 5-142; 6-146; 7-162; 8-165; 9-165; 10-165.
1-18; 2-57; 3-82; 4-87; 5-119; 6-124; 7-173; 8-192; 9-209; 10-210.

NEW SOUTH WALES: BOWLING

	1st Innings				2nd Innings			
	O	M	R	W	O	M	R	W
Lawson	17	5	39	3	0.5	0	4	0
Watson	18	2	61	0				
Clews	13	1	88	2				
Hourn	32	4	114	2				
Border	12.1	2	38	3				

ENGLAND XI: BOWLING

	1st Innings				2nd Innings			
	O	M	R	W	O	M	R	W
Willis	8	3	16	1	15	3	39	2
Hendrick	12	2	33	1	4	2	4	0
Botham	9	2	41	0	17.2	6	51	5
Miller	18.4	3	56	6	24	6	56	0
Emburey	10	4	15	2	22	5	44	2
Gooch					1	0	1	0

Umpires: T. F. Brooks and A. Drake.

QUEENSLAND

Played at Brisbane, November 24th, 25th, 26th, 27th.
England XI won by six wickets. Toss. Queensland.

QUEENSLAND

	1st Innings			2nd Innings	
M. J. Walters	c Gower b Willis	0		retired hurt	4
W. R. Broad	c Taylor b Old	41		lbw b Willis	0
A. D. Ogilvie	retired hurt	43	(7)	c Gower b Willis	45
G. J. Cosier	c Taylor b Botham	32	(3)	b Willis	0
P. H. Carlson	c Miller b Old	1	(4)	b Botham	37
T. V. Hohns	c Taylor b Willis	3	(5)	c Old b Botham	43
*†J. A. Maclean	c Boycott b Botham	1	(8)	c Gooch b Old	94
G. K. Whyte	c Brearley b Old	10	(6)	b Botham	0
G. Dymock	c Brearley b Botham	13		c Taylor b Botham	16
L. F. Balcam	not out	10		b Botham	21
G. W. Brabon	lbw b Old	2		not out	2
Extras	(NB 16)	16		(B 4, LB 2, NB 21)	27
Total		172			289

Fall of wickets: 1-4; 2-90; 3-97; 4-100; 5-129; 6-135; 7-158; 8-159; 9-172.
1-0; 2-0; 3-83; 4-83; 5-121; 6-169; 7-214; 8-268; 9-289.

ENGLAND XI

	1st Innings			2nd Innings		
G. Boycott	c Cosier b Brabon	6		c Maclean b Balcam		60
G. A. Gooch	c Brabon b Dymock	34		c Ogilvie b Carlson		22
D. W. Randall	c Maclean b Balcam	66		b Whyte		47
†R. W. Taylor	c Maclean b Dymock	2				
*J. M. Brearley	not out	75	(4)	not out		38
D. I. Gower	b Balcam	6	(5)	c Cosier b Hohns		1
G. Miller	c Maclean b Dymock	18	(6)	not out		22
I. T. Botham	c Maclean b Dymock	6				
C. M. Old	lbw b Balcam	2				
P. H. Edmonds	c Maclean b Cosier	14				
R. G. D. Willis	b Brabon	6				
Extras	(B 1, LB 3, W 1, NB 14)	19		(B 7, LB 2, NB 9)		18
Total		254		(4 wickets)		208

Fall of wickets: 1-14; 2-75; 3-90; 4-129; 5-148; 6-188; 7-201; 8-208; 9-241; 10-254.
  1-42; 2-117; 3-165; 4-168.

ENGLAND XI: BOWLING

	1st Innings				2nd Innings			
	O	M	R	W	O	M	R	W
Willis	11	1	40	2	11	1	46	3
Old	14.7	4	33	4	14.2	3	63	1
Botham	12	1	66	3	20	3	70	5
Gooch	3	0	11	0	1	0	8	0
Edmonds	5	2	6	0	8	1	35	0
Miller					11	1	40	0

QUEENSLAND: BOWLING

	1st Innings				2nd Innings			
Balcam	13	1	56	3	12	2	25	1
Brabon	10.1	1	45	2	5	0	31	0
Carlson	14	1	48	0	9.3	1	29	1
Dymock	19	3	46	4	17	5	38	0
Hohns	2	2	0	0	8	5	13	1
Cosier	4	0	19	1	5	2	10	0
Whyte	7	3	18	0	15	3	44	1

Umpires: C. E. Harvey and M. W. Johnson.

WESTERN AUSTRALIA

Played at Perth, December 9th, 10th, 11th.
England XI won by 140 runs. Toss: England XI.

ENGLAND XI

	1st Innings			2nd Innings	
G. Boycott	lbw b Clark	4		c Marsh b Yardley	13
G. A. Gooch	c Wright b Alderman	3		c Wright b Porter	15
C. T. Radley	b Alderman	2		c Marsh b Yardley	18
*J. M. Brearley	c Wright b Porter	11		b Yardley	18
D. I. Gower	c Wright b Alderman	0		c Wright b Porter	4
†R. W. Tolchard	not out	61		b Yardley	3
I. T. Botham	c Charlesworth b Porter	4		c Marsh b Yardley	4
P. H. Edmonds	lbw b Porter	21		c Wright b Alderman	27
J. E. Emburey	c Wright b Clark	22		not out	7
J. K. Lever	c Wright b Mann	2		b Alderman	1
M. Hendrick	c Charlesworth b Mann	6		b Clark	8
Extras	(B 1, LB 2, W 1, NB 4)	8		(B 7, NB 1)	8
Total		144			126

Fall of wickets: 1-7; 2-7; 3-13; 4-17; 5-25; 6-31; 7-69; 8-115; 9-121; 10-144.
1-23; 2-41; 3-58; 4-63; 5-69; 6-73; 7-98; 8-115; 9-117; 10-126.

WESTERN AUSTRALIA

	1st Innings			2nd Innings	
G. M. Wood	b Lever	2		lbw b Botham	15
R. I. Charlesworth	c Tolchard b Botham	3		lbw b Lever	6
K. J. Hughes	b Botham	8		lbw b Botham	1
G. R. Marsh	c Tolchard b Botham	0		c Tolchard b Hendrick	9
*R. J. Inverarity	c Tolchard b Hendrick	9		lbw b Botham	2
A. L. Mann	c Botham b Hendrick	3		c Tolchard b Botham	0
G. D. Porter	c Brearley b Hendrick	8		c Tolchard b Hendrick	2
B. Yardley	c Tolchard b Hendrick	8		not out	38
†K. J. Wright	c Brearley b Botham	0		b Hendrick	0
W. M. Clark	not out	2		run out	1
T. M. Alderman	c Botham b Hendrick	1		run out	2
Extras	(LB 3, W 1, NB 4)	8		(LB 2)	2
Total		52			78

Fall of wickets: 1-4; 2-6; 3-10; 4-16; 5-28; 6-39; 7-48; 8-49; 9-49; 10-52.
1-22; 2-22; 3-28; 4-32; 5-32; 6-35; 7-48; 8-64; 9-69; 10-78.

WESTERN AUSTRALIA: BOWLING

	1st Innings				2nd Innings			
	O	M	R	W	O	M	R	W
Alderman	12	4	18	3	9	2	26	2
Clark	16	4	50	2	12	2	22	1
Porter	17	4	37	3	16	9	16	2
Yardley	2	0	7	0	13	1	54	5
Mann	8.3	2	24	2				

ENGLAND XI: BOWLING

	1st Innings				2nd Innings			
Lever	8	3	10	1	7	3	16	1
Botham	9	3	16	4	13.5	4	37	4
Hendrick	5.4	2	11	5	7	2	23	3
Gooch	2	0	7	0				

Umpires: D. Hawks and D. G. Weser.

SOUTH AUSTRALIA

Played at Adelaide, December 22nd, 23rd, 24th.

Match drawn with the scores equal. Toss: S. Australia.

SOUTH AUSTRALIA

	1st Innings			2nd Innings		
J. E. Nash	c Tolchard b Old	10		lbw b Emburey	25
W. M. Darling	c Tolchard b Old	19	(7)	not out	41
I. R. McLean	c Tolchard b Gooch	7	(2)	c and b Emburey	25
B. L. Causby	b Old	87	(3)	c Randall b Emburey	7
R. J. Parker	c and b Edmonds	51	(4)	c Randall b Emburey	42
*R. K. Blewett	c Old b Emburey	19		c Brearley b Emburey	51
P. R. Sleep	not out	31	(5)	c Tolchard b Old	18
†S. R. Gentle	lbw b Lever	1		not out	21
A. T. Sincock	not out	12			
G. R. Attenborough	did not bat				
D. A. Johnston	did not bat				
Extras	(LB 3, NB 1)	4		(LB 1)	1
Total	(7 wickets declared)	241		(6 wickets declared)	231

Fall of wickets: 1-25; 2-36; 3-38; 4-129; 5-174; 6-220; 7-221.
1-45; 2-57; 3-58; 4-96; 5-140; 6-174.

ENGLAND XI

	1st Innings			2nd Innings		
G. Boycott	c Gentle b Sincock	4	(11)	not out	7
G. A. Gooch	st Gentle b Causby	20	(5)	st Gentle b Blewett	64
C. T. Radley	c Gentle b Attenborough	60		lbw b Attenborough	1
†R. W. Tolchard	run out	72		lbw b Johnston	6
D. W. Randall	c Gentle b Attenborough	47	(2)	c Blewett b Johnston	45
*J. M. Brearley	not out	18	(1)	c Parker b Johnston	26
G. Miller	not out	2	(6)	not out	68
C. M. Old	did not bat		(7)	b Attenborough	2
P. H. Edmonds	did not bat		(8)	lbw b Blewett	2
J. E. Emburey	did not bat		(9)	b Blewett	0
J. K. Lever	did not bat		(10)	c Darling b Attenborough	11
Extras	(B 3, LB 4, NB 4)	11		(B 1, LB 2, NB 3)	6
Total	(5 wickets declared)	234		(9 wickets)	238

Fall of wickets: 1-26; 2-32; 3-138; 4-186; 5-231.
1-65; 2-68; 3-74; 4-91; 5-180; 6-187; 7-196; 8-202; 9-223.

South Australia cont'd.

ENGLAND XI: BOWLING

	1st Innings				2nd Innings			
	O	M	R	W	O	M	R	W
Lever	16	1	63	1	10	1	33	0
Old	18	2	55	3	5	0	21	1
Gooch	6	1	16	1	4	0	11	0
Emburey	17	3	48	1	26	3	67	5
Edmonds	17	3	55	1	28	9	91	0
Miller					4	1	6	0
Boycott					1	0	1	0

SOUTH AUSTRALIA: BOWLING

	1st Innings				2nd Innings			
Attenborough	13	5	41	2	16	1	92	3
Johnston	8	2	21	0	7	0	44	3
Sincock	5	0	27	1	5	0	39	0
Causby	6	0	34	1				
Sleep	12	1	58	0	2	0	22	0
Blewett	8	1	41	0	7	0	35	3
Nash	1	0	1	0				

Umpires: R. A. French and M. G. O'Connell.

TASMANIA

Played at Hobart, January 19th, 20th, 21st.
Match drawn. Toss: England XI.

TASMANIA

	1st Innings			2nd Innings	
M. J. Norman	c Taylor b Old	13		b Emburey	43
G. W. Goodman	c Taylor b Old	1		c Taylor b Willis	1
S. J. Howard	c Taylor b Old	13		b Lever	20
J. H. Hampshire	c Taylor b Old	0		not out	46
†R. D. Woolley	b Old	4		c Radley b Miller	0
T. W. Docking	b Emburey	39		not out	2
*J. Simmons	c Miller b Old	1			
D. J. Gatenby	b Willis	1			
G. J. Cowmeadow	c Edmonds b Willis	10			
M. B. Scholes	b Miller	10			
G. R. Whitney	not out	0			
Extras	(B 5, LB 3, NB 5)	13		(B 2, LB 1, NB 3)	6
Total		105		(4 wickets)	118

Fall of wickets: 1-6; 2-20; 3-20; 4-36; 5-47; 6-60; 7-61; 8-75; 9-105; 10-105.
1-3; 2-34; 3-102; 4-107.

ENGLAND XI

	1st Innings	
G. Boycott	not out	90
G. A. Gooch	c Goodman b Whitney	14
C. T. Radley	c Woolley b Cowmeadow	15
D. I. Gower	b Gatenby	30
R. W. Taylor	b Whitney	1
G. Miller	b Gatenby	44
P. H. Edmonds	not out	7
C. M. Old	did not bat	
J. E. Emburey	did not bat	
J. K. Lever	did not bat	
R. G. D. Willis	did not bat	
Extras	(B 4, LB 2, NB 3)	9
Total	(5 wickets declared)	210

Fall of wickets: 1-30; 2-54; 3-99; 4-102; 5-187.

ENGLAND XI: BOWLING

	1st Innings				2nd Innings			
	O	M	R	W	O	M	R	W
Willis	10	1	24	2	4	1	9	1
Old	14	3	42	6	5	2	12	0
Lever	7	3	18	0	8	0	27	1
Emburey	4	3	1	1	6	1	15	1
Miller	3	1	7	1	5	1	18	1
Edmonds					12	3	27	0
Boycott					1	0	4	0

TASMANIA: BOWLING

	1st Innings			
Cowmeadow	16	2	64	1
Whitney	26	3	73	2
Scholes	10	4	40	0
Gatenby	5	1	22	2
Simmons	1	0	2	0

Umpires: K. Connor and A. Edsall.

OTHER MATCHES

Played at Renmark, November 1st. Match drawn. England XI 199 for 4 (dec) (C. T. Radley 64).
South Australia Country XI 137 for 6.

Played at Leongatha, November 8th. England XI won by 71 runs. England XI 130 for 8 (dec)
(C. Aitken 4 for 30). Victoria Country XI 59 (J. E. Emburey 5 for 10).

Played at Canberra, November 15th (40 overs). England XI won by 179 runs. England XI 255 for 2
(40 overs) (G. Boycott 123*, R. W. Tolchard 108). A. C. T. and Districts 76 (33.6 overs) (R. G. D.
Willis 4 for 10).

Played at Bundaberg, November 22nd (35 overs). England XI won by 132 runs. England XI 259 for 5
(35 overs) (R. W. Tolchard 74, J. M. Brearley 59). Queensland Country XI 127 (31.6 overs)
(J. K. Lever 4 for 17).

Played at Albany, December 13th (40 overs). England XI won by 69 runs. England XI 208 for 4 (40 overs) (G. A. Gooch 112). Western Australia Country XI 139 (34.3 overs) (B. Miguel 53, P. H. Edmonds 6 for 53, G. Miller 4 for 68).

Played at Newcastle, January 14th, 15th, 16th. England XI won by nine wickets. Northern New South Wales Country XI 223 for 9 (dec) (C. Beatty 72, J. Gardner 59, P. H. Edmonds 3 for 66) and 166 (C. Evans 64, C. M. Old 4 for 30, J. K. Lever 3 for 24, P. H. Edmonds 3 for 49). England XI 163 (J. M. Brearley 66, R. Holland 4 for 60, K. M. Hill 3 for 49) and 230 for 1 (G. Boycott 117*, C. T. Radley 55*, J. M. Brearley 50).

Played at Launceston, January 18th (40 overs). England XI won by 163 runs. England XI 240 for 8 (40 overs) (I. T. Botham 61, D. W. Randall 60). Tasmania 77 (34.4 overs) (G. Miller 3 for 3).

Played at Melbourne, February 3rd (50 6-ball overs, reduced to 48 overs after rain). England XI won by three wickets. Tasmania (Gillette Cup winners) 131 for 6 (48 overs). England XI 134 for 7 (43.3 overs) (R. J. Sherriff 3 for 16).

Played at Geelong, February 6th (40 overs). England XI won by 48 runs. England XI 165 for 9 (40 overs) (J. Caulfield 3 for 28). Geelong & Districts 100 for 9 (38.6 overs). Match abandoned when children invaded the playing area. Result decided on England XI score of 148 for 8 after 38.6 overs.

TEST AVERAGES

ENGLAND: BATTING

	M	I	NO	Runs	Highest	Average
D. I. Gower	6	11	1	420	102	42.00
D. W. Randall	6	12	2	385	150	38.50
I. T. Botham	6	10	0	291	74	29.10
R. W. Taylor	6	10	2	208	97	26.00
G. Miller	6	10	0	234	64	23.40
G. A. Gooch	6	11	0	246	74	22.36
G. Boycott	6	12	0	263	77	21.91
J. M. Brearley	6	12	1	184	53	16.72
J. E. Emburey	4	7	1	67	42	11.16
R. G. D. Willis	6	10	2	88	24	11.00
M. Hendrick	5	9	4	34	10	6.80

Also batted: P. H. Edmonds 1; J. K. Lever 14, 10; C. M. Old 29*.

ENGLAND: BOWLING

	Overs	Mdns	Runs	Wkts	Average	Best
J. K. Lever	15.1	2	48	5	9.60	4-28
G. Miller	177.1	54	346	23	15.04	5-44
M. Hendrick	145	30	299	19	15.73	3-19
J. E. Emburey	144.4	49	306	16	19.12	4-46
C. M. Old	26.7	2	84	4	21.00	2-24
R. G. D. Willis	140.3	23	461	20	23.05	5-44
I. T. Botham	158.4	25	567	23	24.65	4-42

Also bowled: G. Boycott 1-0-6-0; P. H. Edmonds 13-2-27-0; G. A. Gooch 6-1-15-0.

ENGLAND: FIELDING

20 R. W. Taylor (18 ct, 2 st); 11 I. T. Botham; 9 G. A. Gooch; 6 J. E. Emburey; 5 J. M. Brearley; 4 D. I. Gower, D. W. Randall; 3 M. Hendrick, R. G. D. Willis; 2 G. Boycott; 1 P. H. Edmonds, G. Miller, substitute (J. K. Lever).

AUSTRALIA: BATTING

	M	I	NO	Runs	Highest	Average
A. R. Border	3	6	2	146	60*	36.50
G. N. Yallop	6	12	0	391	121	32.58
K. J. Hughes	6	12	0	345	129	28.75
G. M. Wood	6	12	0	344	100	28.66
W. M. Darling	4	8	0	221	91	27.62
B. Yardley	4	8	1	148	61*	21.14
P..M. Toohey	5	10	1	149	81*	16.55
G. J. Cosier	2	4	0	52	47	13.00
J. A. Maclean	4	8	1	79	33*	11.28
K. J. Wright	2	4	0	37	29	9.25
R. M. Hogg	6	12	0	95	36	7.91
J. D. Higgs	5	10	4	46	16	7.66
P. H. Carlson	2	4	0	23	21	5.75
G. Dymock	3	6	1	28	11	5.60
A. G. Hurst	6	12	2	44	17*	4.40

Also batted: A. M. J. Hilditch 3, 1; T. J. Laughlin 2, 5.

AUSTRALIA: BOWLING

	Overs	Mdns	Runs	Wkts	Average	Best
R. M. Hogg	217.4	60	527	41	12.85	6-74
A. G. Hurst	204.2	44	577	25	23.08	5-28
J. D. Higgs	196.6	47	468	19	24.63	5-148
G. Dymock	114.1	19	269	7	38.42	3-38
P. H. Carlson	46	10	99	2	49.50	2-41
A. R. Border	31	13	50	1	50.00	1-31
B. Yardley	113.2	12	389	7	55.57	3-41

Also bowled: G. J. Cosier 12-3-35-0; T. J. Laughlin 25-6-60-0.

AUSTRALIA: FIELDING

18 J. A. Maclean; 8 K. J. Wright (7 ct, 1 st); 6 G. M. Wood; 5 K. J. Hughes, P. M. Toohey; 4 W. M. Darling, B. Yardley; 3 A. R. Border, G. N. Yallop; 2 P. H. Carlson, G. J. Cosier, A. M. J. Hilditch, T. J. Laughlin; 1 A. G. Hurst.

TOUR AVERAGES

BATTING

	M	I	NO	Runs	Highest	Average
D. W. Randall	10	18	2	763	150	47.68
R. W. Tolchard	3	5	1	142	72	35.50
J. M. Brearley	11	21	5	538	116*	33.62
D. I. Gower	12	20	1	623	102	32.78
G. Boycott	12	23	3	533	90*	26.65
G. Miller	11	18	3	398	68*	26.53
I. T. Botham	9	14	0	361	74	25.78
G. A. Gooch	13	23	1	514	74	23.36
R. W. Taylor	10	15	2	230	97	17.69
P. H. Edmonds	7	9	2	115	38*	16.42
C. M. Old	6	6	1	81	40	16.20
C. T. Radley	6	9	0	138	60	15.33
R. G. D. Willis	10	13	4	115	24	12.77
J. E. Emburey	9	12	2	101	42	10.10
J. K. Lever	6	7	0	67	28	9.57
M. Hendrick	8	12	4	68	20	8.50

BOWLING

	Overs	Mdns	Runs	Wkts	Average	Best
M. Hendrick	184.4	40	399	28	14.25	5-11
G. Miller	277.1	74	607	36	16.86	6-56
J. E. Emburey	261.1	73	563	31	18.16	5-67
I. T. Botham	239.3	44	848	44	19.27	5-51
R. G. D. Willis	210.3	34	696	34	20.47	5-44
C. M. Old	138	24	452	21	21.52	6-42
J. K. Lever	118.1	18	377	13	29.00	4-28
P. H. Edmonds	149	34	397	11	36.09	5-52

Also bowled: G. Boycott 3-0-11-0; G. A. Gooch 26-2-80-1; C. T. Radley 1-0-4-0; D. W. Randall 2-0-9-0.

FIELDING

41 R. W. Taylor (35 ct, 6 st); 14 I. T. Botham; 13 G. A. Gooch, R. W. Tolchard; 11 J. M. Brearley; 9 J. E. Emburey; 8 P. H. Edmonds; 7 D. I. Gower; 6 M. Hendrick, D. W. Randall; 5 G. Boycott, G. Miller; 3 R. G. D. Willis; 2 C. M. Old, C. T. Radley. 2 substitutes (J. K. Lever and D. W. Randall).

CENTURIES

D. W. Randall	(2)	150	v Australia (4th Test) at Sydney
		110	v New South Wales at Sydney
J. M. Brearley	(1)	116*	v Victoria at Melbourne
D. I. Gower	(1)	102	v Australia (2nd Test) at Perth
G. N. Yallop	(2)	121	for Australia (6th Test) at Sydney
		102	for Australia (1st Test) at Brisbane
K. J. Hughes	(1)	129	for Australia (1st Test) at Brisbane
J. E. Nash	(1)	124	for South Australia at Adelaide
G. M. Wood	(1)	100	for Australia (3rd Test) at Melbourne

INDEX